THE POEM AS PROCESS

THE POEM AS PROCESS

DAVID SWANGER

University of California, Santa Cruz

HARCOURT BRACE JOVANOVICH, INC.

New York   Chicago   San Francisco   Atlanta

CREDITS AND ACKNOWLEDGMENTS

ARC MUSIC CORP. for "Rock and Roll Music" by Chuck Berry. © 1957 Arc Music Corp. For "Almost Grown" by Chuck Berry. © 1959 Arc Music Corp. Used with permission of the publisher; all rights reserved.

ATHENEUM PUBLISHERS, INC., for "World War III," from *A Probable Volume of Dreams* by Marvin Bell. Copyright © 1969 by Marvin Bell. Reprinted by permission of Atheneum Publishers.

ATV MUSIC LIMITED for the lyric of "A Day in the Life" by John Lennon/Paul McCartney. © 1967 Northern Songs Limited. Reprinted by permission of ATV Music Limited.

BIG BELLS INCORPORATED for "The Sound of Silence" by Paul Simon. © 1964 Paul Simon. Used with the permission of the publisher.

JOAN BLACKBURN for "The Purse-Seine," from *The Nets* by Paul Blackburn. © Paul Blackburn 1961. Reprinted by permission of the Estate of Paul Blackburn.

JONATHAN CAPE LIMITED for "Naming of Parts," from *A Map of Verona* by Henry Reed. Reprinted by permission of the author and Jonathan Cape Limited.

CONTINENTAL TOTAL MEDIA PROJECT, INC., for "Suzanne" by Leonard Cohen. Copyright 1966 by Project Seven Music, div. of CTMP, Inc. Reprinted by permission of CTMP, Inc.

CORINTH BOOKS INC. for "Preface to a Twenty Volume Suicide Note," from *Preface to a Twenty Volume Suicide Note* by LeRoi Jones. Copyright © 1961 by LeRoi Jones. Reprinted by permission of Corinth Books Inc.

COTILLION MUSIC, INC., for the lyric of "For What It's Worth" by Stephen Stills. © 1966 (unp) and 1967 by Cotillion Music, Inc., Ten East Music & Springalo Toones. International copyright secured; all rights reserved. Reprinted by permission of Cotillion Music, Inc.

THE DIAL PRESS, INC., for "Parents," a found poem, reprinted from *Search for the New Land* by Julius Lester. Copyright © 1969 by Julius Lester. Reprinted with permission of The Dial Press. The original news story, "Coed Kills Herself to Spare Pet Dog Doomed by Father," © 1968 by The New York Times Company. Reprinted by permission.

DODD, MEAD & COMPANY for "We Wear the Mask" by Paul Laurence Dunbar. Reprinted by permission of Dodd, Mead & Company, Inc., from *The Complete Poems of Paul Laurence Dunbar*.

DOORS MUSIC CO. for "Horse Latitudes"—Words by the Doors. © 1969 Doors Music Co. Used by permission of Doors Music Co.

DOUBLEDAY & COMPANY, INC., for "I Knew a Woman" by Theodore Roethke, from *The Collected Poems of Theodore Roethke*. Copyright 1954 by Theodore Roethke. For "My Papa's Waltz" by Theodore Roethke. Copyright 1942 by Hearst Magazines,

Inc., from *The Collected Poems of Theodore Roethke.* For "The Empress No. 5" by Diane Wakoski. Copyright © 1965 by Doubleday & Company, Inc., from the book *A Controversy of Poets,* edited by Robert Kelly and Paris Leary. Reprinted by permission of Doubleday & Company, Inc.

FARRAR, STRAUS & GIROUX, INC. for "Waking in the Blue" by Robert Lowell. Reprinted with the permission of Farrar, Straus & Giroux, Inc., from *Life Studies* by Robert Lowell. Copyright © 1956, 1959 by Robert Lowell.

HARCOURT BRACE JOVANOVICH, INC., for "Buffalo Bill's," "in Just-." Copyright, 1923, 1951, by e. e. cummings. Reprinted from his volume *Complete Poems 1913–1962.* For "The Journey of the Magi," "The Love Song of J. Alfred Prufrock," from *Collected Poems 1909–1962* by T. S. Eliot. Copyright, 1936, by Harcourt Brace Jovanovich, Inc.; copyright © 1963, 1964 by T. S. Eliot. Reprinted by permission of Harcourt Brace Jovanovich, Inc.

HARPER & ROW, PUBLISHERS, INC., for "The Pawnbroker," from *The Privilege* by Maxine Kumin. Copyright © 1964 by Maxine W. Kumin. For "Daddy," from *Ariel* by Sylvia Plath. Copyright © 1963 by Ted Hughes. Reprinted by permission of Harper & Row, Publishers, Inc.

HARVARD UNIVERSITY PRESS for "The Bat is dun, with wrinkled Wings—" by Emily Dickinson. Reprinted by permission of the publishers and the Trustees of Amherst College from Thomas H. Johnson, Editor, *The Poems of Emily Dickinson,* Cambridge, Mass.: The Belknap Press of Harvard University Press. Copyright, 1951, 1955, by The President and Fellows of Harvard College.

ROBERT HERSHON for "Spitting on Ira Rosenblatt," from *Grocery Lists* by Robert Hershon, The Crossing Press (copyright by Robert Hershon 1972). Reprinted by permission of the author.

HODDER & STOUGHTON for "There was rapture of spring in the morning" by G. A. Studdert Kennedy, reprinted from *More Rough Rhymes of a Padre,* published by Hodder & Stoughton. © 1918. Reprinted with the permission of the publisher.

HOLT, RINEHART AND WINSTON, INC., for "The Most of It" by Robert Frost, from *The Poetry of Robert Frost,* edited by Edward Connery Lathem. Copyright 1942 by Robert Frost. Copyright © 1969 by Holt, Rinehart and Winston, Inc. Copyright © 1970 by Lesley Frost Ballantine. For "Stopping by Woods on a Snowy Evening" by Robert Frost, from *The Poetry of Robert Frost,* edited by Edward Connery Lathem. Copyright 1923, © 1969 by Holt, Rinehart and Winston, Inc. Copyright 1951 by Robert Frost. Reprinted by permission of Holt, Rinehart and Winston, Inc.

HOUGHTON MIFFLIN COMPANY for "Ars Poetica" by Archibald MacLeish, from *The Collected Poems of Archibald MacLeish 1917–1952.* Copyright 1952 by Archibald MacLeish. For "Letter Written on a Ferry Crossing Long Island Sound" by Anne Sexton, from *All My Pretty Ones.* Copyright © 1961, 1962 by Anne Sexton. Copyright © 1961 by Harper & Brothers. Reprinted by permission of Houghton Mifflin Company.

THE HUDSON BAY MUSIC COMPANY for "Summer in the City." Words & Music by John Sebastian, Mark Sebastian, Steve Boone. © Copyright 1966 The Hudson Bay Music Company. Used by permission.

INDIANA UNIVERSITY PRESS for "Award" by Ray Durem from *New Negro Poets: USA,* edited by Langston Hughes. Copyright © 1964 Indiana University Press. Reprinted by permission of Indiana University Press.

KAYAK for "The Morning Glory" by Basho, from *The Morning Glory* by Robert Bly. Copyright 1969 by Kayak. For "Morning, Thinking of Empire" by Raymond Carver, from *Kayak #27.* Copyright 1971 by Kayak. For "Prelude, Responsibilities, The Mongoose, Coda," a found poem from *Pioneers of Modern Poetry,* George Hitchcock and Robert L. Peters, eds. Copyright 1967 by Kayak. Reprinted by permission of Kayak.

ALFRED A. KNOPF, INC. for "Peter Quince at the Clavier" by Wallace Stevens. Copyright 1923 and renewed 1951 by Wallace Stevens. Reprinted from *The Collected Poems of Wallace Stevens,* by permission of Alfred A. Knopf, Inc.

LITTLE, BROWN AND COMPANY for "Game After Supper," from *Procedures for Underground* by Margaret Atwood. Copyright © 1970 by Oxford University Press. For "The Dark and the Fair," from *Selected Poems 1928–1958* by Stanley Kunitz. Copyright © 1957 by Stanley Kunitz. Reprinted by permission of Little, Brown

and Co. in association with the Atlantic Monthly Press. The text of Dan Jones'
commentary is from *The Life of Dylan Thomas* by Constantine Fitz Gibbon and
reprinted by courtesy of Little, Brown and Company.

MACMILLAN PUBLISHING CO., INC., for "Hap," from *Collected Poems* by Thomas Hardy.
Copyright 1925 by Macmillan Publishing Co., Inc., & Harper's Magazine, renewed
1926 by Macmillan Publishing Co., Inc. For "A Deep-Sworn Vow," from *Collected
Poems* by William Butler Yeats. Copyright 1919 by Macmillan Publishing Co.,
Inc., renewed 1947 by Bertha Georgie Yeats. For "Leda and the Swan," from
Collected Poems by William Butler Yeats. Copyright 1928 by Macmillan Publish-
ing Co., Inc., renewed 1956 by Georgie Yeats. Reprinted with permission of
Macmillan Publishing Co., Inc.

THE MINNESOTA REVIEW for "Lemming Song" by David Swanger, from *The Minnesota
Review*, Vol. X, No. 3/4, 1970. © 1970 The Minnesota Review and reprinted by
permission of the publication.

MODERN POETRY ASSOCIATION for "Who Hungers for a Face That Fades Away" by Paul
Nemser and Mark Rudman, from *Poetry*, Vol. CXXII, No. 1, April 1973. Copy-
right 1973 by The Modern Poetry Association. Reprinted by permission of the
Editor of *Poetry*.

NEW DIRECTIONS PUBLISHING CORPORATION for "They had come from the place high on
the coral hills" by Daniel Jones and Dylan Thomas, from *The Notebooks of Dylan
Thomas*, ed. by Ralph Maud. Copyright © 1967 by the trustees for the copyright
of Dylan Thomas. For "The Secret" by Denise Levertov, from *O Taste and See.*
Copyright © 1964 by Denise Levertov Goodman. For "Dulce et Decorum Est,"
from *Collected Poems* by Wilfred Owen. Copyright Chatto & Windus, Ltd., 1946,
© 1963. For "In a Station at the Metro," "A Virginal," from *Personae* by Ezra
Pound. Copyright 1926 by Ezra Pound. For "The Advantages of Learning," from
Collected Shorter Poems by Kenneth Rexroth. Copyright 1944 by New Directions
Publishing Corporation. For "Fern Hill," from *The Poems* by Dylan Thomas.
Copyright 1946 by New Directions Publishing Corporation. For "Red Wheel-
barrow," "This Is Just to Say," "To Elsie," from *Collected Earlier Poems* by
William Carlos Williams. Copyright 1938 by New Directions Publishing Corpora-
tion. Reprinted by permission of New Directions Publishing Corporation.

THE NEW YORKER for "The Labors of Thor" by David Wagoner, from *The New
Yorker*, Vol. XLIX, No. 30, September 17, 1973, p. 46. Reprinted by permission.
© 1973, The New Yorker Magazine, Inc.

OCTOBER HOUSE INC. for "The Whipping" by Robert Hayden, from *Selected Poems.*
Copyright © 1966 by Robert Hayden. Reprinted by permission of October House
Inc.

OXFORD UNIVERSITY PRESS, INC., for "The Groundhog," from *Collected Poems 1930–
1960* by Richard Eberhart. © 1960 by Richard Eberhart. Reprinted by permission
of Oxford University Press, Inc.

QUARRY for "How Hippos Make Love" by David J. Swanger, from *Quarry*, No. 1,
Winter 1971/1972. Reprinted by permission of the editor of Quarry.

RANDOM HOUSE, INC., for "In Memory of W. B. Yeats." Copyright 1940 and renewed
1968 by W. H. Auden. Reprinted from *Collected Shorter Poems 1927–1957*, by
W. H. Auden, by permission of Random House, Inc. For "My Parents Kept Me
from Children Who Were Rough." Copyright 1934 and renewed 1962 by Stephen
Spender. Reprinted from *Selected Poems*, by Stephen Spender, by permission of
Random House, Inc. For "What's Inside the Moon?" by Vivien Tuft and Fontessa
Moore, and the collaborative poem "Hooray" from *Wishes, Lies and Dreams:
Teaching Children to Write Poetry*, by Kenneth Koch and the students of P.S. 61
in New York City. Copyright © 1970 by Kenneth Koch. Reprinted by permission
of Random House, Inc.

ARAM SAROYAN for "Crickets" by Aram Saroyan. © 1966, 1967, 1969 by Aram Saroyan.
First printed in *Works* (24 Poems) by Aram Saroyan, Lines Press, 1966. Used by
permission of the author.

CHARLES SCRIBNER'S SONS for "I Know a Man," reprinted by permission of Charles
Scribner's Sons from *For Love* by Robert Creeley. Copyright © 1962 Robert
Creeley. "Ben" (copyright 1929 Charles Scribner's Sons) by Thomas Wolfe, as
adapted in *A Stone, a Leaf, a Door* (1945), is reprinted with permission of
Charles Scribner's Sons.

SIMON & SCHUSTER, INC., for "Rain," from *Miracles* by Richard Lewis. Copyright ©
1966 by Richard Lewis. Reprinted by permission of Simon & Schuster.

SKYWRITING for "Body Mechanics" by Albert Goldbarth, from *Skywriting*, Vol. 1,
No. 1. Copyright by Albert Goldbarth. Reprinted by permission of the magazine.

SMITHSONIAN INSTITUTION PRESS for "The Rising of the Buffalo Men," from *The Osage
Tribe—The Rite of Vigil*, by Francis Laflesche, 39th Annual Report of the Bureau
of American Ethnology, Smithsonian Institution, 1925. Reprinted by permission
of the Smithsonian Institution Press.

THE STERLING LORD AGENCY for "Black People!" by Imamu Amiri Baraka (LeRoi Jones),
from *Evergreen* by Imamu Amiri Baraka (LeRoi Jones). Copyright © 1967 by
LeRoi Jones. Reprinted by permission of The Sterling Lord Agency.

ROBERT SWARD for Robert Sward's "Uncle Dog: The Poet at 9," reprinted from *Kissing
The Dancer & Other Poems*. Copyright © 1964 by Robert Sward and reprinted by
permission of the author, who holds copyright on this poem.

TREE PUBLISHING CO., INC., for "Heartbreak Hotel," words and music by Mae Boren
Axton, Tommy Durden, and Elvis Presley. © 1956 Tree Publishing Co., Inc. Re-
printed by permission of the publisher. For "The Love You Save (May Be Your
Own)," words and music by Joe Tex. © 1965 and 1966 Tree Publishing Co., Inc.
Reprinted by permission of the publisher.

TRO—ESSEX MUSIC, INC., for "A Whiter Shade of Pale." Words & Music by Keith Reid
& Gary Brooker. © Copyright 1967 Essex Music International Ltd., London, En-
gland. TRO—Essex Music, Inc., New York, controls all publication rights for the
USA and Canada. Used by permission.

THE VIKING PRESS, INC., for "Snake" by D. H. Lawrence, from *The Complete Poems
of D. H. Lawrence*, edited by Vivian de Sola Pinto and F. Warren Roberts. Copyright © 1964, 1971 by Angelo Ravagli and C. M. Weekley, Executors of the
Estate of Frieda Lawrence Ravagli. All rights reserved. Reprinted by permission
of The Viking Press, Inc.

WESLEYAN UNIVERSITY PRESS for "Falling," by James Dickey. Copyright © 1967 by
James Dickey. Reprinted from *Poems 1957–1967* by James Dickey, by permission
of Wesleyan University Press. For "The Sheep Child" by James Dickey. Copyright
© 1966 by James Dickey. Reprinted from *Poems 1957–1967* by James Dickey, by
permission of Wesleyan University Press. For "The Jewel" by James Wright.
Copyright © 1962 by James Wright. Reprinted from *The Branch Will Not Break* by
James Wright, by permission of Wesleyan University Press.

WINLYN MUSIC, INC., for "Sally, Go 'Round the Roses" by Lona Stevens and Zel
Sanders. Copyright 1963 by Winlyn Music, Inc. Published by Winlyn Music, Inc.
Reprinted by permission of the publisher.

PREFACE

The assumption underlying *The Poem as Process* is that poetry as art is not something that generates "right" answers, because it is not a form of discourse that makes assertions. On the contrary, poetry evokes rather than asserts, and its range of evocation is certainly beyond the control of the English instructor; indeed, it is often beyond the control of the poet. A poem is not a static object; it is a dynamic form. Books that presume to tell the reader the meaning of a poem, or how to understand a poem, assume *a* meaning, *an* understanding. But a poem can have many meanings, to which the same reader can respond differently at different times.

Some modern aestheticians (psychologists and philosophers of art) have been sensitive to the integrity of poetry as an art form. In a tradition begun by Samuel Taylor Coleridge, aestheticians like I. A. Richards, Monroe Beardsley, Kenneth Burke, and Susanne Langer have attempted to understand poetry as a dynamic form. Instead of taking poetic devices (like meter or diction) as their starting point, these aestheticians have asked basic questions about the function of language in poetry: If poetry, like other discourse, uses words, what then makes it poetry? They have probed the question of meaning in poetry not by classifying poems, but by studying responses to poetry. What is it that poetry does to and with the person who reads or hears it? Two major conclusions emerge, and it is on these that this book is largely based:

(1) The way language is used in poetry (how poetry "means") makes particular demands on the reader; it requires him or her to be, in a sense, co-poet, creating the poem anew as he responds to it.

(2) The way poetry makes meaning is more closely akin to painting or music than to other discourse—that is, although poetry uses the materials of discourse (words), its meaning is produced by evocation in ways that are similar to the meanings created by the nonverbal arts.

A third conclusion, noted by many poets, is important to this book: a poem is never finished, although it may be abandoned. As this is true for the working poet, so it is for the reader as he seeks to know a poem. The reader can never know or understand a poem finally; if he has the resources and energy, he can return again and again to the poem, each time to know it somewhat differently. The poem is a dynamic form for both the poet and his reader, who can no more think he has "done" Shakespeare's "Sonnet 129," Wordsworth's *Lyrical Ballads*, or Frost's "Death of a Hired Man" than he can have "done" Mahler's Fourth Symphony or Picasso's *Guernica*. In this regard, a single poem is a continuing performance, a concert to which we can listen at will.

The content and organization of this book follow from these conclusions. *The Poem as Process* stresses the activity and process common to the reader and the poet. Moreover, it approaches the study of poetry from the vantage point of the aesthetician instead of the literary critic. Finally, the book is concerned with the sharing of poetry. By "sharing" I mean to suggest a variety of activities including, but not limited to, the teaching of poetry. Every conversation about a poem is a sharing; giving someone a book of poetry as a gift is a sharing; teaching, at its best, is a ritualized form of sharing. This book itself is a way of sharing poems and the concerns of poetry. It is therefore not directed solely at the teacher and his students, but at anyone interested in poetry, whether in the classroom or elsewhere.

The book is organized into chapters primarily for the sake of convenience, not because I believe that the various activities poetry inspires are distinct and separate. In fact, they overlap considerably. However, the chapters are designed as a series of activities and discussions that grow in implication: if the progression works, each chapter will not so much answer questions as lead to new ones. The chapters are open-ended and are not meant to provide hard-and-fast rules for responding to poetry. They should, however, provide the reader with at least one man's view of the poetic endeavor.

Preceding each chapter is a "Reconnaissance" section—the term describes an exploratory journey, a kind of scouting mission. The Reconnaissance sections propose activities for the reader that will enable him—experientially, by doing—to form a perspective on the problem to be discussed in the ensuing chapter. It is my hope that each Reconnaissance will help the reader to generate his own questions, independent of the chapter that follows. Implicit in the Reconnaissance is the value of "doing" as a way of "knowing," particularly as a way of learning what it is we need to know. There are no exercise questions or testing mechanisms in the book, for in my view these devices are stifling rather than stimulating.

My greatest hope for this book is that it will encourage the reader to immerse himself in those activities crucial to poetry: making poems, developing a poetic, responding to poems, and sharing responses. One of my intentions, paradoxically, is to eliminate the middleman, the teacher or critic who too often stands between the reader and poetic activity, buffering that activity with a predesigned teaching strategy or a preformulated critical analysis. To this end I have added a small collection of poems without commentary. My hope is that the reader will move from these works to a larger field and find poetry on his own.

This book owes much to two Harcourt Brace Jovanovich editors: Merton Rapp, who encouraged my work on it from the beginning, and Sid Zimmerman, who offered sound criticism as it neared completion. I would also like to thank Brewster Ghiselin, University of Utah; Marie Ohlsen, California State University at Los Angeles; and Thomas R. Steiner, University of California at Santa Barbara, for their helpful suggestions on the text.

The Poem as Process is for Lynn, Ana, and Elissa.

DAVID SWANGER

CONTENTS

RECONNAISSANCE

Write a poem of any length, in any style, about anything. After you have "finished" the poem, think back over the way you got started on it, the difficulties you faced as you wrote it, the kinds of decisions you made as you gave the poem its definition. Write a "process account" of the making of your poem (refer back to earlier drafts in the progress of the poem).

There is no need at this point to assess whether the poem is good or bad, or what its faults may be. The important thing is that you make a poem and consider what is involved in doing so.

I

MAKING A POEM

Most of my readers will have observed a small water-insect on the surface of rivulets, which throws a cinque-spotted shadow fringed with prismatic colours on the sunny bottom of the brook; and will have noticed, how the little animal *wins* its way up against the stream, by alternate pulses of active and passive motion, now resisting the current, and now yielding to it in order to gather strength and a momentary *fulcrum* for a further propulsion. This is no unapt emblem of the mind's self-experience in the act of thinking.

SAMUEL TAYLOR COLERIDGE,
Biographia Literaria

As I went along, thinking of nothing in particular, only looking at things around me and following the progress of the seasons, there would flow into my mind, with sudden and unaccountable emotion, sometimes a line or two of verse, sometimes a whole stanza at once, accompanied, not preceded, by a vague notion of the poem which they were destined to form part of.... Then there would usually be a lull of an hour or so, then perhaps the spring would bubble up again.

A. E. HOUSMAN,
The Name and the Nature of Poetry

Do not save time, but lose it.

JEAN JACQUES ROUSSEAU,
Émile

In the spring of 1972, when the United States launched its unprecedented massive bombing of North Vietnam, I read an item in the paper about "free-fire zones." The reporter explained that a free-fire zone was any place the military declared it had the right to kill everything. By designating an area a free-fire zone, the generals issued an unrestricted hunting license; concurrently, a warning was issued to the populace of that area that they were licensed to be killed.

The brutality of the Vietnam war was no longer news; advocates and opponents alike of United States policy had long since been confronted in the news media by the victims of My Lai. But for some reason the existence of free-fire zones worked itself into my consciousness the way a splinter can burrow increasingly deeper into the skin. I realized I would have to attempt a poem about the free-fire zone. I was not pleased by the prospect because it is very difficult to write a political poem—not just for ad hoc poets like me, but even for expert practitioners.

My first problem was to find a core metaphor for the poem. Here I use the term metaphor broadly rather than technically, to mean an unexpected combination of ideas or images, an incongruent alliance that nonetheless works and produces a whole that is conceptually different and more meaningful than either of the parts. I searched for what Coleridge conceived of as a poetic idea, since poetry must be more than "translations of prose thoughts into poetic language." The idea behind the poem—what I call its core metaphor—had of itself to be poetic.

Finally, after virtually an hour of staring alternately out the window and at the pale glow of the page in my typewriter, my thoughts settled on the idea of license. "License to kill" is already a metaphor, albeit a tired one. I decided to blend this old metaphor with the idea of licenses in general, nonlethal ones like licenses to drive cars, own dogs, remodel homes— the kinds of licenses that every day cross the desks of civil servants into the hands of ordinary citizens. In the poem the generals themselves would be the civil servants, the license-issuers.

I had long been impressed by television appearances of political and military leaders; they are so respectable-looking and articulate. I had my core metaphor. The license to kill would be issued under the most urbane conditions, a business transaction between civilized men. I had no trouble, now, beginning the poem.

> LICENSE
>
> Go along the corridor and do not be afraid
> of the doors' eyes which watch you;
> they are opaque, blurred as cataracts;
> no one will see you enter or leave.
>
> I'll be behind the third door studying
> the gold letters which appear backwards
> from the inside; peeling
> at their edges, they say, "Licenses."
>
> I am not as you imagined, I know: smaller,
> older, looking benign as a senior partner;
> you are surprised I chew Ex-Lax and smell
> faintly like your grandparents—minty, clean.

I liked what I had achieved with the doors inside office buildings, and I was pleased with the effect of an older man who wears cologne and chews mints. But where to go with it? I saw that these lines hinted at the surreptitious quality of the transaction, that despite the familiarity of the setting and the benign license-issuer, there was a Faustian, pact-with-the-devil suggestion. The recipient of the license was apprehensive.

Then something I had read several months ago, but had hitherto not thought about, surfaced and became the image of the next stanza. It was an account of birds at a feeder, the point of which was that the charming scene of birds darting in and out of the bonanza of seeds was actually fraught with terror, as though the birds expected at any moment to meet their doom. Thus the license-issuer would describe his client:

> I understand the delicacy of your mission:
> you are like a bird at a feeder,
> terrified of consequences yet lured
> beyond judgment by the unnatural feast.

From this, the next stanza flowed wih relative ease:

> Calm yourself. This dull wood, these curls
> of dust, my green lampshade are all here
> to give assurance, as are the frail
> diplomas inked in Latin.

Later I changed "This dull wood" to "the wood's patina," and replaced "these curls of dust" (an image I had already used in a poem) with "the corpulent books"—but otherwise, I was satisfied with the stanza. I now had five stanzas:

> Go along the corridor and do not be afraid
> of the doors' eyes which watch you;
> they are opaque, blurred as cataracts;
> no one will see you enter or leave.
>
> I'll be behind the third door studying
> the gold letters which appear backwards
> from the inside; peeling
> at their edges, they say, "Licenses."
>
> I am not as you imagined, I know: smaller,
> older, looking benign as a senior partner;
> you are surprised I chew Ex-Lax and smell
> faintly like your grandparents—minty, clean.
>
> I understand the delicacy of your mission:
> you are like a bird at a feeder,
> terrified of consequences yet lured
> beyond judgment by the unnatural feast.
>
> Calm yourself: the wood's patina, the corpulent
> books, my green lampshade are all here
> to give assurance, as are the frail
> diplomas inked in Latin.

My work up to this point had been joyous, despite my being at it for over an hour. Like Coleridge's water bug, I had won my way against the stream with a pulse of activity. But I was now at the crucial juncture of the poem and faced its most difficult task. The actual business transaction—issuing the license—must take place.

The expression "You scratch my back, I'll scratch yours" came to mind, and I made a start on the next stanza:

> Our business is as simple as scratching . . .

which I then altered and expanded to

> I can see that God, as you say,
> is with you; your credit is good

and you're in real estate; this deal
is as easy as scratching your ear.

But this was wrong. It was too explicit; the use of God was
too easy; the stanza wasn't evocative, it didn't have the power
to go beyond itself. Whereas my activity had been satisfying, it
now became panicked: What if I couldn't finish the poem? I
searched for ideas and images. I thought again of the television
appearances of the generals and tried a variety of lines:

We've no bright lights nor cameras
here; this is not a public ...

Tailored men sign agreements like these
between trips to the barber, and walk away
glistening like foil: the nation is told
and visits their homes with television cameras

You are well tailored; your cheek
is taut as ...

Tailored men sign agreements
like these between trips to the barber;
they walk away glistening like foil
and the nation televises their families

Then, I tried similarly futile efforts using highway and automo-
tive imagery that came from I don't know where:

Well-tailored men often sign agreements
like these: the profits will be relentless;
you will be as a man who lives on a gold highway
where power throbs

Well-tailored men often sign agreements
like these, and their profits
are relentless as trucks on a highway,
a throbbing power of steel pistons.

Real estate, profits, the industrial pulse of highways—none of
it seemed right. These stanzas also were too explicit, almost
satirical in their play on tailors, barber shops, television, gold-
lined highways.

Although I didn't consciously know it, I had now to heed Rousseau's advice and "lose time." Or, like Housman, to allow a lull so that the original source of inspiration might again bubble up. It was imperative that I put the poem out of my mind for a while; I was trying too hard.

I ended up watching a forgettable television program for two hours. Then I returned to the typewriter.

"Eureka!" is an expression that evokes a caricature of the inventor with a light bulb over his head; but eureka is what happened. Staring at what I had written, I suddenly could see a license, complete with the dotted line on which one signs his name. The dotted line looked like a trail of blackened blood on snow. The concluding stanza of the poem emerged as if of its own intelligence. The mechanistic pistons suddenly made sense as did the tailored men; these would be combined with the violence of the hunter and his blooded prey:

> We are well-tailored men, but hunters also;
> sign where the line breaks like a rabbit's spoor
> in the snow: blood explodes and drives the pistons:
> Done! It is a plain license and will serve.

After some minor changes, the poem was mine.

LICENSE

Go along the corridor and do not be afraid
of the doors' eyes which watch you;
they are opaque, blurred as cataracts;
no one will see you enter or leave.

I'll be behind the third door studying
the gold letters which appear backwards
from the inside; peeling
at their edges, they say, "Licenses."

I am not as you imagined, I know: smaller,
older, looking benign as a senior partner;
you are surprised I chew Ex-Lax and smell
faintly like your grandparents—minty, clean.

I understand the delicacy of your mission:
you are like a bird at a feeder,
terrified of consequences yet lured
beyond judgment by the unnatural feast.

10

Calm yourself: the wood's patina,
the corpulent books, my green lampshade
are all here to give assurance
as are the frail diplomas inked in Latin.   20

We are tailored men but hunters also:
sign where the line breaks like rabbit spoor
in the snow; blood explodes and drives the pistons.
Done. It is a plain license and will serve.

It is not finished, in the sense of "final" or "complete" or
"ended"; but the poem is crafted to a point beyond which I
don't feel I can go, at least for the time being. This is not to
say I am satisfied with the poem; on the contrary, it ultimately
fails. It does not convey the bitter shock I felt in learning about
the use of free-fire zones specifically, nor my hatred of the war
in which they were invented. The poem is abandoned rather
than finished—but one can abandon a poem for a variety of
reasons. This poem and I have reached an understanding: it
goes to my limits, and I know approximately what it can do.

Several questions about writing poems emerge from the
making of "License." First, I wonder if my experience is
typical. Are there common elements in the genesis of poems
written by different poets? Are there common elements to
creativity generally, whether the "product" is a poem or a
steam engine? If there is some broad similarity in the way
different poets create, what bearing do actual accounts of the
making of poems have on assumptions and stereotypes about
poets and poems? Finally, what of the person who will hear
or read the poem? How does he enter into the consciousness
of the poet at work on a poem?

Not many poets have written detailed accounts of their
work on poems. Usually it is the critic or biographer who
comes along later, meticulously pieces together the scattered
fragments of a complicated life, and attempts to tell us how
works came into being. For the most part, the poets themselves have remained silent about how they work. Or their
remarks about their poetry have been pronouncements rather
than descriptions (for example, Wordsworth's "Poetry takes its
origins from emotion recollected in tranquility"), which give
only a general and often misleading impression.

There is nothing unethical about the poet's reluctance to

describe his work. He is not like the auto mechanic who keeps his method of adjusting the brakes a secret in order to protect his quota of brake jobs. Many poets don't wish to discuss the details of their work because they feel these are private, even sacred; after all, it's the poem itself that counts.

It is, without doubt, the poem itself that finally matters most. But the poem is no more divorced from its making than it is from its apprehension by the reader. The conventional separation between criticizing and making poems can be seen in the way poetry is taught in schools and colleges: creative writing (where people at least try to talk about the process of making) is divorced from and often subordinated to the other offerings of the English department. The separation is thus institutionalized—as if making poems had nothing to do with studying them, and vice versa. When I was a graduate student, Robert Lowell would come to the campus each autumn to offer two seminars, one on creative writing and the other on criticism. The courses were listed in separate divisions in the catalogue and no one had the temerity to suggest that perhaps making and analyzing poems were not unalterably separate activities.

Those poets who have described the making of their poems confirm my experience of a pattern of initial inspiration and flurry of writing, frustration and enforced idleness, fresh return to the task and its resolution. (Incidentally, the resolution may not be a poem that the poet even keeps; the matter can also be resolved by tearing up the draft and vowing never to attempt that poem again.) All accounts of writing poems attest to the veracity of Coleridge's water bug as a metaphor for the pulse-and-stay of the mind as it creates.

After writing down stanzas that suddenly flowed into his mind, A. E. Housman could only wait and hope "that further inspiration might be forthcoming." And ending the poem seems to be more difficult than beginning it, as Housman recounts:

> I happen to remember distinctly the genesis of the piece which stands last in my first volume. Two of the stanzas, I do not say which, came into my head, just as they are printed, while I was crossing the corner of Hampstead Heath between the Spaniard's Inn and the footpath to Temple Fortune. A third stanza came with a little coaxing

after tea. One more was needed, but it did not come; I had to turn and compose it myself, and that was a laborious business. I wrote it thirteen times, and it was more than a twelve-month before I got it right.[1]

Jean Cocteau once called inspiration "the result of profound indolence." I am convinced that he is right, however counter to our cultural mores it may be to value doing nothing. Probably one can never do nothing. Something is always happening inside. But we can certainly do too much, especially when working on a poem, just as I felt I was trying too hard with the last stanza of "License."

Melville Cane, a notable exception to the rule that poets don't discuss how they write, takes some pains to outline the "slow germination" of a number of his poems:

> One becomes involved with poems that insist on being written eventually. It may take a long time, even years, before one finally surrenders and becomes victorious through the surrender. There are many causes for this obstinacy, but perhaps the most common cause is that the original impulse though recognized lies too deep in the unconscious to be dredged up. One has the feeling that though the climate is right the time is not yet ripe; one lacks that involvement with the material which will either evoke an intuitive kindling hint or lift a definite theme to consciousness.
>
> The condition is one of slow, delayed immersion.[2]

The pattern extends to creators other than poets, as we learn from Henri Poincaré's biography of a mathematical discovery. First, working on Fuchsian functions, Poincaré tells how ideas suddenly "rose in crowds" and he made a discovery. But it was later, on a journey during which "the incidents of the travel made me forget my mathematical work," that "the idea came to me, without anything in my former thoughts seeming to have paved the way for it, that the transformations

[1] "The Name and the Nature of Poetry," in Brewster Ghiselin, ed., *The Creative Process: A Symposium* (Berkeley and Los Angeles: University of California Press, 1954), pp. 49–50.
[2] *Making a Poem—An Inquiry into the Creative Process* (New York: Harcourt Brace Jovanovich, 1953), p. 49.

I had used to define the Fuchsian functions were identical with those of non-Euclidian geometry." [3]

Bertrand Russell, half a century later, was also to describe "the fruitless effort" he expended in trying to push for solutions in mathematics, solutions that could only come of their "own subconscious development." And Darwin recorded in his autobiography that his theory of evolution came to him, after many years of struggle with it, while he was riding one day in his carriage.

There are many accounts of scientific creation (the scientist being less reluctant than the poet to chronicle the way he works) that show that creative work in the sciences proceeds much like creative work in the arts: it may be that art and science are not so antithetical as they are often portrayed, are not warring visions of the world.

A three-stage creative process—surge, dormancy, and resolution—characterizes most creative activity. Of particular interest to me is the dormancy period, for that is the "make-or-break" point not only in my own work, but for my students and colleagues also.

I once heard the poet defined as someone who is always between jobs. The statement referred to the long intervals in a poet's life when he may not write, when he is waiting for inspiration for the next poem. It seems to me that "between jobs" describes the poet's life even while he works on one poem. He, and all of us, must learn to wait through that frustrating time about which we can really do nothing, while the poem in a sense resolves itself. But what is commonly called "writer's block" is not that at all—there is no barricade, no stoppage of the mind's traffic. The traffic has simply gone underground, to the unconscious. "Writer's block" might more appropriately be called the "creative pause" inherent in the making of art. Things are happening; we must have faith to let them happen.

The stereotype of the poet as a person divinely inspired, who writes in trembling ecstasy, is misleading. We all are familiar with the image of the ethereal, passionate poet, the poet who has, as Dryden says, "a faculty wild and lawless." Perhaps the history of literature is indeed racier for its atten-

---

[3] Henri Poincaré, in Jacques Hadamard, *Psychology of Invention in the Mathematical Field* (Princeton: Princeton University Press, 1949), pp. 13–14.

tion to the volatile behavior of the Romantics Byron and Shelley, to the vices of Coleridge and Dylan Thomas, and to the idiosyncracies of Ezra Pound and Robert Frost. Only in passing is it noted that Wallace Stevens led a sober life as an insurance executive, that T. S. Eliot was a businessman, and that William Carlos Williams maintained a successful medical practice all his working life. The poet is not necessarily either a tormented outcast of society nor a sturdy executive—but the nature of the creative process necessitates that he be a hard and careful worker. The poet does not get a free ride on the wings of imagination.

Once the energy of initial inspiration has expended itself, there is a lot of plain hard work—selection and revision. Asked by the interviewer, "Do you revise a very great deal?" Robert Lowell's response was, "Endlessly." He goes on to say:

> It's such a miracle if you get lines that are halfway right; it's not just a technical problem. The lines must mean a good deal to you. All your poems are in a sense one poem, and there's always the struggle of getting something that balances and comes out right, in which all parts are good, and that has experience you value.[4]

And even a poet like Allen Ginsberg, who for many people epitomizes the stereotype of the "wild man," describes his work as "step by step, word by word and adjective by adjective." And there is the comment by Kingsley Amis on hard work:

> To have worked on a poem a lot says nothing about its final merit, but poets are likely not to feel that. "It may not be much good but at least it wasn't easy" is a natural reaction against romantic inspirational attitudes. Regarding poetry as hard work, though perhaps dangerous, strikes me as less dangerous than feeling it ought to possess or obsess one, etc. But don't take my word for it.[5]

We often think of the scientist as epitomizing the meticulous worker, but not the poet; yet Coleridge, in the *Biographia*

---

[4] George Plimpton, ed., *Writers at Work*. The Paris Review Interviews, 2nd ser., vol. 2 (London: Secker & Warburg, 1963), pp. 349–50.
[5] Paul Engle and Joseph Langland, eds., *Poet's Choice* (Boston: Little, Brown, 1962), p. 196.

Literaria, asserts that poetry has a logic of its own as strict as that of science; and the poet–scientist comparison is raised again by Marianne Moore:

> Do the poet and scientist not work analogously? Both are willing to waste effort. To be hard on himself is one of the main strengths of each. Each is attentive to clues, each must narrow the choice, must strive for precision. As George Grosz says, "In art there is no place for gossip and but a small place for the satirist." The objective is a fertile procedure. Is it not? [6]

The precision of the scientist and the passion of the poet are not usually conceived of as allies. Yet, as we have seen, emotion may impel early work on a poem only to be later combined with the goal of precision which guides every choice of noun, verb, and adjective that the poet makes.

But how do we know when a poem achieves precision? We can say that a poem achieves precision when it elicits the desired range of responses from the reader. Precision in poetry links the poet to the reader and consists in the effect a word, a line, a stanza, the entire poem, will have. The poet makes choices on the basis of how he thinks or senses the reader will react to one thing over another.

The poet gauges his reader's response on the basis of a shared language and culture. Both the reader and the poet are to some extent members of the same community, and to that extent can be presumed to have similar reactions to words, phrases, and, possibly, allusions. Of course the notion of community is a complex one, and each of us is in fact a member of several communities simultaneously. But for our purpose it is sufficient to note that a linguistic culture forms the matrix within which the poetic endeavor takes place, enabling the poet to estimate with some precision the effect his work will have on his readers.

There are two counterarguments to this notion of precision in poetry. The first is that precision lies in objective form rather than in gauging response and working for a particular response. Frost's celebrated remark that writing poetry without meter is like playing tennis without a net is pertinent here,

[6] Plimpton, *Writers at Work,* vol. 2, p. 86.

as is Dryden's somewhat lengthier endorsement of the virtues
of rhyme in poetry:

> The great easiness of blank verse renders the poet too
> luxuriant; he is tempted to say many things which might
> better be omitted, or at least shut up in fewer words; but
> when the difficulty of artful rhyming is interposed, where
> the poet commonly confines his sense to his couplet, and
> must contrive that sense into such words, that the rhyme
> shall naturally follow them, not they the rhyme; the fancy
> then gives leisure to the judgment to come in, which
> seeing so heavy a tax imposed, is ready to cut off all un-
> necessary expenses.[7]

The best answer to these arguments is simple fact. Very
good poets are playing very good tennis without the net; even
without the tax of rhyme, poetic economy has not become
inflated. Shakespeare alone refutes Dryden's contention that
blank verse is "too luxuriant." Virtually every modern poet
stands in opposition to Frost. This is not to say that poets
write without form—form is there. Consider e. e. cummings'
"in Just-."

> in Just-
> spring   when the world is mud-
> luscious the little
> lame balloonman
>
> whistles   far   and wee
>
> and eddieandbill come
> running from marbles and
> piracies and it's
> spring
>
> when the world is puddle-wonderful   10
>
> the queer
> old balloonman whistles
> far   and   wee
> and bettyandisbel come dancing
>
> from hop-scotch and jump-rope and

[7] John Dryden, in Ghiselin, *The Creative Process*, p. 78.

it's
spring
and
    the

        goat-footed   20

balloonMan   whistles
far
and
wee

The poem is not anarchic; its form is carefully worked out.
Every line, every word is carefully placed. Even the spaces
between words are carefully thought out. Yet form follows
function rather than existing for its own sake. Form is but one
of the elements with which the poet works to achieve precision.
The precision itself, defined as the poet's accuracy in getting
the effect he desires, has form as a necessary but not a
sufficient component.

The second argument asserts that in the act of creation
the poet does not calculate how people will respond to his
poem. This argument is part of the romantic myth of the poet.
Again he is seen as a soul writing in ecstatic frenzy, aloof from
the opinions of others, worlds apart from the manufacturer of
a new vacuum cleaner who must ask himself whether his
product will sell. Yet it does not diminish the poet to discover
that he takes into account those who will read or hear his
poems, any more than it diminishes the violin virtuoso to say
that he cares about concert hall acoustics. As Melville Cane
says, "The act of creation is twofold":

> ...[It is] an offering and a response, the poet can-
> not be satisfied with merely pleasing himself. If that
> were all, he would not need to be understood by anyone
> but himself; he could indulge his fancies at will for his
> purely private consumption. The poet fails when he fails
> to communicate.[8]

The myth of the poet's distance from the public dies hard.
Recently, we have this self-description by Sylvia Ashton-

[8] *Making a Poem*, p. 25.

Warner: "Maybe they've made a mistake in summoning me, inviting an alien to them. Alien. There's the word. I should reel from it but I don't. I don't dislike being an alien. An artist must be an alien in life. Art must walk alone, a pariah of the human family." [9]

Not so: The artist by definition cannot walk alone—he walks in a parade with his fellow men.

The myth must be discarded in face of the reality of the creative act: that act does not exist in a vacuum, the poet does not speak into a void. The poet must listen for echoes and reverberations as he writes. This is not simply a matter of whether the product will sell; it is a matter of the poem's success or failure as a poem. T. S. Eliot, whose poetry is hardly an effort to cater to popular taste, nonetheless feels strongly about the exigencies of communication:

> And when I speak of modern poetry as being extremely critical, I mean that the contemporary poet, who is not merely a composer of graceful verses,—is forced to ask himself such a question as "what is poetry for?"; not merely "what am I to say?" We have to communicate— if it is communication, for the word may beg the question—an experience which is not an experience in the ordinary sense. [10]

If "communication" begs the question (and I am not sure that it does), universal applicability, as described by Allen Ginsberg, might rest more comfortably:

> Sometimes I do know [the poem] makes complete sense, and I start crying. Because I realize I am hitting some area which is absolutely true. And in that sense applicable universally, or understandable universally. In that sense able to be read through time—in that sense to be read by somebody and wept to, maybe, centuries later. [11]

The poet may be a prophet, but he is not a prophet crying in the wilderness—not if he can help it, at any rate. He seeks to

[9] "Spearpoint," *The Saturday Review* (June 24, 1972), pp. 33–39.
[10] *The Use of Poetry and the Use of Criticism* (Cambridge, Mass.: Harvard University Press, 1933), p. 30.
[11] Plimpton, *Writers at Work*, vol. 3, pp. 290–91.

be understood, to communicate; and the precision of poetry lies in the fulfillment of the twofold nature of the creative act. The poem is precise when the offering and the response correlate, when the poet's joy creates joy, when the poet's tears cause tears to well in the eyes of the reader.

Still, this is abstract; it is time to return to the concrete, to the making of the poem. I use another of my own in order to work with what I know best. Consider the twofold act of creation in the making of "Lemming Song."

> My nerve ends fuse
> as spring heat reaches
> that thermostat in me
> which triggers madness.
>
> On the sea run remembering
> at three weeks old my prime
> —this was not precocious lust
> but timely—seizing sex
>
> in the sharp grass
> newly loosed from the snow   10
> where my mother dropped twelve
> of us like pellets; so small
>
> was our spark then.
> But then before the moon phased
> I was ready and pumping hot
> new lemmings,
>
> cued for haste and self-
> destruction. The tundra
> echoes with procreation
> as it echoes now with death.   20
>
> I would not have my flame
> less hard nor bright: it will take
> the sea to quench me.

During the crafting of this poem I was very much aware of a range of possible responses to almost every word, and aimed for certain specific responses. I first took account of what I. A. Richards in *Practical Criticism* calls "stock responses." These are the standard associations the reader is likely to have with the lemming: the lemming throwing itself over the cliff, the lemming as a symbol of mass hysteria and suicide. Such associations, I decided, could work to my advantage, and thus I did not seek to dam the predictable flow of associations tapped by the mention of lemmings. In fact, since virtually everyone would know what a lemming is and would have these responses, I could proceed rather early in the poem to introduce new ideas about the lemming: haste and lust. The lemming's madness is described in the first stanza, after which the poem devotes itself wholly to the high-speed procreative urge.

Despite his much touted suicidal bent, the lemming is, after all, a small rodent. I expected that the image of this rodent "seizing sex" and making the tundra echo "with procreation" would be slightly incongruous, even humorous, to the reader.

But I was not sure that the reader would get the humor I intended. The seriousness with which we usually approach suicide might overwhelm the nascent humor. For this reason I decided to put what I thought would be an unmistakable signal in the last stanza. "I would not have my flame / less hard nor bright" is a facetious allusion to a line by Walter Pater, whom I consider pretentious. Pater once said that the aim of life is to burn with a "hard, gem-like flame." Thus I intended the reader to associate my lemming's rush to the sea with Pater's pronouncement.

Some months before writing the poem I read an article which observed that, in keeping with their short life span, lemmings are able to reproduce at a very young age: child brides and grooms all. This fact of early sexual prowess became central to the poem; but since the reader could not be assumed to have seen the same article, I decided to make the fact explicit. Hence the phrase between dashes, "this was not precocious lust / but timely."

I worked hard deciding on individual words like "thermostat," "triggers," "pellets," and "cued." Each is rich in connotation: "thermostat" suggests mechanical and electrical devices and denotes an apparatus to regulate heat; "triggers" obviously connotes weaponry as well as the quick impulse to action; "pellets" has a range of connotations from shotguns to dog food; "cued" could suggest images of pool halls, as well as poised readiness.

My choices had to be made not only on the basis of the sounds of words, what might or might not rhyme, what meter is created by what number of syllables; ultimately, I had to decide on the basis of what thoughts, images, and feelings a word or phrase might evoke in the reader.

Conscious decision-making, not simply free-flowing emotional release, was vital throughout the making of "Lemming Song." As Paul Valéry says, there are a "plurality of ways that occur to the author during his labor of production," and choices must be based on "the possible diversity of legitimate effects"—responses the poem might evoke.[12]

I have discussed "Lemming Song" with friends and with students in my classes on poetry, and these discussions have resulted in a remarkable consistency of responses over the years. Some of the decisions I made in gauging responses turn out to have been wise ones; significant others have been shown to be misguided. On the whole, the diction of the poem is successful. "Thermostat," "triggers," "pellets" and "cued"—the painstaking choices of diction—evoke in the readers associations similar to those they possess for me. No one, for example, has complained that "thermostat" too strongly suggests devices on apartment walls and thus is inappropriate in a poem about wild lemmings. "Pellets," about which I was not sure, seems fine. Readers are able to visualize the newborn lemmings as that tiny, that primitive in development. The diction seems to work not because it neatly fits my readers' image of these things and nothing more, but because it fits and enlarges. For them, just as for me, the idea of encroaching madness resembling something like a thermostat registering too intense a heat, is a discovery, a growth in the way we view the phenomenon.

My assumption that the allusion to Pater would be recognized was incorrect. None of the readers has found the lemming's credo suggestive of Walter Pater. Furthermore, in estimating response to that line incorrectly, I misjudged the poem's overall effect on the reader. Everyone has failed to recognize the irony I intended throughout. My image of the lemming's song as grandiose is not shared by others. They take the poem entirely seriously. Taken seriously, the poem is an expression of "seize the day," of living fast and hard. (I

[12] "The Course in Poetics: First Lesson," in Ghiselin, *The Creative Process,* p. 99.

say this realizing that the condensation of any poem into "an expression" or "a meaning" makes it somewhat banal.) But if the reference to Pater is lost, so is the ironic dimension of the poem as a whole. It is intended not only as the expression of a particular vision of life, but also as a comment on that vision—that the lemming's view of the world (or anyone's) should not be taken as solemnly as all that. For the majority of readers my ironic intention was not perceived; therefore I was less precise in gauging response than I hoped.

Finally, my readers tell me I also miscalculated in inserting "this was not precocious lust / but timely" between dashes in the second stanza. There is enough in the rest of the poem to convey the precociousness of the lemming: the reference to its age of three weeks when mating, the description of birth, the moon–month image. For some, the lines between the dashes intrude, a too explicit attempt on my part to clarify. Others have not particularly objected to the lines, but have felt they could just as well be omitted. In either case, as I had over-estimated the probability of the reader's recognizing my allusion to Pater, here I underestimated his ability to perceive one of the poem's premises.

The conversations I was able to have with various individuals about "Lemming Song" are of the sort that should take place about poems generally. It is not often, however, that the poet has the luxury of a sympathetic group of readers who are willing to talk with him in detail about his poem. Poets who are also teachers can be lucky this way. Similarly, we as readers seldom have the poet before us to discuss the making of his poems. (Poetry readings, the usual forum, are typically performances exclusive of dialogue.) It can happen, however, even outside the organized poetry class, that correspondence between reader and poet occurs. A beautiful and powerful instance is reported by Stanley Kunitz. The poem is "The Dark and the Fair."

> A roaring company that festive night;
> The beast of dialectic dragged his chains,
> Prowling from chair to chair in the smoking light,
> While the snow hissed against the windowpanes.
>
> Our politics, our science, and our faith
> Were whiskey on the tongue; I, being rent

By the fierce divisions of our time, cried death
And death again, and my own dying meant.

Out of her secret life, that griffin-land
Where ivory empires build their stage, she came,   10
Putting in mine her small impulsive hand,
Five-fingered gift, and the palm not tame.

The moment clanged; beauty and terror danced
To the wild vibration of a sister-bell,
Whose unremitting stroke discountenanced
The marvel that the mirrors blazed to tell.

A darker image took this fairer form
Who once, in the purgatory of my pride,
When innocence betrayed me in a room
Of mocking elders, swept handsome to my side,   20

Until we rose together, arm in arm,
And fled together back into the world.
What brought her now, in the semblance of the warm,
Out of cold spaces, damned by colder blood?

That furied woman did me grievous wrong,
But does it matter much, given our years?
We learn, as the thread plays out, that we belong
Less to what flatters us than to what scars;

So, freshly turning, as the turn condones,
For her I killed the propitiatory bird,   30
Kissing her down. Peace to her bitter bones,
Who taught me the serpent's word, but yet the word.

Kunitz tells us that

after I first published the poem ... a stranger wrote to me
that there were lines in it that "beat the hell" out of him
... the best praise I ever heard. I have his generous letter,
dated October 1, 1958, before me as I write, and I am
disarmed again by the fresh candor of my correspondent's
voice, as in his offer of an interpretation: " 'The Dark and
the Fair,' it seems to me, is the story of a love affair and
also, how Art came to you." In a passage that follows he
incorporates his stage directions: "... After the first two
stanzas, which I read with an obvious energy, I pause for
about three seconds; then I begin pianissimo with 'Out

of her secret life' and build to a quiet sustained, intense thing ending on 'colder blood.' I pause for about four seconds and resign (sic) proudly for the rest of the way."

And now it seems clear to me that my final reason for choosing this poem [for an anthology] is that it was favored by Anthony Bove of Pittsburgh, Pennsylvania, stone mason and poet, who died untimely in Madrid at the age of twenty-eight.[13]

In the twofold act of creation, the ultimate goal, the epitome of precision, is the kind of communion shared by Anthony Bove and Stanley Kunitz. Bove provided Kunitz with the "best praise," and the best praise a poet can receive is that he judged correctly, that the response has become one with the offering.

I have argued in this chapter for a different view of making poetry and, hence, of the poet himself. This requires that we abandon two widely held assumptions about the poet: that his work is a passionate explosion of ideas, feelings, and images onto the page before him; and that he is a self-ordained outcast, hurling his words at a world assumed to be indifferent if not unsympathetic to his art.

One danger in breaking old molds is that they are too readily succeeded by new ones no less rigid. We should not replace the poet-as-pariah image with that of the poet as a man whose every word is chosen in deference to its effect on a body of real or imagined readers. Quite simply, the polarities are misguided. The poet creates neither wholly for himself nor wholly for others. As he creates, the poet *is* the others. The creative act requires that the poet cease to be a private person, much less an outcast, and embrace "otherhood" as part of himself. Furthermore, one of the principal criteria of a poem's success is how well the poet achieved otherhood as he wrote it: as we read the poem, it will succeed insofar as the poet has been able to be *us*, to look on his work not only as its creator but as its reader.

If the poet can be—has to be—us, he really is not so totally aloof and distant a figure; he is not, whatever the romantic descriptions tell us, a different species of mortal. And if the

[13] Engle and Langland, *Poet's Choice*, pp. 67–69.

poet can be us, why can we not be the poet? In the same sense
that the act of making requires the poet to respond as a reader
of that poem, is it not possible that responding to the poem
may require us to be the poet?

As we view the poet in a different way, so must we view
the poem. If we accept my argument thus far, it no longer
makes sense to think of the poem as a fixed, immutable work.
The only thing that is fixed about a poem is the sequence of
words and lines on the page. These are important, but essentially as a vehicle to transmit the poet's intention. They are
symbols and symbols depend on intentions. Think, for example,
of the American flag. It is a prodigious symbol, yet its meaning
is almost totally dependent on the intentions of both the user
and the perceiver. A member of the veterans of Foreign Wars
intends one thing as he marches down the street carrying the
flag; the pacifist intends another. Similarly, the veteran and
the pacifist, watching a parade in which the flag is carried by
a Cub Scout, are likely to interpret its meaning differently. To
pursue the analogy a bit further, the poet is a man waving
many different flags, sending out signals. The poem occurs
when we respond to his flags with our own, which ideally will
be able to duplicate and enlarge on the message he is sending.

What follows are successive versions of a poem I wrote,
inspired by an engraving of a pensive young man sitting with
his legs crossed, and dressed in Renaissance costume. As poet,
I consciously strove to imagine the effect of my words on the
reader. I offer as an experiment these versions of the poem as
it moves toward its last incarnation. Without explanatory notes
by me, can a reader empathetically re-create my writing process
and understand why the poem progressed as it did?

VERSION I:

> To a Young Man in Tights and Tunic,
> Posed Seated, Looking Moody
>
> That calf which angles, leads
> Us to you, a silvered long fish
> Caught in a net of fingers
> ~~Resting~~ on your knee beneath
> The tunic which arcs also parallel,

In parallel obedience across
~~Your breast frail as a soufflé~~
Does not belie your breast,
Frail as a soufflé
Hardly a pediment for such
A head, somehow both large
And small-featured, a sun-
Flower in shadow, waiting
For some miracle of heliotropism
Or eclipse . . .

VERSION II:

Rienzi: Etching of a Young Man

That calf which angles, leads
Us, a silvered long fish
Caught in a net of fingers
On your knee, the ~~parallel~~ diagonal
Arc of tunic
                                ~~ribs torso~~
Does not belie your ~~breast~~ frame
Frail as a soufflé,
Doubtful pediment for such
A head, ~~both large~~ magnificent and
Small-featured, ~~a sunflower~~

A sunflower in shadow
Waiting for science
Or miracle, heliotropism
Or another source
Of light.

But the shade
Is as sure as ink.

VERSION III:

Rienzi: Etching of a Young Man

That calf which angles, leads
Us, a silvered long fish
Caught in a net of fingers
On your knee; the diagonal
Arc of tunic
Does not belie your frame,

Frail as a soufflé,
Doubtful pediment for such
A head, magnificent and
Small featured,

A sunflower in shadow
Waiting for science
Or miracle, heliotropism
Or another source
Of light.

But the shade
Is sure as ink.

2

RECONNAISSANCE

crickets
crickess
cricksss
cricssss
crisssss
crssssss
cssssss
ssssssss
ssssssts
ssssssets
sssskets
sssckets
ssickets
srickets
crickets

Is this a poem? If you think it is, why? If you think it is not, why not?

II

SHAPING A POETIC

ARS POETICA

A poem should be palpable and mute
As a globed fruit

Dumb
As old medallions to the thumb

Silent as the sleeve-worn stone
Of casement ledges where the moss has grown—

A poem should be wordless
As the flight of birds
        *   *   *   *   *
A poem should be motionless in time
As the moon climbs   10

Leaving, as the moon releases
Twig by twig the night-entangled trees,

Leaving, as the moon behind the winter leaves,
Memory by memory the mind—

A poem should be motionless in time
As the moon climbs
        *   *   *   *   *
A poem should be equal to:
Not true

For all the history of grief
An empty doorway and a maple leaf   20

For love
The leaning grasses and two lights above the sea—

A poem should not mean
But be.

Archibald MacLeish's "Ars Poetica" has been the focal point of animated discussions by poets and teachers; it has been railed against passionately and defended as gospel. The antagonists draw their artillery from the last two lines, "A poem should not mean / But be." "How true!" exclaim the poem's defenders. "That's it exactly; a poem does not have to explain itself, does not have to be anything other than free, free to be itself." "Absolutely false!" counters the other side. "In fact, do not the last two lines contradict in practice the very point they make? They say a poem should not mean, yet they mean something." [1]

The participants in this dispute fail to realize that they are basically in agreement about the nature of poetry: both assume that what is said in a poem can be judged "true" or "false."

Before one can debate whether a poem "should not mean / But be," there is a prior question. Is it valid to debate the truth or falsity of something said in a poem? Can a poem tell the truth? Can a poem lie?

Historically, it has been assumed that poetry indeed can lie. This assumption stems from the writings of Plato, in Book X of *The Republic*, and has put poetry and poets on the defensive ever since.

Plato wished poetry banned from the Republic because the poet "stimulates and strengthens an element which undermines the reason." [2] He supports this contention by noting the poet's place in a hierarchy of three levels of being. The highest level is the ideal or essential truth created by a god. Next comes man's approximation of truth, the representation of the ideal or essential, which is made by a craftsman. At the third level is the work of a poet, a sorry creature who can only make a representation of the representation. Using a bed as his example, Plato argues that the ideal or essential bed is that which exists in the mind; the one we lie on is that made by a carpenter; and the one written about is that of the poet. Poetry then is "at the third remove from the essential nature of the thing" and "a long way from reality." [3]

---

[1] See Donald Stauffer, in Francis X. Connolly, *Poetry: Its Power and Wisdom* (New York: Charles Scribner's Sons, 1960), p. 69.
[2] *The Republic*, trans. Francis MacDonald Cornford (New York: Oxford University Press, 1945), p. 331.
[3] Ibid., pp. 327–28.

The poet is therefore a liar. Although Plato is too genteel to use that term, he does speak strongly:

> We may conclude, then, that all poetry, from Homer on-wards, consists in representing a semblance of its subject, whatever it may be ... the poet, knowing nothing more than how to represent appearances, can paint in words his picture of any craftsman so as to impress an audience which is equally ignorant and judges only by the form of expression.... Strip what the poet has to say of its po-etical colouring, and I think you must have seen what it comes to in plain prose. It is like a face which was never really handsome, when it has lost the fresh bloom of youth.[4]

The falseness of poetry leads to excessive emotion, which is debilitating, appeals to what is weak in man, even "womanish":

> We have, then, a fair case against the poet and we may set him down as the counterpart of the painter, whom he resembles in two ways: his creations are poor things by the standard of truth and reality, and his appeal is not to the highest part of the soul, but to one which is equally inferior.[5]

Reason is the sphere of truth and the ideal; poetry, being false, appeals to the passions, watering their growth until they, like weeds in a hitherto productive garden, destroy pos-sibilities of fruitfulness. The "goodness and happiness of our lives," according to Plato, depend on the passions' "being held in subjection." Clinching his argument, Plato reminds us that philosophy (truth) has always been opposed to poetry:

> But, lest poetry should convict us of being harsh and un-mannerly, let us tell her further that there is a long-standing quarrel between poetry and philosophy.[6]

Given the opposition of philosophy and poetry invoked by Plato, it is interesting to see that another famous rational philosopher, John Stuart Mill, undertook to defend poetry.

[4] Ibid., p. 331.
[5] Ibid., p. 336.
[6] Ibid., p. 339.

Mill's fame as a logician is legendary; in his autobiography, he tells how at age twelve his proudest accomplishment was dissecting a bad argument, discovering where the fallacy lay. As a logician, he, like Plato, finds philosophy and poetry in opposition:

> By logic . . . I mean the antithesis of Poetry or Art: in which distinction I am meaning to perceive a twofold contrast: the *literal* as opposed to the *symbolical*, and *reasoning* as opposed to *intuition*. Not the *theory* of reasoning but the *practice*. In reasoning I include all processes of thought which are *processes* at all, that is, which proceed by a series of steps or links.[7]

This hardly looks like a defense of poetry; Mill seems to be denying the poet reason; the poet cannot put two ideas together by "steps or links." Since Mill allies the poet and the painter as men who have "a tendency to conceive things in pictures . . . richly clothed in attributes and circumstances," precisely as Plato had done, there is good reason to wonder just what kind of "defense" this will be.

Departing from Plato, Mill defends the poet on the basis of human feelings:

> Let our philosophical system be what it may, human feelings exist: human nature, with all its enjoyments and sufferings, its strugglings, its victories and defeats, still remain[s] to us; and these are the materials of all poetry. Whoever, in the greatest concerns of human life, pursues truth with unbiased feelings, and an intellect adequate to discern it, will not find the resources of poetry are lost to him because he has learned to use and not to abuse them. They are as open to him as to the sentimental weaklings, who have no test of the true but the ornamental. And when he once has them under his command, he can wield them for purposes, and with a power, of which neither the dilettante nor the visionary have the slightest conception.[8]

[7] *Earlier Letters*, ed. Francis E. Mineka, in *Collected Works*, vol. 12 (Toronto: University of Toronto Press, 1963), p. 173.
[8] "Tennyson's Poems," in J. W. Gibbs, ed., *Early Essays* (London: G. Bell and Sons, 1897), pp. 266–67.

As its defender, Mill is nonetheless wary of poetry. If he were not, why the mention of the "sentimental weaklings," and the emphasis on using but not abusing poetry (as if it were some sort of minor vice)? On the whole, though, Mill affirms poetry's humanizing power. We might wonder how Mill, starting from virtually the same premises as Plato, could reach such different conclusions.

The answer lies in Mill's life story and the role poetry played in it. As a young man, Mill experienced a severe intellectual and emotional crisis. All his skill as a logician was doing him no good; in fact, it was wearing away his feelings. He felt he was losing touch with humanity. Desperate, he turned to poetry, and in Wordsworth found expressions of beauty that were medicinal. Poetry rescued Mill from the abyss created by his devotion to analysis and logic. Later, he had to defend poetry even if he could not reconcile it with philosophy.

Mill does not so much deny that the poet tells lies, as praise the salubrious effect of the poet on mankind, lies notwithstanding. In this sense, the difference between Plato and Mill is simply one of degree. For Plato, poetry lies, and the lies are pernicious; for Mill, there are lies in poetry, but these are "white lies," exaggerations undertaken in the service of beauty.

In our day, philosophy has been replaced by science as the domain of truth; but poetry is still the odd man out. We divide learning into the arts and sciences; and of the arts, poetry is the least respectable. Anyone who doubts this needs merely to inquire how many schools and universities have poets on their faculties and, of those that do, how many treat their poet-teachers as regular faculty, entitled to rank and tenure privileges. Worse yet, how many English departments are not guilty of dealing with the creative arts generally and poetry specifically as interlopers? Creative writing, the practice of the art, is generally considered—from Harvard to Berkeley—as a lesser activity within the English department. "Knowledge" resides not in writing poetry, but in being a literary historian steeped in facts and chronology. Even the defenders of poetry are too often uneasy; like Mill, they profess a "weakness" for poetry, a susceptibility. Or what is even less helpful, they—like those mentioned in the first chapter—aggrandize and mystify poetry; it becomes a magic practiced by sorcerers. The poet on the faculty is encouraged to be "colorful," and is viewed with a mixture of awe and bemused tolerance.

In the world outside the university, poetry is no less suspect. To discover that someone writes poetry comes as a surprise and makes him at least a little strange. Eugene McCarthy, as a presidential aspirant, revealed to the press that he wrote poems. He was already an anomalous candidate for president, and poetry-writing added to his unsuitability, to his image as the impractical dreamer. That some of his poems were displayed in major magazines did not improve his chances of being elected.

We know that volumes of poetry rarely if ever make the best seller list. Nor are they selected by the Book-of-the-Month Club. The average literate American, choosing a book on a winter evening, is almost sure to find what he is looking for in a novel. In fact, most readers would rather read anything than poetry.

None of this is to say, "Poor poetry, neglected stepchild of the literary world!" Nor do I mean to indict as philistine schools, universities, and the reading public. These observations point not toward accusation or chastisement but toward genuinely perplexing questions that need to be pursued in establishing a working poetic: What is it about poetry that sets it apart from other literature? Why is it that poetry isn't read by people who read newspapers, novels, and biographies? Why has poetry, historically, been the object of attack and defense as no other genre of literature?

Condensed, these questions become one: What are the distinguishing characteristics of poetry? The question does not admit of an easy answer, and no definition per se will do. Defining poetry, the first chapter in many a textbook, is an exercise in futility. For example, "A poem is a formal structure in which many elements operate at the same time." [9] Or, "Poetry is a form of speech, written or spoken." [10] Suppose someone said to you, "Define Carla, your closest friend." I hope you would reject the task as ridiculous. "Describe Carla," is a more reasonable request. Definition stultifies; it makes rigid

[9] John Ciardi, *How Does a Poem Mean?* (Boston: Houghton Mifflin, 1959), p. 1.
[10] Cleanth Brooks and Robert Penn Warren, *Understanding Poetry* (New York: Holt, Rinehart and Winston, 1960), p. 1.

that which is fluid, it treats as product that which is process. We might be able to describe poetry—as difficult a task as describing the complexities and the mobile characteristics of a person—but we shall not set out to define it.

Where to begin? In this instance, the obvious is also the best: poetry uses words, and a discussion of poetics ought to begin with this fact. Because all literature, including poetry, uses words as its medium, poetry in effect has no medium of its own. The painter, the sculptor, the musical composer, all have established, discrete media with which they work. Currently, many artists are creating new media—a painter I know of experiments with vegetable juices on wrapping paper, a sculptor shapes gargantuan mounds of earth, a composer arranges electronic bleeps. But whether they use the media traditionally associated with their art or create new media (or, as has become common, mix media), there is in each instance a medium capable of being separated from the everyday communications of men. Not so the poet: he began centuries ago with words of common usage and has continued to use such words to make poems. It thus becomes all the more perplexing to observe the status of poetry among the arts.

We can only conclude that what the poet does with words is very different from what other people—even other literary artists, like novelists or playwrights—do with words. But if the poet's use of words is so different, how can he also be, as I contended in the first chapter, a man speaking to other men?

Our investigation of these questions can begin with a study of the poetics of Coleridge, the first modern aesthetician. Like Plato and Mill, Coleridge seeks to describe the workings of poetry; unlike them, and unlike most of his predecessors, Coleridge has no axe to grind—his is neither a defense nor an attack. And he brings a panoply of skills—as poet, critic, psychologist, and philosopher—to his conversations about poetry. Most important, Coleridge does not start with the effect of poetry on men's morals; he begins with the making of poetry and proceeds to discuss how it works as art, not as moral philosophy.

The poet himself is the nucleus of Coleridge's discussions. For him, "What is poetry? is so nearly the same question with, what is a poet? that the answer to the one is involved in the solution of the other." [11]

The first characteristic of the poet and poetry that Coleridge identifies is excitement. The quality of excitement—in the poet as he writes, in the poem, in the person reading—sets the language of poetry apart from other uses of language: "The very assumption that we are reading the work of a poet supposes that he is in a continuous state of excitement; and thereby arises a language in prose unnatural, but in poetry natural." [12] The reader becomes aware of "that pleasurable emotion, that peculiar state and degree of excitement that arises in the poet himself in the act of composition." [13]

We can be happy that Coleridge does not confront us with a definition. Nor does he identify features of the poem-as-object: its meter, subject matter, figurative language, or stanzaic form. He discusses the poem as a process in which the poet and reader participate.

"Excitement" in Coleridge's lexicon becomes more significant as he equates it with passion:

> Now poetry . . . does always imply PASSION: which word must be here understood in its general sense, as an excited state of feelings or faculties. And as every passion has its proper pulse, so will it likewise have its characteristic modes of expression. But where there exists that degree of genius and talent, which entitles a writer to aim at the honors of a poet, the very *act* of poetic composition *itself* is, and is *allowed* to imply and to produce an unusual state of excitement, which of course justifies and demands a correspondent difference of language, as truly, though not perhaps in as marked a degree, as the excitement of love, fear, rage, or jealousy. [14]

All men are capable of excitement, of passion. A man becomes a poet when he is able to convey his passion to another

[11] Samuel Taylor Coleridge, *Biographia Literaria*, ed. George Watson (London: J. M. Dent, 1917, 1956), p. 564.
[12] Samuel Taylor Coleridge, *Coleridge's Shakespearean Criticism*, ed. Thomas Middleton Raysor, vol. 2 (Cambridge, Mass.: Harvard University Press, 1930), pp. 67–68.
[13] Ibid., p. 77.
[14] Coleridge, *Biographia Literaria*, p. 564.

through language. No, he must do more than "convey"—that term sounds too much like simple transport. The poet's use of language, language "correspondent" with his emotion, must be capable of re-creating the emotion within the reader. The poet's is an "unusual statement of excitement," but not a mysterious or unearthly passion: Coleridge carefully points out that the poet's emotion is like the excitement of our most basic emotions.

Coleridge's poetics contain contradictions. He is pulled on one side by a democratic impulse, and does not wish to set the poet apart from other men. The poet's passion can be shared by all of us; poetry can be understood by "the principles of grammar, logic, psychology and *good sense.*" Yet Coleridge also describes the poet as a man possessing "vision and the faculty divine," a species of demigod.

Whether the poet is demigod, man among men, or both, his work cannot be sustained solely by passion. Coleridge recognizes this, and broadens his characterization of poetry to include not only the poet's excitement but also his craftsmanship:

> [Poetry] is the art of communicating whatever we wish to communicate, so as to express and produce *excitement,* but for the purpose of immediate pleasure; and each part is *fitted to afford as much pleasure,* as is compatible with the largest sum of the whole.[15]

The emphasis in that passage is mine, to underscore the dual nature of the poet's work and hence poetry. As we discovered empirically in the first chapter, after the burst of creative excitement in writing a poem, comes a time of slower, painstaking weighing and balancing of words. The words unleashed initially, no matter how emotion-laden they may be, may not be the right words. The poem is not fulfilled, we said, unless it is precise.

Our notion of precision, based on the process of writing the poem, was that of realized intentions, in which the poet's and the reader's apprehension of the poem become one. Coleridge describes this phenomenon somewhat differently, and refines our thinking about the "right" word or line in a

[15] Coleridge, *Coleridge's Shakespearean Criticism,* vol. 2, pp. 67–68.

poem. It's right, he says, if it is absolutely untranslatable, if it could not be replaced by any other word:

> In poetry, in which every line, every phrase, may pass the ordeal of deliberation and deliberate choice, it is possible, and barely possible, to attain that ultimate which I have ventured to propose as the infallible test of the blameless style; its *untranslatableness* in words of the same language without injury to the meaning. Be it observed, however, that I include in the *meaning* of a word not only its correspondent object, but likewise all the associations which it recalls.[16]

The key sentence is the last. Coleridge is not speaking simply of denotative meaning ("dog" is the right word because the poem requires reference to a four-legged hunting companion of man), but of the cluster of connotations or associations that orbit around the word ("dog" is right because it connotes a certain kind of loyalty, submission, manginess, or whatever). The poem will be precise and untranslatable when any other word would evoke associations detrimental to the whole.

Think of the opening lines of T. S. Eliot's "The Love Song of J. Alfred Prufrock" (see p. 189).

> Let us go then, you and I,
> When the evening is spread out against the sky
> Like a patient etherized upon a table

Would "night" do as well as "evening"? Would "cast across" reasonably replace "spread out"? Could "sick man" be substituted for "patient," or "anesthetized" for "etherized"? If a reader accepts any of these possible substitutions (or thinks of others that would suffice), then for him the poem is not working. I will go further: it is not truly a poem (for that reader) if it or any part of it can be translated into other words.

For me, these lines are perfect. In Coleridge's terms, I find that they, as a part of a larger whole, "pass the ordeal of deliberation and deliberate choice"—none of the words I suggested can be substituted for those chosen by Eliot. "Evening"

[16] Ibid., p. 611.

is right because it suggests an eerie half-light, a foreboding of total darkness. "Night" would be too absolute, too black; nothing could be seen across a pitch-black sky. "Spread out" reminds me of torture by spread-eagling a victim; it also connotes a kind of passivity—for example, jam is spread; it doesn't spread itself. "Cast across" would lose these suggestions and bring in less desirable ones like a fisherman casting his line, or bread cast upon the waters. The poem needs the irrevocable anonymity of "patient." We don't know the gender nor the particular illness of a "patient"; "sick man" would be too explicit. The "patient" could and should be anyone-everyone, not a particular person. One can have a *local* anesthetic; and "anesthetic" has certain positive, healing connotations. "Etherized," on the other hand, is total in its effect on a human being and sinister in its explicit gaseous nature—therefore it is the superior choice.

Such word-by-word testing of the poem by no means accounts for its total effectiveness. But it serves to corroborate Coleridge's assertion that one important characteristic of poetry is its untranslatableness. And I might add that I am speaking of *all* poetry, not just lyric poetry, for example, nor of poetry of a specific historical period. The test of untranslatableness can be put to the first four lines of Shakespeare's Sonnet 73 (see p. 192) as well as to the poetry of T. S. Eliot.

> That time of year thou mayst in me behold
> When yellow leaves, or none, or few, do hang
> Upon those boughs which shake against the cold,
> Bare ruined choirs, where late the sweet birds sang.

Try "season" for "time," "ochre" for "yellow," "shudder" for "shake," or "once" for "late." Meter and rhyme introduce new strictures on the choices made, but the test of untranslatability remains valid.

Having railed against the proclivity of many critics to define poetry, what can I say as we come to what Coleridge calls his "final definition"? First, that I wish he had called this a description instead of a definition; but that seems petty. Besides, it is a definition. Its saving grace as a definition is, I think, that Coleridge formulates it not at the outset, but midway through his poetics, long after he has described, through the poetic process, how language in poetry differs from its other uses. Also, there is nothing "final" at all about the definition. It is a marking point, a summing up of observations so far; Coleridge goes on to say much more about poetry. Here it is:

> The final definition then, so deduced, may be thus worded. A poem is that species of composition, which is opposed to the works of science, by proposing for its *immediate* object pleasure, not truth; and from all other species (having *this* object in common with it) it is discriminated by proposing to itself such delight from the *whole*, as is compatible with distinct gratification from each component *part*.[17]

This is a difficult passage. However, unlike poetry, it *is* translatable into different words in the same language. First, Coleridge opposes poetry and science, following the line of reasoning expounded by both Plato and Mill. It is the business of science to reveal and assert truth, hard facts. Truth is secondary or incidental to poetry. Since Coleridge emphasizes that truth is not poetry's *"immediate* object," I take him to mean that there is no reason why poetry cannot be true; but truth is not its prime concern. Coleridge leaves open the issue of the truth or falsity of poetry; in effect he does not belabor the matter, except to propose that poetry must, above all, achieve pleasure.

The latter part of the passage distinguishes poetry from other "species" that also propose pleasure as their object (I think of plays or the novel in this context) and argues that poetry differs in the degree of precision it must attain.

We have discussed poetry's precision thoroughly enough to translate these remarks liberally. My interpretation is that they mean that poetry is all style. We cannot say of a poem, as we can of a novel, "The writing style leaves something to be desired, but it is a powerful work of art"—the kind of statement that can, for example, apply to the work of Theodore Dreiser or Thomas Wolfe. The very fact that we comment on a novelist's writing style at all, positively or negatively, indicates that it is a quality of his art separable from the whole. (One of my favorite remarks on style is attributed to Alfred Kazin,

[17] Ibid., p. 557.

talking about Norman Mailer: "Mailer is as fond of his style as an Italian tenor is of his vocal cords.") We cannot speak of a poet's style. A poet cannot be a good stylist or a poor stylist: if his writing style is not good, he cannot make a poem, for a poem is all style. And since it is *all* style, a poem's every part, down to the last word, must be precise.

Being all style, a poem is not *only* style, I hasten to add. Style is one way of describing the precision of poetry; and precision, in turn, is one of three characteristics Coleridge identifies. Passion, a continuous undercurrent of feeling in the poem, and the pleasure to be derived from the poem are the other two.

A shortcoming in Coleridge's analysis of poetry is that he never adequately describes how and why poetry gives pleasure. Coleridge has often misled critics on this point because he does discuss how and why meter, specifically, creates pleasurable response. Meter has the capacity "to increase the vivacity and susceptibility both of the general feelings and of the attention" by producing "the continued excitement of surprise" and "the quick reciprocations of curiosity still gratified and still re-excited." [18] This description is rightly famous; nowhere else in literary criticism do we find such a succinct and perceptive account of meter in poetry.

But meter is not, according to Coleridge, a fundamental attribute of poetry. Not only do his descriptions of how poetry works make no mention of meter, but his debate with Wordsworth (which we shall examine shortly) manifestly declares that Coleridge considers meter to be a device of poetry (like rhyme) rather than one of its essential characteristics.

The assumption that Coleridge defines poetry in terms of meter is widely enough held to deserve explicit rebuttal. One critic tells us that "Coleridge expressly defines a poem in such a way as to make meter an essential attribute." [19] This contention is supported by the same "final definition" we have just discussed, and in which we find no mention of meter. It is simply not the case that Coleridge considers meter to be "an essential attribute" of poetry.

Critics have also devoted some attention to the seeming paradox of Coleridge's argument that the poet and poetry are

[18] Ibid., pp. 558–59.
[19] M. H. Abrams, *The Mirror and the Lamp* (New York: Oxford University Press, 1953), p. 117.

at once excited and precise. They argue that emotion and intellect (excitement and precision) are never fully reconciled in Coleridge's poetics. Coleridge is accused of having bequeathed to later generations of literary critics a "fatal legacy" of indecision.[20] And we hear that Coleridge, by using "two controlling analogues, one of a machine, the other of a plant [divided] the process and products of art into two distinct kinds." [21]

Coleridge, however, contends that the poet is able to reconcile "a more than usual state of emotion with more than usual order":

> The poet ... brings the whole soul of man into activity, with the subordination of its faculties to each other, according to their relative worth and dignity. He diffuses a tone and spirit of unity, that blends, and (as it were) *fuses*, each into each, by that synthetic and magical power, to which we have exclusively appropriated the name of imagination. This power ... reveals itself in the balance of reconciliation of opposite or discordant qualities: of sameness, with difference; of the general, with the concrete; the idea, with the image; the individual, with the representative; the sense of novelty and freshness, with old and familiar objects; a more than usual state of emotion, with more than usual order.[22]

There is, it seems to me, only one way to verify Coleridge's description of the poet's synthesizing capability. Write a poem. The experience of making a poem brings the faculties of which Coleridge speaks into play. A self-conscious analysis of the act of making the poem will reveal whether in fact opposites are reconciled, whether the imagination balances discordant qualities. To speak of how the poet-poem works without working on a poem is speculation, armchair poetics.

Coleridge's debate with Wordsworth forces him to assert his poetic vigorously and explicitly, for each man was both a poet and an aesthetician, and each was fully convinced that he was accurately revealing the essence of poetry.

In addition, not only were Coleridge and Wordsworth

---

[20] Alan Tate, *Reason in Madness* (New York: G. P. Putnam's Sons, 1941), p. 51.
[21] Abrams, *The Mirror and the Lamp*, p. 176.
[22] *Biographia Literaria*, p. 524.

friends and colleagues who understood each other well, but they shared a desire to liberate poetry from the sway of clever but not truly passionate practitioners. Wordsworth insists that poetry be made of the "language really used by men":

> Such a language, arising out of repeated experience and regular feelings, is a more permanent, and a far more philosophical language, than that which is frequently substituted for it by poets, who think that they are conferring honour upon themselves and their art in proportion as they separate themselves from the sympathies of men, and indulge in arbitrary and capricious habits of expression, in order to furnish food for fickle taste and fickle appetites of their own creation.[23]

Speaking to the same point, Coleridge advises that "the passion and passionate flow of poetry" must not be subordinated to the "subtleties of intellect." Coleridge's "subtleties of intellect"—intellect divorced from feeling—and Wordsworth's "arbitrary and capricious habits of expression" are virtually the same.

Coleridge and Wordsworth worked so closely together over so many years that at first Coleridge could only half sense that there was a fundamental difference between them concerning the nature of poetry. Wordsworth declares his poetic in the "Preface" to his *Lyrical Ballads*, of which Coleridge says in a letter to the poet Robert Southey, "Although Wordsworth's 'Preface' is half a child of my own brain, [I] rather suspect that somewhere or other there is a radical difference in our theoretical opinions concerning poetry; this I shall endeavor to get to the bottom of." [24]

The "radical difference" lies in how the two men perceived the function of meter in poetry. For Wordsworth, it is meter which makes poetry:

> It would be a most easy task to prove to [the reader] that not only the language of a large portion of every good poem, even of the most elevated character, must necessarily,

---

[23] "Preface 1800" (to the edition of the *Lyrical Ballads*), *The Poems of Wordsworth*, ed. Andrew J. George (Boston: Houghton Mifflin, 1932), p. 791.

[24] Abrams, *The Mirror and the Lamp*, p. 116, quoting *The Letters of Samuel Taylor Coleridge* (London, 1950), pp. 386–87.

except with reference to the metre, in no respect differ from that of good prose, but likewise that some of the most interesting parts of the poems will be found to be strictly the language of prose when prose is well written.[25]

Even without my added emphasis, the meaning of this passage is clear. Wordsworth tells us that the only thing that distinguishes poetry from anything else well written is meter.

Before considering Wordsworth's supporting argument, I suggest we try out his contention for ourselves. If what he says is true, we should be able to make a poem by taking a well-written prose passage and arranging it so that the lines become metrical. I will work with a paragraph from the "Foreword" of Robert Coles' *Children of Crisis:*

I can still feel myself standing there, benighted, frightened, seized with curiosity, suddenly quite restless. I was not morally outraged. I did not want to join in the Negroes' protest for equal access to the essentially useless, shallow bit of seashore. Eventually, I simply wanted to go away; and I did. Riding home I condemned *all* the antagonists—for fighting, for choosing to fight for such absurd stakes, for being the kind of people who *would* fight. I am not now very proud of those minutes. Yet if I forgot them, I would be even more ashamed.[26]

Good prose. I shall try for trochaic meter; the accent falling on the first syllable of each two-syllable foot. Each line will have three feet, and should sound approximately like this: DA dum DA dum DA dum. (Some of course will not fit the pattern exactly.)

I can still feel myself
standing there, benighted,
frightened, seized with curiosity,
suddenly quite restless.

I was not morally
outraged. I did not want
to join in the Negroes'

[25] "Preface 1800," p. 792.
[26] *Children of Crisis* (New York: Delta Publishing, 1964), p. 5.

> protest for equal access
> to that essentially useless,
> shallow bit of seashore.
>
> Eventually, I simply
> wanted to go away;
> and I did. Riding home I
> condemned *all* the antagonists—
> for fighting, for choosing
> to fight for such absurd
> stakes, for being the kind
> of people who *would* fight.
>
> I am not now very
> proud of those minutes. Yet
> if I forgot them, I
> would be even more ashamed.

My metrical success is modest at best; I had some difficulty realizing the rhythm I attempted. Certain words, like "curiosity," do not yield readily to the demands of superimposed meter. I also took some liberty in breaking the passage into four stanzas. Despite the hazards of the enterprise, Coles' prose passage does emerge metrical, and looks on the page very much like a poem. Is it therefore a poem?

Wordsworth takes a different tack to demonstrate that poetry is essentially good prose made metrical. He starts with a poem, rather than prose, and attempts to show that certain lines in the poem, except for their metrical form, are no different from prose. Using a sonnet by Thomas Gray, Wordsworth emphasizes those lines on which he bases his case.

> In vain to me the smiling mornings shine,
> And reddening Phoebus lifts his golden fire;
> The birds in vain their amorous descant join,
> Or cheerful fields resume their green attire.
> These ears, alas! for other notes repine;
> *A different object do these eyes require;*
> *My lonely anguish melts no heart but mine;*
> *And in my breast the imperfect joys expire.*
> Yet morning smiles the busy race to cheer,
> And newborn pleasure brings to happier men:
> The fields to all their wonted tribute bear,
> To warm their little loves the birds complain.

> *I fruitless mourn to him that cannot hear,*
> *And weep the more because I weep in vain.*

The "only part of this Sonnet, which is of any value, is the lines printed in italics," says Wordsworth, and "except in the rhyme, and in the use of the single word 'fruitless' for 'fruitlessly,' which is so far a defect, the language of these lines does in no respect differ from that of prose." [27] Knowing what we do of Wordsworth's objections to affected, artificial writing, we can understand his condemnation of high-flown phrases like "reddening Phoebus" and "amorous descant." We can also imagine why he objects to notes that "repine" and fields that "resume their green attire." In fact, we might agree that the lines Wordsworth italicizes are the best in the poem; but that is not to say that they are best because they in no way differ from the language of prose.

Wordsworth, however, is so convinced of the correctness of his view that he rushes to generalization. What holds for the lines of this sonnet holds for all poetry:

> We will go further. It may be safely affirmed that there neither is, nor can be, any *essential* difference between the language of prose and metrical composition. [28]

Coleridge counters that the issue is not whether this or that sequence of words can occur in prose as well as poetry— "The true question must be, whether there are not modes of expression, a *construction* and an *order* of sentences, which are in their fit and natural place in a serious prose composition, but would be disproportionate and heterogeneous in metrical poetry; and vice versa. [29] By "construction" and "order," I take Coleridge to mean diction and syntax. And he later remarks on figures of speech that work in poetry but weaken prose.

Fully appreciative of the powerful effects of meter, Coleridge still insists that it is not the defining characteristic of poetry:

> For any *poetic* purpose, metre resembles (if the aptness of the simile may excuse its meanness) yeast, worthless

[27] "Preface 1800," p. 793.
[28] Ibid., p. 793.
[29] *Biographia Literaria*, pp. 556–57.

or disagreeable by itself, but giving vivacity and spirit to the liquor with which it is proportionally combined.[30]

The "liquor" is the language of poetry, as it were, *before* meter —it can be enlivened by meter, but requires for its essence other ingredients. Coleridge had no way of anticipating what we now call "free verse" (poetry that has no formal meter although, like all poetry, it is rhythmic). Yet his apprehension of the function of meter in poetry is almost prophetic of free verse. If one believes that free verse is true poetry, it is, in the terms of Coleridge's analogy, like bread made without yeast— but it is genuine bread nonetheless.

In the sense that it relies on broadly conceived notions of passion, precision, and the achievement of pleasure, Coleridge's poetic is less definitive than Wordsworth's. No matter how fully we may explore what Coleridge intends by his three criteria, we can never reduce them to a formula, to strict definition (although "precision equated with untranslatableness" approaches a definition). Wordsworth, in contrast, offers a formula: poetry is the speech of men, or good prose, made metrical. Clear formulation has its appeal; Wordsworth, seduced by a basically narrow view, overestimated its validity.

It is clear to me that Coleridge's poetic is more profound than Wordsworth's. Moreover, Coleridge's poetic is a major advance in the study of poetry. Although he does not question the old dichotomy between poetry and science (or philosophy), Coleridge is the first aesthetician to go beyond classification and defense-attack strategies and into a study of the dynamics of poetry. He considers language, and the way language is used in poetry, as a way of understanding poetry. It is Coleridge whom we can credit with the concept of a special use of language as the distinguishing feature of poetry. Further, the use of language in poetry as Coleridge conceives it does not comprise the usual classification of surface features: figures of speech, similes, rhyme, and so forth. Coleridge is a geologist, not a cartologist; he takes core samplings of the ore of poetry and finds that beneath the surface are special emotional qualities infused in the language that makes poetry.

For all his insights, Coleridge leaves us with a dilemma.

He does not adequately describe the pleasure we receive from poetry. Granted that the pleasure of which he speaks is more profound than what would bring a smile to our faces; granted, also, that the aim of poetry is pleasure insofar as poetry, unlike an auto mechanic's manual or a scientific treatise, is not "useful" and does not lead to "results," yet we must still ask what is meant by the particular kind of pleasure attributed to poetry. The effect of poetry has been damned by Plato, exalted by Mill, and singled out as a uniquely created pleasure by Coleridge—understanding how poetry works requires that we explore this particular idea of pleasure further.

I should remark that for those who agree with Wordsworth, Frost, and others that meter is essential to poetry, the task of understanding poetry's effect is more straightforward. A convincing poetic can be based on life rhythms—the seasons, days, heartbeats, rhythms of speech—within which the meter of poetry embodies a condensation, a focusing and organizing form that gratifies our ear and pulse because it articulates, replicates, and transforms that which is already necessary and pleasurable to us. Those of us who believe meter is the yeast but not the grain of poetry have a more difficult task before us.

Modern aestheticians, inheritors of Coleridge's legacy, have based their work on the same bipartite philosophy of language: on the one hand, there is the language of science, made up of facts, asserting truths; on the other, the language of poetry, emotional and, while not necessarily false, certainly not responsible for truth in the same way as is the language of science. The poetic use of language is not usually restricted to poetry, but includes emotional language generally. It is symptomatic of the general perception of poetry that poetry is singled out as the repository of emotional language. The term "poetic language" can encompass everything from vivid writing to epithets.

The division of language into two functions becomes repetitive in modern aesthetic theory, but if we attend to how each aesthetician defines the two kinds of language use, we inch closer to an understanding of how the language of poetry affects the respondent.

Here is C. K. Ogden and I. A. Richards' account of language use, from *The Meaning of Meaning:*

A twofold division of language function is convenient, the division being between the *symbolic* use of words and the *emotive* use. The symbolic use of words is statement; the recording, the support, the organization and the communication of references. The emotive use of words is a more simple matter, it is the use of words to express or excite feelings and attitudes.[31]

In *Aesthetics,* Monroe C. Beardsley diagrams the two ways language works (creates meaning):

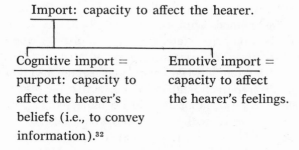

Import: capacity to affect the hearer.

Cognitive import =	Emotive import =
purport: capacity to	capacity to affect
affect the hearer's	the hearer's feelings.
beliefs (i.e., to convey	
information).[32]	

And Kenneth Burke, in *The Philosophy of Literary Form,* gives examples of semantic as contrasted with poetic meaning:

> Semantic meaning would be a way of pointing to a chair. It would say, "That thing is a chair." And to a carpenter it would imply, in keeping with his organized technique, "By doing such and such, I can produce this thing, a chair." Poetic pointing, on the other hand, might take many courses, roughly summed up in these three sentences:
>
> "Faugh! a chair!"
> "Ho, ho!! a chair!"
> "Might I call your attention to yon chair?"
>
> Of these, the third style of pointing obviously comes nearest to the semantic ideal. The first two, most strongly

[31] *The Meaning of Meaning,* 4th ed., rev. (London: K. Paul, Trench, Trubner & Co., 1936), p. 149.
[32] *Aesthetics* (New York: Harcourt Brace Jovanovich, 1958), p. 118.

weighted with emotional values, with *attitudes*, would be farther off.[33]

Symbolic and emotive use of language, cognitive and emotive import, semantic and poetic meaning—these are various ways of saying the same thing: meaning in language comprises two modes, factual and emotional. The structure of this theory no longer interests us, except historically. The details and nuances are what count.

Even in the brief excerpts quoted, we should note that the division is not simply between fact and feeling, but hints at a contrast between a more passive and a more active role on the part of the reader. With Ogden and Richards, words used symbolically comprise statement and recording, whereas the emotive use of words *excites* feelings and attitudes. In Beardsley, the distinction between beliefs and feelings is a distinction between the relatively static and the active faculties: beliefs are *held*, feelings cannot be. Burke underscores "attitudes" that are contrasted with beliefs and knowledge; later in the same passage Burke says that "an attitude contains an implicit program of action."

Here are further samples from the three poetic theories:

OGDEN AND RICHARDS: The difference between the two uses of language may be ... exactly characterized as follows: In symbolic speech the essential considerations are the correctness of symbolization and the truth of references. In evocative [emotive] speech the essential consideration is the character of the attitude aroused.[34]

BEARDSLEY: Two basic types of import are to be distinguished. On the one hand the linguistic expression may have a tendency to cause certain beliefs.... On the other hand, the linguistic expression may have a tendency to evoke certain feelings or emotions in the hearer. This capacity I shall call its *emotive import*. For example, among a certain group of people, an Anglo-Saxon four-letter word may tend to arouse a feeling of horrified shock or disgust;

[33] *The Philosophy of Literary Form*, rev. ed. (New York: Vintage Books, 1957), p. 125.
[34] *The Meaning of Meaning*, p. 239.

certain sentences about Home, Mother, or Alma Mater may tend to arouse a warm glow of affection.[35]

BURKE: The semantic ideal would attempt to *get a description* by the *elimination* of attitude. The poetic ideal would attempt to *attain a full moral act* by attaining a perspective *atop all the conflicts of attitude.*[36]

Burke is the most explicit, but the same emphasis pervades the other theories and leads to a consensus on the poetic itself: language used emotively (poetry is the prime example of this) requires an activity different at least in degree and perhaps in kind from that required by language used symbolically.

We may tentatively conclude that the special pleasure created by poetry is a function of this activity.

One question leads to another (we must have faith in the existence of a bull's-eye if we are to aim at increasingly smaller circles). If the pleasure of poetry may be a function of the particular kind of activity created by language as it is used in poetry, what is this activity?

It is the *making of meaning*. Using Burke's chair example, we can ask, "When told, 'That thing is a chair,' what is there for the hearer to do himself?" Very little. The object is named; the utterance is a statement of fact. If the hearer is confronted by "Faugh! a chair!" there is a great deal he must do to give the utterance meaning. He must be attentive to the facial expression and the tone of voice of the speaker, to the object designated (if there is one)—to the total context of the utterance as well as the utterance itself (what does *faugh* mean?). In sum, the hearer must make meaning out of "Faugh! a chair!" He, as well as the speaker, is responsible for realizing the intentions of the utterance.

What makes meaning of "To be, or not to be—that is the question"? Shakespeare? Hamlet? *Hamlet*, the play? The reader? All four?

It would appear that a considerable share of "meaning-making" in poetry is borne by the reader. The activity is called forth by language that evokes rather than asserts, bringing into play what the aestheticians call attitudes. The activity

[35] *Aesthetics*, p. 117.
[36] *The Philosophy of Literary Form*, p. 128.

is given momentum by "how many and how different may be the tendencies awakened by a situation, and what scope there is for conflict, suppression and interplay," according to Richards,[37] or "the maximum *heaping up* of all these emotional factors, playing them off against one another, and seeking to make this active participation itself a major ingredient of the vision," as Burke puts it.[38] Beardsley defines literature as discourse in which "an important part of the meaning is implicit" and it is the "language of poetry," of all literary genres, in which implicit meaning "is most fully actualized."[39] Implicit meaning creates a "semantic thickness," according to Beardsley: in plumbing the strata of this thickness, the reader must contend with a variety of meanings, each championing its own supremacy. The process is as difficult and as pleasurable as growth:

> Hence the experience of coming to understand a literary discourse is a kind of growth; not, as with a simple symbolism, that either we have it or we don't, but a matter of more or less, of depth or shallowness. *All this is especially true of poetry.*[40]

The modern aestheticians all evince a change of tone. They may accept the bipartite division of language function that characterized earlier poetic theory, but they do not accept the defensive posture of their predecessors. Poetry does not "tell the truth" in the same way as other discourse, but this is hardly cause for apology. Richards and Burke go so far as to initiate offensive action, asserting that the "truth" of poetry is more essential and the repository of a more powerful morality than that of science and other endeavors that use language symbolically or referentially.

In *Science and Poetry*, Richards warns that "reliance on scientific, symbolic statements is one of the great new dangers to which civilization is exposed.... [The truths of poetry] about human nature, the relations of mind to mind, about the soul, its rank and destiny... which are pivotal points in the

---

[37] *Principles of Literary Criticism* (London: K. Paul, Trench, Trubner & Co., 1925), p. 48.
[38] *The Philosophy of Literary Form*, p. 128.
[39] *Aesthetics*, pp. 125–26.
[40] Ibid., p. 129 (emphasis added).

organization of the mind, to its well being, have suddenly become, for sincere, honest and informed minds, impossible to believe." [41]

Burke's contention is similar but more specific. We need attitudes, mental and emotional turmoil, to reach moral vantage points; the language of science, which offers close-ended definition instead of provocation, extinguishes the activity required of the moral man. "Perception without feeling" can detail, for example, a theory of ballistics as a physical science. Perception with feeling, with emotionality—the poetic ideal—requires men to consider what it means to use ballistic theory in the world of their fellow men.

I think Richards and Burke are overzealous in attaching moral values to the poetic use of language. Both uses of language, scientific and poetic, neutral and emotion-laden, can be perverted. One need merely read *Mein Kampf* to see the truth of this. Just as those who assailed poetry as immoral were wrong, so are the more recently arrived opponents of the language of science.

Burke and Richards may go too far, but their point of view is instructive. Poetry has long lived with the thesis that it is somehow immoral; the antithetical view is probably a sign of an emerging, valid synthesis.

Having said so much about how different the language of poetry is from the language of other discourse, we might well wonder why poetry is compared to other discourse at all. The answer suggested at the outset of this chapter is no longer adequate. Then I said that poetry, like all discourse, uses words. But if words can be used in such disparate ways, why use these to make comparisons? Why compare an article in *Popular Mechanics*, "How to Build a Picnic Table," with "Lycidas" or "Ode on a Grecian Urn"? Yet this is precisely what we have been doing. In our attempt to understand what characterizes language in poetry, we have been wholly dependent on other discourse as a basis of comparison. The further our investigation has gone, the more dissimilar, it seems to me, we have found these different language uses to be.

Language in poetry "means" differently than it does in prose; what it requires of the reader—and what it returns to

[41] *Science and Poetry* (New York: W. W. Norton, 1928), pp. 71–72.

him in pleasure—is remarkably unlike other uses of language. Imagine, for example, what life would be like if every time someone spoke to us we experienced the maelstrom of associations, attitudes, and emotions that poetry evokes. The "blooming buzzing confusion" would exhaust us. We simply cannot *make* meaning of everything. In fact *most* discourse must not possess semantic thickness but be capable instead of being immediately and simply comprehended.

Susanne Langer, in *Philosophy in a New Key*, offers the first departure from the centuries-old practice of contrasting poetry with science or philosophy. We may still understand two ways generally of creating meaning, she says, but these comprise not scientific and poetic use of language but discursive and presentational symbolism. For the most part, "discursive symbolism" is the symbolism of language, words used to refer to things. "Presentational symbolism" is the symbolism of painting, dance, music, sculpture—of nonverbal modes of communication. Our previous discussion implicitly equated "meaning" with meaning created by *words*. Langer expands our notion of meaning to include all symbolism.

Discursive symbolism uses denotative language; it is what the other aestheticians refer to as the symbolic or the semantic —information-conveying—use of language. Discursive symbolism has definite limitations:

> Everybody knows that language is a very poor medium for expressing our emotional nature. It merely names certain vaguely and crudely conceived states, but fails miserably in any attempt to convey the ever-moving patterns, the ambivalences and intricacies of inner experience, the interplay of feelings with thoughts and impressions, memories and echoes of memories, transient fantasy, or its mere traces, all turned into nameless emotional stuff.[42]

Yet it is the "nameless emotional stuff" that poetry is all about. And poetry uses language, the "poor medium for expressing our emotional nature." How then can poetry be within the realm of discursive symbolism? It follows that it is not, and here we have Langer's most substantial contribution to our

[42] Susanne Langer, *Philosophy in a New Key* (New York: Mentor Books, 1951), p. 92.

poetic: poetry, although it uses words, the usual medium of discursive symbolism, is more properly conceived of as being in the realm of presentational symbolism. Poetry "means" in a way more like music or the visual arts than like other forms of discourse:

> For though the *material* of poetry is verbal, its import [meaning] is not the literal assertion made in words, but *the way the assertion is made,* and this involves the sounds, the tempo, the aura of associations of the words ... the wealth or poverty of the transient imagery that contains them. . . .
>
> The material of poetry is discursive, but the product —the artistic phenomenon—is not; its significance is purely implicit in the poem as a totality, as a form compounded of sound and suggestion, statement and reticence.[43]

This poetic casts into limbo our discussion of the truth or falsity of poetry. The issue of truth is no more (or no less) relevant to a discussion of poetry than it is to a discussion of Beethoven's Fifth Symphony or Monet's paintings of water lilies.

In *Feeling and Form,* the sequel to *Philosophy in a New Key,* Langer's stance is just as emphatic. The poet's business is with experience. He takes the semblance of real events and organizes them into a new reality, the reality of "virtual life"— the life created by the poem and the reader in interaction; together they establish an experience that may have very little to do with truth or reality, or even with reasoning—for according to Langer, in poetry there is only the semblance of reasoning.

We are therefore misguided when we expect great truths or profound ideas from poetry and measure the worth of any poem by these criteria. The important thing is the experience created by the interaction between the poem and the reader. If poetry were essentially a means of stating ideas (as many have contended), it should be reasonably compared to logic or mathematics. But poetry is art and must therefore be seen in the context of all art.

[43] Ibid., pp. 220–21.

What of poems traditionally thought to be funds of wisdom?—for example, those from which the following excerpts are taken (see pp. 214–15).

> The world is too much with us; late and soon,
> Getting and spending, we lay waste our powers
>
> WILLIAM WORDSWORTH

> Let me not to the marriage of true minds
> Admit impediment. Love is not love
> Which alters when it alteration finds,
> Or bends with the remover to remove
>
> WILLIAM SHAKESPEARE

> Leave me, O Love which reachest but to dust;
> And thou, my mind, aspire to higher things
>
> SIR PHILIP SIDNEY

> Oh, how much more doth beauty beauteous seem
> By that sweet ornament which truth doth give!
>
> WILLIAM SHAKESPEARE

Of these, Langer says, "Their messages are familiar to the point of banality ... there is no interesting literal content." [44] She is perhaps too harsh in her judgment, but the insight is profound. It is wrong to expect great philosophy or new ideas from a poem. Rather than the idea itself, it is *the experience of having the idea* that matters.

Seduction scenes are as old as Eve and Adam, and themes of mortality have been sung for ages—yet when Marvell tells his mistress and us, "But at my back I always hear / Time's wingèd chariot hurrying near," we may delight in revelation— not because the idea is new to us, but because we may for the first time be experiencing the idea (which we already "know") emotionally.

Francis X. Connolly opposes Langer's view, as we might surmise from just the title of his book: *Poetry: Its Power and*

[44] *Feeling and Form: A Theory of Art* (New York: Charles Scribner's Sons, 1953), p. 233.

Wisdom. Connolly would have it that all great poems are also sources of wisdom; he explains how:

> In the past most educated readers treasured their classics for their wisdom. They read the ancient writers, Virgil and Horace, the medieval poets of Christendom, Dante and Chaucer, the Renaissance Englishmen, Shakespeare and Milton. . . . In all these poets readers found wisdom.[45]

If Connolly meant something like the wisdom of the human heart, his pronouncement might be defensible. But the wisdom he attributes to poetry is reasoned and judgmental. Thus he says, "At its best, a great poem is a just criticism of life—the utterance of a great mind pronouncing judgment on the affairs of men." [46]

We should reject the premises of Connolly's argument: terms like "just criticism" and "judgment" are misleading when applied to poetry. They set up the wrong criteria for understanding, experiencing, and evaluating poetry. William Blake and LeRoi Jones offer very different views of urban life in their poems. Yet one is no more "just" than the other, and both present experience, not "judgment." If we regard the poems of Blake and Jones as judgmental, we are likely to disagree with their judgments, to argue, to treat the poems as we would articles in a journal of the social sciences.

Take this poem by Yeats.

A DEEP-SWORN VOW

Others because you did not keep
That deep-sworn vow have been friends of mine;
Yet always when I look death in the face,
When I clamber to the heights of sleep,
Or when I grow excited with wine,
Suddenly I meet your face.

To my mind this is a fine poem. However, as an "educated reader," to use Connolly's term, I find immense significance in this poem simply because it creates in me the experience of the vow. I too have felt betrayed, and have at times been the

[45] *Poetry: Its Power and Wisdom*, p. 110.
[46] Ibid., p. 111.

betrayer; on the edge of sleep I have been stirred by the appearance of a face from the past.

But I do not "learn" from the poem; it does not represent "wisdom"; most certainly, it does not "pronounce judgment." If the poem were judgmental, its power would diminish for me. I don't know from the poem what the vow was or under what circumstances it was sworn. Hence I don't know who wronged whom. How can I judge? The poet neither pronounces "judgment on the affairs of men" nor sets forth a "criticism of life." A host of unknowns is essential to the poem; they leave room for my imagination, my experience of the broken vow. As a great architect once said, "Less is more"—I think so, particularly in "A Deep-Sworn Vow."

If we applied Langer's logic, we should indeed find that the "message" of this poem is banal (if we could find some message like "vows must be kept or suffering ensues"). Of course the very process of reducing poems to messages banalizes them. As Coleridge says, poetry is untranslatable. We should apply Coleridge's poetic very seriously, it seems to me. If poetry is untranslatable, it cannot be made into wisdom or judgments or even knowledge. It can and does evoke emotions, and these are part of an experience the reader has because of and with the poem; there is no translation necessary, since the created experience is something new, not something transposed or transmitted.

And not only must we abjure seeking "wisdom" in poetry, we must (finally) stop insisting that poetry makes statements. We must not fall into the error of the textbook author who first gives us this poem by Henry Reed and then asks the student to interpret the "statement" the poem makes about war.

NAMING OF PARTS

Today we have naming of parts. Yesterday,
We had daily cleaning. And tomorrow morning,
We shall have what to do after firing. But today,
Today we have naming of parts. Japonica
Glistens like coral in all of the neighbouring gardens,
        And today we have naming of parts.

This is the lower sling swivel. And this
Is the upper sling swivel, whose use you will see,

When you are given your slings. And this is the piling
    swivel,
Which in your case you have not got. The branches   10
Hold in the gardens their silent, eloquent gestures,
    Which in our case we have not got.

This is the safety-catch, which is always released
With an easy flick of the thumb. And please do not let me
See anyone using his finger. You can do it quite easy
If you have any strength in your thumb. The blossoms
Are fragile and motionless, never letting anyone see
    Any of them using their finger.

And this you can see is the bolt. The purpose of this
Is to open the breech, as you see. We can slide it   20
Rapidly backwards and forwards: we call this
Easing the spring. And rapidly backwards and forwards
The early bees are assaulting and fumbling the flowers:
    They call it easing the Spring.

They call it easing the Spring: it is perfectly easy
If you have any strength in your thumb: like the bolt,
And the breech, and the cocking-piece, and the point of
    balance,
Which in our case we have not got; and the almond-
    blossom
Silent in all of the gardens and the bees going backwards
    and forwards,
    For today we have naming of parts.   30

There is a poetic in all this, in the theory of Coleridge,
Richards and Ogden, Beardsley, Burke, Langer, and our own
thoughts. Yet for me, extracting a formulated poetic from the
flow of ideas is a little like transforming a summer rich in
adventure and harvest into the caricature of the essay assignment: "What I Did Last Summer." Nonetheless, there is a
symbolic value in summing up. The assigned essay doesn't so
much recount the summer as signal the fact of autumn and
a new school year.

First, if we agree with Coleridge, poetry is to be distinguished from other discourse by its special use of language—
not by its meter, nor by its subject matter. This use of language
is excited, precise, and designed primarily to produce pleasure
in the reader—not to teach him or preach to him.

Next, in keeping with the work of Beardsley and other contemporary aestheticians, we have been able to expand the notion of pleasure that Coleridge initiated. The reader's pleasure comes in large part from his active role in making meaning of the poem. The poem does not say, "This is the way it is." It suggests, evokes, inspires the interplay of attitudes and emotions; what emerges from this interplay is the reader's meaning as well as the poet's. The poem becomes in a sense the reader's. The pleasure created may thus be said to be the pleasure of ownership as well as that of activity.

Langer's departure from the basic conception of two kinds of language use, scientific and poetic, serves as much to validate as to alter our prior conclusions. By making poetry more akin to forms of presentational, rather than discursive, symbolism, her aesthetic suggests that the "meaning" of poetry is within the realm of the evocative and experiential. Language as it is used in poetry becomes still more distinctive when conceived as presentational symbolism, even though it uses the medium—words—of discursive symbolism. We are once and for all, if we agree with Langer, freed of looking for significant philosophy or ideas in poetry. There are ideas in poetry, but poetry does not exist to put forth ideas. It is the experience of the idea, our experiencing the idea as readers, that counts—not admiring the idea, agreeing with the idea, or being taught by the idea.

What now of the Reconnaissance that precedes this chapter? The same question obtains: Is "crickets" a poem?

Applying the poetic developed in this chapter, I would say—and this goes only for me, since even if the poetic is agreed to and conceived of similarly by others, their interpretation of its application could differ widely—"crickets" isn't a poem. The language is mildly evocative of the sounds crickets make, of a whole field of chirrupping, hissing crickets, but I miss the process described by Kenneth Burke as "attaining a perspective atop all the conflicts of attitude." For me, no conflict of attitude, no interplay of emotions, is evoked by "crickets." I admire the cleverness of the manipulation of sound; I like the way the poem looks on the page as its *s*'s move about and, in the middle, take over. But admiring a cleverly made object and participating actively in the apprehension and experiencing of a vision are very different.

We might ask the same question of "Ah, How Sweet It Is to Love!" by John Dryden. Because of its formal aspects—the six-line stanzas rhyming *a b a b c c* and the meter—it does not take us aback as "crickets" probably did. Nonetheless, the criteria of our poetic can be applied just as they were in assessing "crickets": Is the language at once precise and evocative? Are there words, phrases or lines which could be altered or translated into other words? Does it inspire in us the interplay of attitudes and emotions which results in our making our own meaning of it? Although it is clearly verse, is "Ah, How Sweet It Is to Love!" a poem?

> Ah, how sweet it is to love!
> Ah, how gay is young Desire?
> And what pleasing pains we prove
> When we first approach Love's fire!
>   Pains of love be sweeter far
>   Than all other pleasures are.
>
> Sighs which are from lovers blown
> Do but gently heave the heart:
> Ev'n the tears they shed alone
> Cure, like trickling balm, their smart: 10
>   Lovers, when they lose their breath,
>   Bleed away in easy death.
>
> Love and Time with reverence use,
> Treat them like a parting friend;
> Nor the golden gifts refuse
> Which in youth sincere they send:
>   For each year their price is more,
>   And they less simple than before.
>
> Love, like spring-tides full and high,
> Swells in every youthful vein; 20
> But each tide does less supply,
> Till they quite shrink in again:
>   If a flow in age appear,
>   'Tis but rain, and runs not clear.

3

RECONNAISSANCE

What does this poem mean to you, how does it achieve its effects, and why do you or do you not consider it to be a successful poem?

I KNEW A WOMAN

I knew a woman, lovely in her bones,
When small birds sighed, she would sigh back at them;
Ah, when she moved, she moved more ways than one:
The shapes a bright container can contain!
Of her choice virtues only gods should speak,
Or English poets who grew up on Greek
(I'd have them sing in chorus, cheek to cheek).

How well her wishes went! She stroked my chin,
She taught me Turn, and Counter-turn, and Stand;
She taught me Touch, that undulant white skin;   10
I nibbled meekly from her proffered hand;
She was the sickle; I, poor I, the rake,
Coming behind her for her pretty sake
(But what prodigious mowing we did make).

Love likes a gander, and adores a goose:
Her full lips pursed, the errant note to seize;
She played it quick, she played it light and loose;
My eyes, they dazzled at her flowing knees;
Her several parts could keep a pure repose,
Or one hip quiver with a mobile nose   20
(She moved in circles, and those circles moved).

Let seed be grass, and grass turn into hay:
I'm martyr to a motion not my own;
What's freedom for? To know eternity.
I swear she cast a shadow white as stone.
But who would count eternity in days?
These old bones live to learn her wanton ways:
(I measure time by how a body sways).

THEODORE ROETHKE

III

THE DILEMMA OF RESPONSE

This is a fine poem written with deep,
emotional feeling and choice of words that
is only possible for the genuine poet.

I will declare the whole poem to be
sentimental rubbish. More detailed
criticism would be foolish and futile.
One reading gave me this opinion.
I never hope to read it again.

TWO COLLEGE STUDENTS
RESPONDING TO THE SAME POEM

It is difficult to talk about poems. Almost no one does, except
the captive participants who are required to during the
specified hours of an English course. Students capable of
animated and articulate conversations about history, politics,
auto mechanics, fashions, love, and athletics become tongue-
tied when asked to discuss a poem. I have given my students
a copy of a poem, read it aloud, and then waited for a conversation about the poem to ensue. Hitherto lively persons sat
in uncomfortable silence, hoping someone else (preferably the
teacher) would make the first comment.

In part, this dilemma is present for all the arts. In response to paintings and music, people have difficulty going
beyond "I like it" or "I don't like it." Yet with poems the
problem is intensified. The lever into conversation is harder
to find. The poem is read; after a long silence, someone may
resort to a comment on the poem's form: "Well, this is a

traditional sonnet." Such a remark is well intentioned—the person who makes it hopes he will provide an opening for other, more substantive, comments.

I have been surprised to discover that the difficulty my students have talking about poetry is shared even by poets talking with one another. In fact, it has been my experience that poets very seldom talk about their poems with each other. They will readily recount their successes and failures at the hands of publishers and they will discuss the lives of fellow poets; but a genuine conversation about poems themselves does not come easily. An editor-writer associated with a major magazine once said he chose poems by whether or not they caused his knees to tingle. The statement is symptomatic of much poetry talk: the poem either "gets to you" or it doesn't.

What I have learned is that conversations about poetry are difficult. They are also rewarding. Just as we may want and need to be able to talk with friends about a person we love, and just as sharing our feelings about someone we love can immensely please us, so it is with poetry. We can experience poetry privately, never attempting to share our excitement with others, and be content. The poem is then like the damsel in the high tower who lets her hair down just for us, a private love that I by no means intend to disparage. But for those of us who wish to bring the damsel down from the tower and have her dance and converse among our friends, there is the challenging task of learning to build the ladder.

Quite simply, we need to study response to poetry, to learn what happens when people express their reaction to poems. Knowledge about how others respond to poetry will help us to articulate and share our own responses.

A major study of response to poetry, made by I. A. Richards some forty years ago, is exceptional. It is the first of its kind, and it is also the most thorough and comprehensive of such studies. The findings are reported in Richards' book *Practical Criticism.*

In the introduction to *Practical Criticism,* Richards tells us that "it is as a step towards . . . training and technique in discussion that I would best like this book to be regarded." And so we shall regard it.

Richards was teaching at Cambridge University, England, at the time he conceived of his experiment with response to poetry, and the students who participated in it were all Cambridge undergraduates. The experiment itself was straight-forward. Richards gave his students poems to read and take away with them. He asked that the students write careful responses to the poems and return these written responses to him. Aware that judgments of poems are often made on the basis of who the poet is, rather than on the poem itself, Richards omitted the titles of the poems and the names of the authors. He also modernized the spelling in some of the older poems. Thus the poems presented to the students were as anonymous as possible; the students could not rely on clues of authorship or historical period and had to look closely at the poems themselves.

The poems that Richards used range from some very good ones (my judgment, using the criteria developed in the pre-ceding chapter) to some clearly passionless, empty pieces of verse. Among the former, for example, is John Donne's "Holy Sonnet VII"; among those I personally don't like is one by Christina Rossetti, which begins

> Gone were but the Winter,
>   Come were but the Spring,
> I would to a covert
>   Where the birds sing.

Whether the students judged individual poems as good or bad, they were, on the whole, enthusiastic about their assignment. Most of the students gave each poem at least four readings; and although no student in Richards' classes was required either to read the poems or write responses to them, 60 percent chose to do so.

In *Practical Criticism*, Richards shows us the poems he used, gives samples of the responses (which he calls "proto-cols"), and discusses them. At the end of the book, he general-izes about the problems that have emerged in responding to poetry. Although Richards edited the protocols somewhat, he assures us that he has tried to present them as fairly as possi-ble, perhaps slighting only those that did not take a strong position on a poem. As we will notice, the protocols Richards cites are left in their original state, with spelling and punctua-tion errors unchanged.

Richards used thirteen poems in all, and it is surprising

to see that response to many of them was fairly equally divided
between those he labels "favourable" and those he labels
"unfavourable." Response to Poem 4, which we shall look
at here, evoked roughly 53 percent favorable and 42 percent
unfavorable response. Five percent of the protocols about this
poem Richards describes as "noncommittal."

Poem 4, we learn (although this information was kept from
the protocol-writers), is from *More Rough Rhymes of a Padre*,
by G. A. Studdert Kennedy. Richards disguised a reference to
the First World War in the first line of the second verse and
omitted a fifth verse; here is the poem as presented to his
students.

> There was rapture of spring in the morning
> When we told our love in the wood.
> For you were the spring in my heart, dear lad,
> And I vowed that my life was good.
>
> But there's winter now in the evening,
> And lowering clouds overhead,
> There's wailing of wind in the chimney-nook
> And I vow that my life lies dead.
>
> For the sun may shine on the meadow lands
> And the dog-rose bloom in the lanes,
> But I've only weeds in my garden, lad,
> Wild weeds that are rank with the rains.
>
> One solace there is for me, sweet but faint,
> As it floats on the wind of the years,
> A whisper that spring is the last true thing
> And that triumph is born of tears.

I think we can readily predict along what line response
to this poem was divided. Do we like, "For you were the
spring in my heart, dear lad," or don't we? Does it express
genuine sentiment, evoking fresh, youthful companionship, or
is it sentimental, bereft of genuine feeling? The following
protocols illustrate how Richards' students felt (the numbering
system is Richards': the first number refers to the poem, the
second, to the protocol-writer):

4.1   It's a *sham*. Sentimentality recollected in a very sentimental tranquillity. *If the girl's life indeed lay dead* she

would *not* write like that. Why, *she's thoroughly enjoying herself—more than I am.* Not one tear in the whole piece. It's PSEUDO, it PRETENDS, its values are worthless. False coin. Low, mimic, stuff.[1]

4.11 A sigh—a great sigh, despairing and tremulous. That is what these lines seem to mean. The sigh though is put into words and these seem to convey to us *a sense of some ineffable sorrow,* too deep for words. Blighted hopes which seemed in the spring so rapturous now have sunk into the hopelessness—*the utter hopelessness of the words* "And I vow that my life lies—dead."

It is the very fact that *the words are so quiet and yet hopeless* that lends such poignancy to it. No passionate utterance but a stony blank grief. And yet despite this in the last stanza a faint trembling hope is put forth *and this must be so for* "hope springs eternal in the human breast."

Above all in this piece one feels a keen sense, as it were, of some *deserted ruins,* stark and bare, the wind moaning, the sky lowering and a *vivid sense of decayed splendour.*

Richards observes that seldom has the adage one man's meat is another man's poison been so beautifully demonstrated:

4.12 An invitation to a debauch which one can hardly claim credit for declining.

4.13 This is a fine poem written with deep, emotional feeling and a choice of words that is only possible for the genuine poet.

Two more of the antiphonous protocols deserve quoting:

4.16 This piece alone of all the four got me straight away. It is very effective indeed—obviously sincere and very pleasant to read. The theme, though somewhat obvious is one that can never be hackneyed, especially when

[1] This and the following protocols are from I. A. Richards, *Practical Criticism* (New York: Harcourt Brace Jovanovich, 1929, 1952), pp. 50–58.

so originally and pleasantly treated as in this case. The ending is very good and strong which always is a strong point. It has a *lilt* in it which is *very pleasant when reading provided it is not overdone.*

4.61   As
   (1) I am only 19.
   (2) I have never been in love.
   (3) I do not know what a dog-rose is.
   (4) I consider that spring has no rapture.
   (5) _____ the alliteration is bad and unnecessary.
   (6) _____ this symbolism is utterly worthless.
I will declare the whole poem to be sentimental rubbish. More detailed criticism would be foolish and futile. One reading gave me this opinion. I never hope to read it again.

These results, and the many more protocols similar to these, unsettled Richards. He is dismayed to find that "poetry should seem such a remote, mysterious, unmanageable thing to so large a majority of readers," and weeps doubly because his protocol-writers were "with few exceptions . . . the products of the most expensive kind of education." [2]

Other eminent critics commiserate and agree. Stanley Edgar Hyman tells us that "what the protocols reveal, by and large, is probably the most shocking picture, exhaustively documented, of the general reading of poetry ever presented." [3] Most recently, in an article entitled, "On Rereading I. A. Richards," René Wellek affirms that the protocols manage "conclusively to prove the disorientation which affects students as soon as they are deprived of names, their authority, and their anchorage in history." [4] The list could go on. To my amazement, I have been unable to discover anyone who takes issue with this interpretation of the protocols. Most literary questions find advocates on both sides.

Strangely, I find myself virtually in complete disagreement with Richards, Hyman, Wellek, and the others. I say "strangely" because the opening of this chapter asserted pre-

---

[2] *Practical Criticism*, pp. 291–92.
[3] *The Armed Vision*, abr., rev. ed. (New York: Knopf, 1955), p. 291.
[4] "On Rereading I. A. Richards," *Southern Review*, 3, No. 3 (July 1967), p. 550.

cisely what we are told the protocols demonstrate—that talking about poems is very difficult to do and usually not done well. However, in this case I think Richards' students did very well indeed.

I don't know where the vitality, humor, and insight of the protocols comes from, but it is clearly there. It may be peculiar to British grammar school and university education, or it may be a product of Richards' own teaching. But the poem is not lost on any reader who can write the series of "As's" we find in protocol 4.61, or the succinct, abrasive summing up of 4.12.

As I understand it, Richards and the others for whom the protocols are a display of poetic insensitivity are reacting to two facts about the protocols: (1) they show widely divergent opinions of a single poem, and (2) they are emotional rather than closely reasoned. I would maintain that these two facts are precisely what make the protocols vital and encouraging.

First of all, why should we expect art to be apprehended in a similar manner by different people? We do not have to get into the issue of critical relativism here, although I admit the question hints at it. If we speak just of poetry, and are loyal to the poetic of the last chapter, we do not have to get into broad historical questions of shifting taste, combative critics, and the like. Language as it is used in poetry requires of the reader that his response be subjective, based on his own attitudes. Assuming that each of us is unique in important ways, each of us will respond differently to a poem that by its very nature brings out what is individual and personal in us.

The next matter is inseparable from the first. If response is to be subjective, it will also be emotional—this too is basic to how poetry means. Poetry "means" by making us make meaning of it; and for us to make meaning of the poem, we must experience conflicts of attitudes and strong emotions. Perhaps the protocols written in response to Poem 4 are a bit heavy on the emotional side (remember that Burke urges, finally, "a perspective atop the conflicts of attitude"), but they most certainly do not portray readers who find the poem "remote," "mysterious," or "unmanageable." The passion with which the protocol-writers leapt to their task, underlining and capitalizing words and phrases when they felt they could not get enough of themselves into more conventional prose, is testimony to the fact that the poem was immediate and certainly manageable as a stimulus of discussion.

The students did not disagree about the poem because they *misunderstood* it; this, I think, is an important point. Sometimes we simply don't "get" a poem. Its vocabulary may be too remote (by the time we've looked up enough words in the dictionary, we find we are responding to Webster rather than to the poem). Or its symbolism may be too learned, too arcane for those outside a particular kind of scholarship (T. S. Eliot's "The Wasteland," for example, presents many readers with this problem). Or the poem's structure may be too complicated or experimental; it thus becomes as much puzzle as poem. But such is not the case here—all the protocol-writers "got" the poem. They knew what it is about, in the sense that a poem can be about anything. Apart from the humorous confession by the nineteen-year-old that he does not know what a dog-rose is, there is no indication that the poem baffled the protocol-writers. They felt they understood it and were qualified to comment on it—which means that the differences among the protocols are profound, not to be eliminated by providing each reader with a "key" to the poem (as in the endless footnotes that accompany some poems, and the actual manuals that have been produced to help readers "understand" poems).

If we think in terms of semantic thickness, the protocols are products of the deepest levels of meaning; they represent response to the evocative power of the language in the poem. In virtually every instance, we are confronted by the reader's attitudes and associations.

The poem's reference to seasons was particularly evocative. Protocol writer 4.41, not previously quoted, says, "Seasons and sun affect me more than anything, and *in this I can feel the spring, the best season of life and nature*"; and 4.5, "*A little poem like this does do for my feelings, what spring does for flowers.*" And, returning to 4.61, we have the forthright if iconoclastic attitude that "spring has no rapture."

If "truth" has any meaning in poetry, that meaning must be closely related to the passion described by Coleridge; a poem is "true" when its genuine feelings can be perceived and shared by the reader. The protocol-writers are quick to respond to whether or not the emotion of the poem is genuine. The line "And I vow that my life lies dead" is "sham" for writer 4.1 because the feeling is false; someone who was truly suffering would not describe his life in that fashion. For the author of 4.11, the same line creates an emotion "too deep for words," an expression of "utter hopelessness."

The last two lines of the poem—"A whisper that spring is the last true thing / And that triumph is born of tears"—was similarly divisive. Protocol-writer 4.5 finds that *"one's feelings rush out* to endorse those last two lines," whereas 4.23 tells us that the whole poem is a conglomeration of *"conventional trappings and catchwords of romance"* capped by closing lines that rhyme but are devoid of feeling: " 'Thing' " means exactly nothing but it rhymes with spring so there it is." Yet another protocol-writer (4.27) attributes the poem's perfection in large part to "the last two lines. . . . It leaves no final impression of sadness, but of greatness."

So that there will be no effort wasted in speculating about how I respond to the poem, I will state that I agree with those students who found it empty of genuine emotion, conventional in the extreme, and riddled by phrases and words that exist to maintain the rhyme and metrics of the poem but that add nothing to its evocative power.

But more important than the "favourable," "unfavourable," or "noncommittal" categories is the *how* of the protocols. It is how the students were able to talk about the poem, and not whether they liked or did not like it, that informs us. And in this regard I maintain that they responded to the poem as one must respond to all poems—allowing attitudes and emotions free play, understanding why such attitudes and emotions were evoked by the poem, and achieving a perspective on the poem from the interplay of these feelings.

It occurs to me that there might be a third reason, in addition to the lack of unanimity and the emotionalism of the protocols, for Richards' disappointment in them. He may have been disheartened because the students did not echo *his* feelings about the poems he presented to them. A friend of mine once set up an exhibit of modern paintings at a gallery, paintings that were, I think, surrealistic. (I can still see the one that depicted a series of gas stations over which hovered an olive [pimento-stuffed] floating in space.) I asked her something like, "Where did you get this junk?" My question, intended to be funny, proved tactless and offensive. These were not my friend's paintings, yet she had a great stake in them, having set up the exhibit. So it is with poems we offer others. We want those with whom we share poems to share our response to them. From the editorial comments interspersed among the protocols, I gather that in many instances Richards was more appreciative of certain rhetorical devices and of a kind of formalism in the poetry than were his students.

The fact remains that the protocols demonstrate the veracity of a poetic to which Richards himself contributes. They corroborate that the language of poetry is, in Richards' own term, "emotive." Further, the protocols show that it is the meaning of poetry, that meaning co-created by the poem and the reader, that matters most. In almost every case, the protocol-writers spoke of what the poem meant to them—what meaning the seasons, friendship, love, and sorrow were given by their experience with the poem. Significantly absent are comments about meter, figures of speech, the stanzaic organization of the poem. In the instance when rhyme is mentioned, it is because the rhyme appears to that protocol-writer as an impediment to meaning. I don't think Richards' students avoided talking about the poem's meter, for example, because scansion and metrical analysis is especially difficult (this particular poem, in fact, is uncomplicated metrically). The protocols dealt with the poem's meaning because that is its most basic quality: making meaning is what responding to poetry is all about.

Before moving from *Practical Criticism* to other examples of response to poetry, I must, in fairness to Richards, say something of his general contentions. At the end of the book, he classifies various kinds of obstacles that present themselves to the reader of poetry. Among these are "Irrelevant Associations and Stock Responses," "Sentimentality and Inhibition," "Doctrine in Poetry" and "Presuppositions and Preconceptions." Out of context—that is, apart from interpretation of specific protocols—I find all of Richards' general concerns valid and immensely helpful.

For example, having developed a poetic that asserts that the stuff of poetry is not ideas per se, but the experience of an idea, we can well understand how doctrine should not be allowed to impede our understanding and appreciation of a poem. Dante should not be lost to atheists, nor Shakespeare to anarchists. Five-star generals should be open to appreciation of Wilfred Owen's poems, and Ku Klux Klansmen should be able to read Langston Hughes. My "should" is emphatic and idealistic. In point of fact, I cannot imagine a Klansman responding to the *poetry* of any black writer. On the other hand, many, many non-Catholics are enormously moved by the poetry of Dante. Obviously the reader who allows doctrinal differences to bar him from a poet's work does not believe in the poetic established here. For he is treating the poem as though it were a political speech, as strictly discursive rather than presentational symbolism.

The categories including irrelevant associations, sentimentality, and preconceptions are more difficult to apply. How do we know whether an association is irrelevant or relevant? Or if we are being sentimental? Or when our preconceptions are acting as an impediment? Each of us has private associations, sentimental attachments, and preconceptions. Since these are to some degree emotional and subjective elements of response, how can we judge them rationally? After all, our response to poetry should be emotional and subjective.

Consider, for example, the protocol-writer who stated that for him spring held no rapture. We might imagine that his assertion was born of past associations with springtime; perhaps a love affair was shattered in June or a death occurred, or, less specifically, spring may simply never have lived up to its promise of flowers and sunshine. Confronted by a poem in which a central image is that of joyous spring, what is he to do? The reader cannot disown his past, a part of himself. And yet he may lose something if he dismisses the poem *solely* on the basis of his past association. (The protocol-writer in question, it will be remembered, invoked several other reasons for his dislike of the poem.)

Or there is the associational problem reversed with "The Wasteland," which begins, "April is the cruelest month, breeding / Lilacs out of the dead land...." Imagine how this line affects the multitude of readers who are imbued from earliest childhood with the most positive associations with spring. How do these readers ever come to share Eliot's vision?

We have here the dilemma of response. Our poetic tells us to be emotional, personal, and subjective in responding to poetry. Yet somehow we must be more than this if we are ever to experience those poems that don't fit our preconceptions, that jar our associations, that go contrary to our attitudes.

This dilemma confronts readers often, except perhaps those who have found a favorite poet who "fits" and confine themselves to his work only. The dilemma may be raised by a single word or image in the poem, or by a line, as well as by the meaning made of the poem in its entirety. I have even seen the title of a poem alone cause grave associational difficulties for a reader. The dilemma can also be raised by factors not strictly within the poem at all: knowledge about the poet and the context in which the poem was written (dimensions that Richards eliminated in *Practical Criticism*) can have a profound effect on the reader.

Among my students, "Daddy," by Sylvia Plath, has been immensely problematic; it has produced all the kinds of response which Richards warns against.

DADDY

You do not do, you do not do
Any more, black shoe
In which I have lived like a foot
For thirty years, poor and white,
Barely daring to breathe or Achoo.

Daddy, I have had to kill you.
You died before I had time—
Marble-heavy, a bag full of God,
Ghastly statue with one grey toe
Big as a Frisco seal   10

And a head in the freakish Atlantic
Where it pours bean green over blue
In the waters off beautiful Nauset.
I used to pray to recover you.
Ach, du.

In the German tongue, in the Polish town
Scraped flat by the roller
Of wars, wars, wars.
But the name of the town is common.
My Polack friend   20

Says there are a dozen or two.
So I never could tell where you
Put your foot, your root,
I never could talk to you.
The tongue stuck in my jaw.

It stuck in a barb wire snare.
Ich, ich, ich, ich,
I could hardly speak.
I thought every German was you.
And the language obscene

An engine, an engine
Chuffing me off like a Jew.
A Jew to Dachau, Auschwitz, Belsen.
I began to talk like a Jew.
I think I may well be a Jew.

The snows of the Tyrol, the clear beer of Vienna
Are not very pure or true.
With my gypsy ancestress and my weird luck
And my Taroc pack and my Taroc pack
I may be a bit of a Jew.

I have always been scared of you,
With your Luftwaffe, your gobbledygoo.
And your neat moustache
And your Aryan eye, bright blue.
Panzer-man, panzer-man, O You—

Not God but a swastika
So black no sky could squeak through.
Every woman adores a Fascist,
The boot in the face, the brute
Brute heart of a brute like you.

You stand at the blackboard, daddy,
In the picture I have of you,
A cleft in your chin instead of your foot
But no less a devil for that, no not
Any less the black man who

Bit my pretty red heart in two.
I was ten when they buried you.
At twenty I tried to die
And get back, back, back to you.
I thought even the bones would do.

But they pulled me out of the sack,
And they stuck me together with glue.
And then I knew what to do.
I made a model of you,
A man in black with a Meinkampf look

And a love of the rack and the screw.
And I said I do, I do.
So daddy, I'm finally through.
The black telephone's off at the root.
The voices just can't worm through.   70

If I've killed one man, I've killed two—
The vampire who said he was you
And drank my blood for a year,
Seven years, if you want to know.
Daddy, you can lie back now.

There's a stake in your fat black heart
And the villagers never liked you.
They are dancing and stamping on you.
They always *knew* it was you.
Daddy, daddy, you bastard, I'm through.   80

      Even a reader who has never heard of Sylvia Plath is likely to view this poem as autobiographical. What of the reader who knows something of Plath's life—her difficult marriage to the poet Ted Hughes; her several attempts to kill herself, culminating in suicide at age thirty-one? The student who brought "Daddy" to the poetry class was concurrently taking a course on women's literature and had learned a lot about Sylvia Plath. To share the poem with the rest of us, she began by recounting some of the details of Plath's relationship with men—in particular, her husband and her father.

      Another student, a believer in "New Criticism," which allows discussion only of the poem, interjected that knowledge of Plath's life was irrelevant or, worse, an obstacle to our experiencing the poem for ourselves. In the ensuing battle it also came to light that the student who brought the poem to us had an investment in it larger than her studies of women's literature. In Plath's "Daddy" she saw her own father, and had first read the poem at a critical point in her feelings toward him. Thus the issue was complex: strands of New

Criticism versus traditional criticism, interwoven with objective distance versus personal identification. The argument was not so issue-oriented as this, however, and the emotions that erupted brought about a volatile and important exchange.

Even if there were a right and a wrong in matters of this sort, I am not sure I could pronounce a winner. The processes of response are different in each instance.

For the student who knew Plath's biography, it was clear that the "daddy" in the poem had not literally been a Nazi, no more than Plath was Jewish. The last four stanzas refer to Plath's first emotional breakdown and suicide attempt, to her marriage (the second man in the poem), and to the fact that her marriage was poisoned by destructive emotions similar to those she felt for her father.

The student ignorant of the biography had more work to do. Was "daddy" a Nazi, literally, and had his daughter by some quirk been Jewish? Or had she converted to Judaism? What is meant by "And I said I do, I do" and "If I've killed one man, I've killed two"? Why does the poem seem to begin in the United States ("Frisco seal," "freakish Atlantic") and then draw its images from Germanic cities and countries?

We might infer that the reader who had not previously read of Plath's life was the more fortunate, because without certain factual details there was more meaning to make of the poem. But it can also be argued that knowledge of certain facts helps the reader move easily into the more wholly emotive realm of the poem. He does not have to figure out details that make the poem a bit like a puzzle, and can deal from the outset with its emotive import.

As often happens in discussions about a poem, one line emerged as emblematic of the whole. In the case of "Daddy," that line was "Every woman adores a Fascist." All the students experienced a strong reaction, often a mixed, conflicting reaction, to the line. What does it mean? What does it say about women and men? I will accept the risk of repetitiveness by emphasizing again that the question of meaning is not synonymous with the question of truth as we usually define it. The students did not say, for example, "Why of course the statement is nonsense; all the women I know are appalled by Fascism." They properly did not treat the line as an assertion of fact but as a presentational symbol—words used to evoke rather than to state a meaning. But then what does the line evoke? Plath's masochism? Feelings of guilt on the part of the readers, either because as women they have enjoyed or tolerated brutal treatment by men, or because as men they have been brutal toward women? A recognition of the ambivalence, the mixture of love and hate, that infuses most complex relationships?

To the members of the class, the line, in the context of the whole, meant all of these things. That is, the students were able to make many meanings, each somewhat different but none necessarily incompatible with the others. From these a further, more complex, meaning was drawn that can be put in the form of a question: Who can tell the persecuted from the persecutor? "Every woman adores a Fascist" is an immensely rich line, and one that brought the students together, whether they were of the suasion of New Criticism or more traditional in their approach. Sharing response, they achieved collectively what each of us aims for individually—the heaping of meaning on meaning, drawing meanings out of the poem as a whole, attending to the single line, returning those meanings to the broader context.

In the process, the division between the more dispassionate and scholarly and the more emotionally involved students broke down: Who can be objective, confronted by the word "Fascist"? Who can be objective about the images, memories, and associations of his father evoked by a poem? There was no consensus reached in terms of Richards' "favourable," "unfavourable," and "noncommittal" categories (except that no one was "noncommittal"), but each participant had to confront his own conflicts of attitude and truly attain that moral "perspective atop" these conflicts of which Kenneth Burke speaks. I think "moral" is an appropriate term here, not to designate a superior or righteous vision, but as a marking point in the difficult struggle to understand human passions.

The dilemma of response, of how to go beyond our personal associations was, I must add, not resolved. Struggle alone is not enough, although it is a fine beginning.

With another group of students I was startled to find that we were bogged down by personal associations evoked by simply the title of a poem.

TO ELSIE

The pure products of America
go crazy—
mountain folk from Kentucky

or the ribbed north end of
Jersey
with its isolate lakes and

valleys, its deaf-mutes, thieves
old names
and promiscuity between

devil-may-care men who have taken   10
to railroading
out of sheer lust of adventure—

and young slatterns, bathed
in filth
from Monday to Saturday

to be tricked out that night
with gauds
from imaginations which have no

peasant traditions to give them
character   20
but flutter and flaunt

sheer rags—succumbing without
emotion
save numbed terror

under some hedge of choke-cherry
or viburnum—
which they cannot express—

Unless it be that marriage
perhaps
with a dash of Indian blood   30

will throw up a girl so desolate
so hemmed round
with disease or murder

that she'll be rescued by an
agent—
reared by the state and

sent out at fifteen to work in
some hard-pressed
house in the suburbs—

some doctor's family, some Elsie—   40
voluptuous water
expressing with broken

brain the truth about us—
her great
ungainly hips and flopping breasts

addressed to cheap
jewelry
and rich young men with fine eyes

as if the earth under our feet
were   50
an excrement of some sky

and we degraded prisoners
destined
to hunger until we eat filth

while the imagination strains
after deer
going by fields of goldenrod in

the stifling heat of September
Somehow
it seems to destroy us   60

It is only in isolate flecks that
something
is given off

No one
to witness
and adjust, no one to drive the car

WILLIAM CARLOS WILLIAMS

Who could have predicted that there would be a student
unable to read this poem without a vision of the Borden's
milk trademark grinning before his eyes? Yet there it was,
Elsie the cow, forever jolly and wearing a wreath of daisies
around her horns. The rest of us were not amused. We immediately attacked this student, accusing him of falling prey

to one of the principal vices outlined by Richards: Elsie the cow was an "irrelevant association."

On the contrary, he contended; the name is there, and it's not a common name. In fact, throughout his life he had never known an Elsie other than Borden's. Furthermore, his initial response is lent support by the poem's first line, "The pure products of America." Milk is a product and we are inundated by dairy advertisements which claim that milk is the one pure food, nature's own. Why couldn't the meaning of this poem be conceived as a satirical presentation of Elsie the cow's infusion into American life? But most of all, the student argued, there was nothing he could do about his association; for him a cow was evoked, and that was that.

The person who had brought the poem in to us was wounded by this (judging only by the fates of "Daddy" and "Elsie," sharing poems is a risky business). He regarded the association as no less than a profanation of the poem. The poem's meaning was not only endangered for the student haunted by Borden's cow, but for the rest of us now that we had been exposed to that association.

Is the association irrelevant to the poem? Probably yes, since the poem is not satirical and seems to present a somber if not tragic situation. In other words, there is little in the body of the poem to support such a way of making meaning of it. I would not judge Borden's Elsie as unequivocally irrelevant, however. Who knows? That symbol, so corny and still so ingrained in the culture of America, could mean many things for a reader, could even evoke a sense of despair (for someone who has seen the large plastic Elsies that used to be part of billboard advertisements, the plastic cow is not incompatible with one of the poem's meanings).

Beyond Borden's, who is Elsie? Is she a "pure product of America" who has gone crazy? Or is she one of the "young slatterns, bathed / in filth"? Both? If Elsie is the "pure product" gone bad, corrupted by "cheap jewelry," who are the "degraded prisoners"? Is Elsie us? Or are we part of "some doctor's family" in the suburbs, hiring domestic help—and if so, again, who are the "prisoners"?

To answer these questions is to make meanings of the poem. It is not to "puzzle" it out—there are no symbols, references, or allusions that require more information. This is a more profound process than figuring something out. It is putting something in: ourselves. Making meaning requires a great deal of our imaginative resources as responsive readers.

One of the meanings that can be made of this poem is expressed by the same question inspired by "Daddy": How can we tell the persecuted from the persecutor? We can view Elsie—as the poetry class did—as a victim of cumulative forces of exploitation: the inbreeding of her mountain folk, seduction by railroad men, lack of cohesive traditions, state welfare agencies, the middle class. We are still left with the ominous "we degraded prisoners." It may be a system in which all are victims.

No matter how far we go in making meanings, we cannot say, "This is what it means." Even if we accept generally the meaning I just spoke of, and somehow take account of the immensely evocative closing stanzas of the poem as well, we have not made *the* meaning. A Marxist can come along and say the poem means that capitalism is dead, that the poem is "about" the destruction of the class system and the materialism it breeds. Someone else can make a racial meaning of the poem, or can talk about it as illustrative of the failure of agrarian society. Another can decide that the poem portrays the evils of industrialism. It would appear to be impossible to define the boundaries of response.

As a further example of the readers' dilemma, consider this poem.

THE SHEEP CHILD

Farm boys wild to couple
With anything   with soft-wooded trees
With mounds of earth   mounds
of pinestraw   will keep themselves off
Animals by legends of their own:
In the hay-tunnel dark
And dung of barns, they will
Say   I have heard tell

That in a museum in Atlanta
Way back in a corner somewhere   10
There's this thing that's only half

Sheep   like a woolly baby
Pickled in alcohol   because
Those things can't live   his eyes
Are open   but you can't stand to look
I heard from somebody who...

But this is now almost all
Gone. The boys have taken
Their own true wives in the city,
The sheep are safe in the west hill   20
Pasture   but we who were born there
Still are not sure. Are we,
Because we remember, remembered
In the terrible dust of museums?

Merely with his eyes, the sheep-child may

Be saying   saying

> *I am here, in my father's house.*
> *I who am half of your world, came deeply*
> *To my mother in the long grass*
> *Of the west pasture, where she stood like moon-*
> > *light*   30
> *Listening for foxes. It was something like love*
> *From another world that seized her*
> *From behind, and she gave, not lifting her head*
> *Out of dew, without ever looking, her best*
> *Self to that great need. Turned loose, she dipped*
> > *her face*
> *Farther into the chill of the earth, and in a sound*
> *Of sobbing   of something stumbling*
> *Away, began, as she must do,*
> *To carry me. I woke, dying,*
>
> *In the summer sun of the hillside, with my eyes*   40
> *Far more than human. I saw for a blazing moment*
> *The great grassy world from both sides,*
> *Man and beast in the round of their need,*
> *And the hill wind stirred in my wool,*
> *My hoof and my hand clasped each other,*
> *I ate one meal*
> *Of milk, and died*
> *Staring. From dark grass I came straight*
>
> *To my father's house, whose dust*
> *Whirls up in the halls for no reason*   50

> *When no one comes   piling deep in a hellish*
> *mild corner,*
> *And, through my immortal waters,*
> *I meet the sun's grains eye*
> *To eye, and they fail at my closet of glass.*
> *Dead, I am most surely living*
> *In the minds of farm boys: I am he who drives*
> *Them like wolves from the hound bitch and calf*
> *And from the chaste ewe in the wind.*
> *They go into woods   into bean fields   they go*
> *Deep into their known right hands. Dreaming*
> *of me,*   60
> *They groan   they wait   they suffer*
> *Themselves, they marry, they raise their kind.*

JAMES DICKEY

The first problem confronted by most readers is making meaning of the narrative persona, that is, the speaking voice. Who's talking at the beginning, before the indentation? One of the farm boys now grown and in the city? The sheep-child itself? A third party, telling about both the farm boys and the sheep-child from the outside? Readers have argued for all these alternatives. I think it's a farm boy looking back, and rest my case on the lines "Are we, / Because we remember, remembered / In the terrible dust of museums?" But why then does this persona refer to "the boys," instead of saying "we" throughout? Many readers contend that it is the sheep-child who speaks and no one else; that before the indentation, the sheep-child describes the context of the story that begins, *"I am here, in my father's house."*

Apart from the meaning we must make of the narrative persona, and the obviously startling drama of the events presented by the poem, what has intrigued me most in talking about this poem with other readers is a specifically Christian interpretation of its meaning. What if we take the sheep-child to be Christ?

To make meaning of the poem this way may strike us as outlandish, if not sacrilegious, but it is nonetheless within the realm of possibility. Christ is after all the Lamb of God. Moving through the poem from the beginning, let me suggest how a Christ-as-sheep-child meaning may be drawn from it.

It is a legend of conception, birth, death, and afterlife with which we're presented. The sheep-child speaks from his *"father's house"* and belongs only half to the world of men. The sheep-child, like Christ, was conceived in *"something like love / From another world."* Christ knew he must die for the sins of men; the sheep-child *"woke, dying,"* for man's sins. Dead, the sheep-child is returned to his *"father's house,"* whence he views the world through *"immortal waters."* Dead, he is *"most surely living";* dreaming of him, mankind goes on: *"they suffer / Themselves, they marry, they raise their kind."*

If we accept this meaning at all, we must recognize that in terms of semantic thickness it is one of the lower layers. At the surface, using Coleridge's working principles of "grammar, logic, psychology and *good sense*," we can make a much simpler meaning. The poem presents the phenomenon of sodomy between boys and sheep. Out of this union a freak is born that for genetic reasons cannot live. The freak is consigned to a bottle of formaldehyde (*"immortal waters"*) that preserve it in a museum (*"my father's house"*). Dead and pickled, the freak yet lives in the minds of the boys who committed sodomy with sheep or knew of the act. It is an emblem of the great societal taboo.

There is a maxim of logic—"Occam's razor"—which says that when alternative solutions present themselves, the simplest is best. The truth of this is incontestable—in logic. But a poem is not logical discourse, nor do we seek a solution. We seek meanings, and it would appear that many can coexist. Is there no such thing then as a maverick reading, an absolutely untenable meaning of a poem? Of "The Sheep Child" alone, there are meanings upon meanings that can be made. In addition to the two I've just outlined, I have heard readers venture meanings based on the legend of Atlantis (the museum is in Atlanta), racial miscegenation (offered by a reader who knew of the poet's Southern origins and alleged racial attitudes), and women's liberation (the sheep is the passive woman). Can we say one of these is to be preferred over the others?

It may be objected at this point that all the poems we have discussed are relatively long ones and that shorter poems do not spawn such a prodigy of meanings. The objection can be met by considering one of the shortest poems I know.

IN A STATION AT THE METRO

The apparition of these faces in the crowd;
Petals on a wet, black bough.

                    EZRA POUND

The title alone carries us considerably into making meanings
of this poem. The faces in the crowd are those of subway
passengers. They are the petals; perhaps the subway car itself
is the black bough. Or the black bough may be the tunnel; the
passengers may be standing on the platform. There are meanings to be made of the dominant metaphor: faces presented
as petals, the subway car or station as a "wet, black bough"—
but the metaphor is not, I think, as rich in meanings as the
word "apparition."

Is "apparition" used positively or negatively here? An
apparition can be frightening, ghostly, as well as pleasing. It
can be a haunting specter or a beatific vision. How the reader
makes meaning of "apparition" must be consonant with the
meaning made of the rest of the poem; but more important,
it will determine the meaning of the poem as a whole. If
"apparition" is made to mean something ghostly, the "wet,
black bough" becomes ominous, even slimy. If the reader
makes a positive meaning of "apparition," the petals become
rosy faces and the bough is wonderfully glistening, as if after
a rainfall. It is not overblown, if we take the metro station to
mean the world, to say that the poem can be a vision either of
the hope or of the failure of humanity. Or it can be a vision
of both: the two meanings are not mutually exclusive; the
positive and negative connotations of "apparition" can collaborate to create a complex and possibly ambivalent virtual
reality.

Knowing, as I do, what the author of the poem himself
says about its meaning, it would be disingenuous of me not
to include his comment. Here is what Ezra Pound tells us:

> Three years ago in Paris I got out of a "Metro" train at
> La Concord, and saw suddenly a beautiful face, and then
> another and another, and then a beautiful child's face,
> and then another beautiful woman, and I tried all day to
> find words for what this had meant to me, and I could

not find any words that seemed to me worthy, or as lovely as that sudden emotion. . . . I wrote a thirty-line poem and destroyed it because it was what we call work "of second intensity." Six months later I made a poem half that length; a year later I made the following . . . sentence:

> "The apparition of these faces
> in the crowd: Petals on a wet,
> black bough."

I daresay it is meaningless unless one has drifted into a certain vein of thought. In a poem of this sort one is trying to record the precise instant when a thing outward and objective transforms itself, or darts into a thing inward and subjective.[5]

Does Pound's account limit the meanings the poem can evoke? It is likely to, if we read his account before we read the poem itself—just as a knowledge of Sylvia Plath's life served somewhat to direct response to "Daddy." But I don't think we should necessarily take a poet's word for what his poem means. Or at least that should not be the final word. Poets consistently find that their poems mean things they did not know they meant; and, further, the poem does not have meaning only for the poet. Meaning ultimately resides with the reader, who must select among the factors he will permit to influence the meanings he makes and who must choose among meanings.

Here is a poem by William Carlos Williams, only slightly less brief than Pound's.

RED WHEELBARROW

so much depends
upon
a red wheel
barrow
glazed with rain
water
beside the white
chickens.

---

[5] Cleanth Brooks and Robert Penn Warren, *Understanding Poetry* (New York: Holt, Rinehart and Winston, 1960), p. 90, quoting Ezra Pound, *Gaudier-Brzeska* (London: John Lane, 1916), pp. 100, 103.

We cannot avoid the obvious: "What depends?" The meanings the reader makes of this question determine the meanings of the poem. Even so short, so seemingly matter-of-fact, so immediate a poem as this requires that the reader make meanings.

What could "depend" on the vision—really like a stark, even primitive painting—that Williams presents? For me, one possible meaning has to do with color. So much of our visual world depends on the kind of contrast of color presented in this poem by the red of the wheelbarrow and the white of the chickens. Another meaning could be that of order; the integrity of order in the world rests on just such simple arrangements as these. Or a meaning could be implicit in the juxtaposition of the mechanical and metallic (the wheelbarrow) and the natural and organic (rainwater, chickens). These meanings, the meanings I make in response to the poem, hardly answer the question "What depends?" But we seek meanings, not answers, and I'm certain the meanings I offer are only beginnings.

Let me anticipate another objection to all this making of meanings. The poems discussed thus far have been modern ones. We have not tried our poetic out on more traditional poetry. Let us then look at a poem by Shakespeare.

SONNET 35

No more be grieved at that which thou hast done.
Roses have thorns, and silver fountains mud,
Clouds and eclipses stain both moon and sun,
And loathsome canker lives in sweetest bud.
All men make faults, and even I in this,
Authorizing thy trespass with compare,
Myself corrupting, salving thy amiss,
Excusing thy sins more than thy sins are.
For to thy sensual fault I bring in sense—
Thy adverse party is thy advocate—
And 'gainst myself a lawful plea commence.
Such civil war is in my love and hate,
    That I an accessory needs must be
    To that sweet thief which sourly robs from me.

With all of Shakespeare's work, and perhaps more so with the sonnets, there is the temptation to be a historian concerned with facts rather than a reader who brings his "whole soul" into the activity of making meaning. The historian's approach is lauded, for example, by A. L. Rowse: "The proper method [of understanding the sonnets] is an historical one: to take each poem one by one, to follow it humbly line by line, watching for every piece of internal information and for its coherence with what is happening in the external world, checking for consistency at every point, accumulating patiently every fact and what may legitimately be inferred, until the whole structure stands forth clear." [6]

If we trust our poetic, we must abjure Rowse's "proper method." We counter that a poem is not a repository of "facts" and "information," but a form of presentational symbolism that creates with us its own virtual world. For those who agree with Rowse, and this includes most Shakespearean scholars, the process of response is not one of making meaning. It is historical research into the most intimate details of Shakespeare's life (for example, was he a homosexual?). Note that the criterion of success is quite different from ours. Rowse, supremely rational, believes he can make "the whole structure [stand] forth clear." We who do not accumulate "every fact" but instead explore every possible way of meaning do not expect a clear answer so much as possibilities.

The historical method is not invalid as part of literary study; I would not be so foolish as to rail against any form of knowledge. But it is hardly the single proper method—on the contrary, it should be considered a supplementary method, one that may buttress but can neither supersede nor dispossess primary emotional response.

But to the sonnet itself.

Is it the presentation of a lover's lament, the poet-as-lover grieving over the sins of his loved one and over his own tolerance of his loved one's sins? If so, what could the "sensual fault" of the loved one be? Does the sonnet seem to be addressed to a woman or a man? Or doesn't it matter? Who is "that sweet thief"? Is the thief the loved one? the poet's own weakness? Is the thief a rival lover? Or is it something more abstract like original sin ("Roses have thorns," Eden has the serpent)? It would seem to me that much of the meaning we make of the poem resides in the meanings we make of "that sweet thief."

In my case, response demands that I push aside some of the scholarly research with which I am familiar. I know that literary historians maintain this sonnet was written to a man, Shakespeare's patron, the Earl of Southampton. I know that historians have chronicled the ups and downs of Shakespeare's relationship with his patron, and place Sonnet 35 in that context. But I also know that even the most meticulous historical research on the subject comprises for the most part inference rather than acknowledged fact. In short, Shakespeare himself tells us nothing; he bequeathed no diary to the historians, who in fact occasionally debate whether Shakespeare actually existed. Alternatively, we could say that Shakespeare tells us everything—but not as fact and not as biography.

The meanings I make of Sonnet 35 include a sense that the sins it presents are a break in a pact between lovers and are specifically sexual, not just sensual. Yet so in love is the speaker of the poem—and I confess to a limit in my sensibilities; for me, love and sex can best be imagined as heterosexual —that he, despite himself, understands and forgives. But he cannot forgive himself for what he has gotten into. His is a liaison with a profligate, promiscuous mistress; she is not only destructive herself but brings out the worst in him. My own self-esteem is never lower than when I feel I have permitted someone to bring out the worst in me. Thus my attitudes about my own behavior come into play in making the meanings of the sonnet.

The couplet with which the sonnet ends supports all these meanings. "That sweet thief" is not necessarily only the unfaithful mistress; it can also be the speaker's susceptibility to his mistress' charms; and it can possess a wider meaning suggestive of mankind's vulnerability to self-corruption. These are multiple and compatible meanings, and I am sure there are more that other readers could make.

Here is another poem from the same era, although not quite as loaded with historical weight as is the work of Shakespeare.

THE LOVER SHOWETH HOW HE IS FORSAKEN OF SUCH AS HE SOMETIME ENJOYED

They flee from me, that sometime did me seek,
With naked foot stalking in my chamber.

I have seen them gentle, tame, and meek,
That now are wild, and do not remember
That sometime they put themselves in danger
To take bread at my hand, and now they range,
Busily seeking with a continual change.
Thanked be fortune it hath been otherwise,
Twenty times better; but once in special,
In thin array, after a pleasant guise,   10
When her loose gown from her shoulders did fall,
And she me caught in her arms long and small,
And therewith all sweetly did me kiss,
And softly said, "Dear heart, how like you this?"
It was no dream, I lay broad waking.
But all is turned, thorough my gentleness,
Into a strange fashion of forsaking;
And I have leave to go, of her goodness,
And she also to use newfangleness.
But since that I so kindly am served,   20
I fain would know what she hath deserved.

THOMAS WYATT

There is one quite explicit meaning described by the title
of the poem itself. But why did the women leave him? Is he
just an aging roué bemoaning the inevitable, or is he a man
truly wronged? If the women in the poem are presented as
deer, first tame, then turned wild, what kind of gamekeeper
do we make of the narrative persona? Do we take him at his
word that he was too gentle for his own good, and, if so, does
this mean he might have kept his mistress if he had been less
kind? (Echoes of "Every woman adores a Fascist.") Or do we
conceive of the women as fickle, mindless creatures, drawn to
any "new fangleness"? Are the last two lines ironic? That is,
does the persona really mean that he is very unkindly served
and that he knows exactly what these women deserve?

On the one hand, the poem would appear not to be multi-
stratified, not to demonstrate semantic thickness. Yet on the
other, we see that there is a great deal of meaning to make.
I know that among readers different meanings are made by
proponents of women's liberation, by bachelors, and by the
middle-aged as compared with the young. These are not different meanings based on different information, but on the
attitudes different readers hold.

Sometimes we encounter a poem that does not immediately offer possibilities of making meaning. The poem may
appear at first not to possess layers of meaning, semantic
thickness. It may be in fact that the poem is not semantically
thick, and we would therefore designate it as verse rather than
poetry (more to be said on this in Chapter V). Or it may be
that, even more so than with "Elsie" or "The Lover Showest,"
we need to work hard to discover the semantic thickness of the
work.

For me, Milton's Petrarchan sonnet "On the Late Massacre
in Piemont" is a poem that needs to be worked at to uncover
its various levels of meaning.

Avenge, O Lord, thy slaughtered saints, whose bones
   Lie scattered on the Alpine mountains cold,
   Even them who kept thy truth so pure of old
   When all our fathers worshiped stocks and stones.
Forget not; in thy book record their groans
   Who were thy sheep, and in their ancient fold
   Slain by the bloody Piemontese that rolled
   Mother with infant down the rocks. Their moans
The vales redoubled to the hills, and they
   To heaven. Their martyred blood and ashes sow
   O'er all the Italian fields, where still doth sway
The triple tyrant: that from these may grow
   A hundredfold, who, having learnt thy way,
   Early may fly the Babylonian woe.

At first the sonnet seems to tell rather than evoke. Once
we know a few historical facts and references, available in any
edition of Milton and in most anthologies containing the poem,
it would appear that Milton is simply portraying the event of
the massacre and asking for divine vengeance. The poem
emerges from a specific historical context: during the religious
struggles of the Reformation, members of an ancient heretical
sect closely identified with early Protestantism were massacred
by Roman Catholic troops. "Stocks and stones" refer to the
wood and stone images found in Catholic churches prior to the
Reformation; the "triple tyrant" is the pope, who wore a triple
crown; and the reference to Babylon can be both political and
biblical. Biblical Babylon was regarded by the ancient Hebrews

as a city of sin; the political reference could be to Rome, the center of the Catholic Church, which was viewed by Protestants as a "modern" Babylon. Knowledge of this sort is helpful, but it does limit somewhat our ability to make meanings.

It is generally agreed by literary historians that "On the Late Massacre in Piemont" is a "political" poem. Milton was closely associated with the Cromwellian government in England, and is even regarded by many historians as its chief literary propagandist. The question thus becomes whether there is any meaning-making for us in this work so obviously rooted in a particular political, historical, and religious period.

For me the answer to the question is yes; but the meaning-making is of a different kind from what I find in the poems we have previously discussed. It inheres not in the evocative power of specific words or lines, but rather in the tone of the poem— specifically, in the manner in which the persona addresses God.

There seem to me to be three possibilities inherent in the persona's way of addressing God in the sonnet: (1) the persona's voice is arrogant, demanding, and righteous; (2) the voice is one of supplication, asking rather than demanding, but asking with a conviction so strong as to make the request seem undeniable; (3) Milton is using a rhetorical device, which assumes the tone it does primarily for evocative effects.

There is a great deal of meaning-making in choosing among these three alternatives, and the meaning of the sonnet as a whole depends on which we choose. If we choose the first meaning, we must deal with the implication of man commanding God and, especially, of man commanding God to be an instrument of national policy. The second meaning also invokes God in pursuit of political ends, but with an approach something like a plea. The rhetorical emphasis requires that we atune ourselves to the relationship between Milton and us, rather than between Milton and God. Why, in considering his readers, would Milton decide to speak with this voice?

Implied in the meaning the reader makes of "On the Late Massacre in Piemont" are his religious attitudes and possibly his political beliefs. I think politics must be considered not only because the sonnet is political, but, more to the point, because twentieth-century political leaders constantly invoke God as the protector and sanctifier of national policy. Not simply our religious beliefs, but the way we regard the use of

God's name to justify and condone national enterprises rang-
ing from war to economic policy, is bound to affect our response to Milton's poem. This does not mean we should fall
into the trap I. A. Richards has called "doctrinal adhesion"—
one does not have to be a theist to appreciate Milton. But it
does mean that even so public a poem as "On the Late Massacre in Piemont" can possess semantic thickness, can tap our
deeply rooted attitudes and beliefs. Ultimately, of course, we
must strive for Kenneth Burke's "perspective atop all the conflicts of attitude; and therein lies the antidote to doctrinal
adhesion.

In responding to "On the Late Massacre in Piemont," I am
besieged by conflicting attitudes and values. On the one
hand I am appalled by the meaning that focuses on Milton's
desire to use God as an instrument of political and religious
vengeance. Yet I can also make meaning of the poem as a
masterful appeal for justice; and I am aware that in the
seventeenth century there was no division between Church and
state. In the end, or at least as of my most recent reading of
the poem, I find that its merits triumph; the tone of the poem
seems compelling and its sheer oratorical resonance transcends
its propagandistic qualities. But to come to this persuasion—
to come to terms with the poem—I had genuinely to plumb my
own attitudes and achieve the kind of perspective Burke
describes.

My personal response to the poem is only to the point
here, however, if it illustrates that even so seemingly forthright
a work as Milton's sonnet may "mean" in a plurality of ways.
And it is the plurality of meanings that poems offer which
makes them elusive, which contributes to the difficulty people
have in talking about poems—it can be like grabbing a jellyfish.

But talking about poems with others is also difficult because the jellyfish has a sting. The poem may mean so deeply
and personally for a reader that he is reluctant to risk his
response before the company of others. Responding to poetry
is difficult but not for the reasons that are generally given: the
remoteness or strangeness of poetry. Our poetic and our study
of response have shown that the sheer imaginative and emotional labor exerted by the reader is very great; it may be
nearly as great as the work of the poet in the first place.

The cutting edge of the poetic is double-edged; the poet

makes meanings as he creates the poem, the reader makes meanings as he seeks to apprehend the poem. For this reason unresolved difficulties remain. Response is making meanings, yet I don't think every meaning is equally valid for a given poem. In a world where anything goes, nothing goes. For our poetic to be useful it must help us discriminate among responses, among meanings. We should be able to say with some assurance that the poem of Reconnaissance 3, Theodore Roethke's "I Knew a Woman," does not have praise of misogyny as one of its meanings. Yet how can we deny this as a valid meaning, any more than we can refute a sheep-child-as-Christ meaning made of James Dickey's poem?

This is a frightening question for those of us who make a living as teachers or critics of poetry. And it provides me with yet another explanation of why Richards was unable to accept the protocols written by his students even though those protocols corroborated his own poetic. Two seemingly contradictory mandates emerge side by side: (1) poetry by its very nature requires emotional, subjective response; (2) we must learn how to respond *properly* to poetry (or even be taught to do so). The contradiction mirrors that of Coleridge's demand that poetry be both passionate and precise.

The reasoning of Louise Rosenblatt in *Literature as Exploration* epitomizes the problem. First, she announces a tenable manifesto of response:

> The reader brings to the work personality traits, memories of past events, present needs and preoccupations, a particular mood of the moment, and a particular physical condition. These and many other elements in a never-to-be-duplicated combination determine his response to the peculiar contribution of the text.

Then she finds Richards' students "at the mercy of personal obsessions, chance association, and irrelevant conventional opinions about poetry." [7]

Response is the product of "needs and preoccupations," yet the reader is condemned for his "personal obsessions." Response derives from "personality traits" and "memories,"

[7] Louise Rosenblatt, *Literature as Exploration* (New York: Appleton-Century-Crofts, 1938), pp. 64–65.

yet the "associations" and "opinions" of the reader are denigrated. The situation is as absurd as that of the schoolteacher who tells his students he respects their maturity yet requires that they obtain a pass from him each time they wish to go to the bathroom.

In sum, we have to learn how to use the poetic that frees readers from the tyranny of "the right response." We have to learn to use it without reneging on it or abandoning it. This means we can neither resort to the old rules, as Rosenblatt does, nor leave response to the mercies of anarchy. New criteria by which to understand and evaluate response are in order.

Before undertaking this formidable task, here's a small poem as an envoy to our venture.

> The morning glory—
> another thing
> that will never be my friend.
>
> BASHO

4

RECONNAISSANCE

I

You post a sign,
"We have gone to the cellar to die."

Ready to descend,
you hear the motors of airplanes.

You look up to see
the American right wing.

You think of the euphemism for pay:
"This is the day the eagle craps."

II

All the planes are driven
by suicide pilots.   10

The young fliers are ready to drown,
to fill the oceans, if need be,

while the fish cough
on dry land.

Mountains will fill valleys,
the beaches fuse.

III

You decide against shelter.
Instead, you stand on your porch.

In the sun,
that old fireball,   20

you stand on your porch with your family.
You tell them not to worry.

It's a nice day, you say,
such a warmth on your skin.

MARVIN BELL

Think about "World War III" as if you were its author. Try
to explain decisions you made about form and meaning. For
example, why did you choose three sections for the poem, each
numbered and each containing four two-line stanzas? Why
use the second person singular, "you," in the poem? Who is
this "you"? Why use phrases like "the American right wing,"
" 'This is the day the eagle craps,' " and "that old fireball"?
Most important, what meanings do you, as poet, intend?

IV

INTEGRATING PRINCIPLES

POET TO CRITIC: "I don't know what makes you think you can judge poetry; you've never written a poem."

CRITIC: "I've never laid an egg, either, but I'm a better judge of an omelette than any hen."

We are convinced that making meanings is what poetry is all about. We are further convinced that such meanings result from the interaction between the poem and the reader's emotional and attitudinal disposition. The problem thus becomes that of distinguishing among the variety of meanings evoked by any given poem. Is one meaning "better" than another? Can certain meanings be more faithful to the poem than others? Is there any meaning made of a poem that should be dismissed as illegitimate for that poem? In short, how do we judge meanings made by the reader?

If we conceived of the meanings that comprise response as *interpretations* of the poem, the difficulty of our task might be diminished. To interpret something assumes that there is a stable, identifiable *thing* that is, in effect, being translated by the interpreter. An interpretation offers another version of something. We have already agreed with Coleridge that one of the important characteristics of poetry is its untranslatability. Therefore it will serve us well to note now the subtle but crucial difference between responding by interpreting a poem and responding by making meanings of it.

Those who offer interpretations of a poem assume that the poem is a fixed entity whose limits may somehow be established (by the words on the page, by dictionary definitions, by common usage, by established codes of symbols). For example, an interpretation of "On the Late Massacre in Piemont" explains the historical event on which the poem is based, and offers "translations" of terms like "stocks and stones" and "triple tyrant." Those of us who make meanings of a poem regard the poem as a series of relationships between the poet, the poem, and the reader, the reader and himself, the reader and the world. The difference is essentially one of process.

Interpretation involves an attempt to "extract" meaning from the poem, meaning ascribed to the poet exclusively; meaning-making infuses the poem with meaning from all the sources just mentioned.

Think of this poem by Robert Frost (which unfortunately has become one of the trusties of most poetry courses and therefore is often treated too patly).

STOPPING BY WOODS ON A SNOWY EVENING

Whose woods these are I think I know.
His house is in the village, though;
He will not see me stopping here
To watch his woods fill up with snow.

My little horse must think it queer
To stop without a farmhouse near
Between the woods and frozen lake
The darkest evening of the year.

He gives his harness bells a shake
To ask if there is some mistake.
The only other sound's the sweep
Of easy wind and downy flake.

The woods are lovely, dark, and deep,
But I have promises to keep,
And miles to go before I sleep,
And miles to go before I sleep.

It is a commonplace that Frost's poems have implications beyond the simple pastoral scenes they present. Most critics interpret this poem as depicting the conflict between nature and society. The "woods and frozen lake" pull the narrative persona toward them, but he has "promises to keep" in the world of men. Some critics have gone so far as to interpret the "lovely, dark, and deep" woods as representing some unconscious longing for oblivion; the persona could even be expressing a suicidal bent.

Making meanings of the poem may produce similar accounts of the poem's implications. But how we come by these meanings is different. It is not just that the persona describes the woods as "lovely, dark, and deep"—we must be able to feel the soft darkness, the seemingly endless recession of trees and snow. If we ourselves can sense the suicidal pull, if we associate times we've buried ourselves in snow and, paradoxically, found the cold snow warm, then that meaning holds. If we cannot, if the woods are redolent for us only of wet feet and a closed sky, then the poem will not mean that way for us, no matter how persuasively another reader argues for a "suicidal" interpretation.

The interpreter will note that the wind is "easy," the snow is "downy," and the woods are "lovely," and will offer an interpretation of the poem that includes the allure of nature, of the dark winter woods. The reader making meanings will draw on his own experience and associations in response to the same presentation of images and make a meaning that includes himself and how he feels about the woods in winter and these particular woods that are filling up with snow.

Two different interpreters of the poem, arguing about whether the woods are a symbol of the womb, can look closely at the text of the poem. One will say that the womb, like the woods, is "lovely, dark, and deep." The other will say that many things, besides wombs, possess those characteristics, but most definitely, wombs do not fill up with snow. He will contend that a return-to-the-womb interpretation requires more evidence than this single line about the woods, and that such evidence is not to be found in the poem. Suddenly a maker-of-meanings appears on the scene. He supports the first interpretation with the confession that snowflakes and sperm cells have always been linked in his world of associations. Therefore, since the snow fills the woods, this reader will make a meaning that includes sperm cells filling the womb—the persona of the poem wishes to join them and return to his origins.

So we are, after a short excursus, back to our question: How do we judge meanings made by the reader? The question assumes an answer; that is, it assumes that judgment is possible, that there are more and less legitimate meanings that can be made of a given poem.

If our poetic has a guiding spirit, it is Coleridge's. Here are two passages from his work, one of which I quoted at the outset of the book:

> Now let a man watch his mind while he is composing.... Most of my readers will have observed a small water-insect on the surface of rivulets ... and will have noticed, how the little animal *wins* its way up against the stream, by alternate pulses of active and passive motion, now resisting the current, and now yielding to it in order to gather strength and a momentary *fulcrum* for a further propulsion. This is no unapt emblem for the mind's self-experience in the act of thinking.[1]

> The grandest efforts of poetry are where the imagination is called forth, not to produce a distinct form, but a strong working of the mind, still offering what is still repelled, and again creating what is rejected; the result being what the poet wishes to impress, namely, the substitution of a sublime feeling of the unimaginable for the mere image.[2]

The first passage describes the poet making the poem; the second, the reader making meaning. But observe that although the protagonists are different, the process described is remarkably similar for both. In both instances, the mind flexes and relaxes, accepts and rejects alternatives. It is always in motion, fulfilling itself creatively, whether in the sense of "self-experience" or substituting "a sublime feeling of the unimaginable for the mere image."

Coleridge is telling us that to make a poem and to make meanings of a poem require similar mental and emotional labor—both bring "the whole soul" of man into activity. If we have any doubt that this is Coleridge's contention, we need only hear his explanation of the effect of Shakespeare's poetry. Why is it that Shakespeare so enthralls us? Coleridge quotes the lines from "Venus and Adonis"

[1] *Biographia Literaria*, ed. George Watson (London: J. M. Dent, 1917, 1956), p. 524.
[2] *Coleridge's Shakespearean Criticism*, ed. Thomas Middleton Raysor, vol. 2 (Cambridge, Mass.: Harvard University Press, 1930), p. 118.

> Look! how a bright star shooteth from the sky,
> So glides he in the night from Venus' eye

and says: "You feel him to be a poet, inasmuch as for a time he has made you one—an active creative being." [3] The poetry works because it makes a poet of the reader—not in the literal sense (Shakespeare is obviously *the* poet), but in the sense of participation in the poetic process. The poet creates the work of art; the reader re-creates it. This, I think, is the point: the making of meanings re-creates the poem.

Not surprisingly, psychologists, in an attempt to analyze the act of re-creation, compare the work of art to a dream, the meaning of which must be made by the dreamer. The "participation mystique," according to Carl Jung, is "the secret of artistic creation and of the effectiveness of art"; it is unique to presentational symbolism, of which the dream is the paradigm:

> A dream never says: "You ought," or: "This is the truth." It presents an image in much the same way as nature allows a plant to grow, and we must draw our own conclusions. If a person has a nightmare, it means either that he is too much given to fear, or else that he is too exempt from it; and if he dreams of the old wise man it may mean that he is too pedagogical, and also that he stands in need of a teacher. In a subtle way both meanings come to the same thing as we perceive when we are able to let the work of art act upon us as it acted upon the artist. To grasp its meaning, we must allow it to shape us as it shaped him. [4]

This is exactly what our poetic tells us about poetry! The multiplicity of possible meanings, different but not contradictory, created by the reader as he allows the poem to "act upon" him—our discovery about poetry parallels in every detail Jung's account. The starting points are different; Jung begins with dreams, we began with language and how language "works" in poetry. Yet the poetic that emerges is similar—with one

[3] Ibid., p. 213.
[4] "Psychology and Literature," in Brewster Ghiselin, ed., *The Creative Process: A Symposium* (Berkeley and Los Angeles: University of California Press, 1954), p. 231.

addition. Jung, more explicitly than we until now, allies the person who responds to the work of art and the artist who creates it: "...we must allow [the work of art] to shape us as it shaped him."

Another psychologist, Hanns Sachs, underscores Jung's notion of the "participation mystique," while adding the proviso that the respondent becomes an artist only for the time that he is under the sway of the work of art; he is obviously not transformed for all time into a poet, painter, or composer:

> Responding to art we are led in a ... subtle way toward a much higher degree of participation. In a sense we are creating the work out of our own person while we are looking at it. The work, or rather the artist who produced it, has been able to change us into artistic creators, of course only for the time that we are able to take his work and all its values with our senses as well as with the rest of our mind.[5]

Our study of poems must qualify our acceptance of Sachs' assertion that "we are led" somehow into a "higher degree of participation." On the contrary, we are not so much led as impelled: the poem virtually requires of us that we re-create it by making meanings. Our "higher degree of participation" is the sine qua non of response to poetry—there is no other way; and I, for one, would hardly call the process "subtle." If we don't make meanings our response to the poem can only be a mechanical, surface description of form, meter, and the like. To immerse ourselves in a poem is to leap, feet first, into the currents, countercurrents, and tides that carry the poem's meanings.

While we are considering the psychologist's view of art, we cannot omit Freud. His description of the poet is well known and, I think, misguided. Freud, like Jung, makes an analogy between art and dreams. But he goes further and calls the poet a daydreamer: the child daydreams and the poet—the childlike man—creates art of his daydreams. But a daydream is uncontrolled fancy; it is all play. We learned in Chapter I that the poet's activity cannot accurately be described as play. It

---

[5] *The Creative Unconscious* (Cambridge, Mass.: Sci-art Publishers, 1942), p. 195.

is hard work, disciplined, and requiring a great deal of control. Freud's comparison might be used to inform the first stage of poetic creation, but that is only the beginning. The poem is really made, not of the initial play of the mind, but of the careful attention to detail, of the working and reworking required to effect a precise range of meanings.

In an essay not on poetry at all, Freud surprises us with a revelation profoundly relevant to our investigation. He is writing about his response to Michelangelo's statue of Moses, before which he stood for a number of weeks in unabashed awe. Freud attempts to understand why the statue evoked such a strong emotional response, and writes:

> In my opinion, it can only be the artist's intention, insofar as he has succeeded in expressing it to us in his work and conveying it to us, that grips us so powerfully. I realize it cannot be merely a matter of intellectual comprehension; what he aims at is to awaken in us the same emotional attitude, the same mental constellation as that which in him produced the impetus to create.[6]

The artist brings us into the "same emotional attitude, the same mental constellation as that which in him produced the impetus to create"—that's the point. It is another way of describing the "participation mystique." We participate in the creation by re-creating; but in order to re-create we must share the impulse that impelled the work originally.

In adding the concept of the participation mystique to our poetic, we seem to veer toward "intentionalism" in response to poetry. Intentionalism is not one of the kinds of malpractice mentioned by Richards; but it is so clearly a habit of response among my own students, and so clearly, to my way of thinking, an error in response, that we must be careful to distinguish between bringing response into "the same mental constellation" of the poet, and requiring that that response take account of the poet's known or supposed intentions.

Intentionalism is not a difficult concept to understand. It means exactly what it says: to understand a poem we must understand the poet's intentions. Readers might, for example,

[6] *On Creativity and the Unconscious* (New York: Harper & Row, 1958), p. 12.

assert that Kenneth Rexroth, in the following poem, intends us to feel sorry for him.

THE ADVANTAGES OF LEARNING

I am a man with no ambitions
And few friends, wholly incapable
Of making a living, growing no
Younger, fugitive from some just doom.
Lonely, ill clothed, what does it matter?
At midnight I make myself a jug
Of hot white wine and cardamon seeds.
In a torn grey robe and old beret,
I sit in the cold writing poems,
Drawing nudes on the crooked margins,
Copulating with sixteen year old
Nymphomaniacs of my imagination.

In addition to noting the plaintive effect of "few friends," "lonely," "ill clothed," and other images of poverty, students have supported their intentionalism with the photograph of Rexroth on the cover of the volume from which the poem comes. In the photograph, Rexroth looks like the persona of his poem, morose, eyes downcast, wearing somewhat shabby clothes. But how do we know the poem is about Rexroth himself? The narrative persona, the "I" of the poem, could be someone else. The persona could be drawn from an acquaintance of Rexroth's, or it could be imaginary. Or it could be Rexroth portraying himself: we simply don't know. All we do *know* is that there is an "I" speaking in the poem, who may be *a* poet, since he tells of writing poems.

What if we had a statement from Rexroth attesting that the poem is indeed autobiographical? Would we then be able to say he intends us to feel sorry for him? I think not. The poem of course makes no assertion. A reader can argue that the last three lines present a triumph of the imagination over the physical world. For this reader, the title is not ironic: the advantage of learning is that it avails a man of other worlds, it provides a feast for the imaginative life. Another reader can maintain that the last three lines present the sorriest dimension of the whole poem; the poor poet must resort to masturbatory fantasies. For him the title is thus ironic; there are no advantages to learning at all, and the learned man ends up in a cold room, lonely and abandoned.

It could still be asked: what if the intentions are not supposed but known? What if Rexroth told us—not only that the poem was about himself but that he intended it as a portrait of self-pity? Admittedly, given such testimony, our capacity to make meanings of the poem by re-creating it might be restricted. (And poets are usually too wise to impose such restrictions; hence they seldom tell what they intend by a poem.) But even so I would argue that to base our response on the poet's stated intentions would be wrong. I refuse to equate intentions with meanings. The poet can quite honorably intend one or several meanings and create a poem that has others quite different. If Rexroth told us he intended this poem to be self-pitying, it could still have as one of its meanings an affirmation of individual strength. In this sense the meanings that can be made of a poem truly are beyond the poet's control or intention. This fact is demonstrated by the numerous instances in which an eager reader offers a poet a new meaning for his work. The poets I have seen in this situation candidly acknowledge that the new meaning had not occurred to them; nonetheless they admit or even are enthusiastic about the reader's meaning as supplementing their own range of meanings. Perhaps we can recall Kunitz's reaction on pages 21 and 22 to one reader's meaning, and here we can read a poem by Denise Levertov celebrating new meanings made by her readers.

THE SECRET

Two girls discover
the secret of life
in a sudden line of
poetry.

I who don't know the
secret wrote
the line. They
told me

(through a third person)
they had found it   10
but not what it was
not even

what line it was. No doubt
by now, more than a week
later, they have forgotten
the secret,

the line, the name of
the poem. I love them
for finding what
I can't find,   20

and for loving me
for the line I wrote,
and for forgetting it
so that

a thousand times, till death
finds them, they may
discover it again, in other
lines

in other
happenings. And for   30
wanting to know it,
for

assuming there is
such a secret, yes,
for that
most of all.

To return to our previous discussion—I have used "The Advantages of Learning" to articulate two of the problems inherent in intentionalism: (1) we usually don't know what the poet intended; and (2) even when we do, we should not let his intentions restrict the meanings we can make of the poem. To these, a third problem can be added: that for the majority of poems, we have no way of knowing the poet's intentions; the poet is dead and has not left a declaration of intentions to accompany his poems.

Literary historians will of course speculate about a poet's intentions. It may very well be that Emily Dickinson longed for an unattainable lover and intended the poem "Hope" to be a message to him. But she doesn't say so, and the intentionalist argument must be built on speculation.

In the arena of literary criticism, intentionalism is at worst a mild vice; at best, a way of attempting to gain a fuller picture of a poet's life and work. In the "real world," the world of the personal and political destinies of men, intentionalism can be pernicious. We have all heard of poets punished by totalitarian governments because their work was branded dangerous or subversive. In such cases, the government officials assume a specific intention on the part of the poet. As recently as 1968, a poem was used against a poet in a court of law in this country. The poem is "Black People!" by LeRoi Jones (Imamu Amiri Baraka).

BLACK PEOPLE!
What about that bad short you saw last week
on Frelinghuysen, or those stoves and
     refrigerators, record players, shotguns,
in Sears, Bambergers, Klein's, Hahnes',
     Chase, and the smaller joosh
enterprises? What about that bad jewelry, on
     Washington Street, and
those couple of steps on Springfield? You
     know how to get it, you can
get it, no money down, no money never,   10
     money dont grow on trees no
way, only whitey's got it, makes it with a
     machine, to control you
You cant steal nothin from a white man, he's
     already stole it he owes
you anything you want, even his life. All the
     stores will open if you
will say the magic words. The magic words
     are: Up against the wall mother
fucker this is a stick up! Or: Smash the   20
     window at night (these are magic
actions) smash the windows daytime,
     anytime, together, lets smash the
window drag the shit from in there. No
     money down. No time to pay. Just
take what you want. The magic dance in the
     street. Run up and down Broad
Street niggers, take the shit you want. Take
     their lives if need be, but
get what you want what you need. Dance up   30
     and down the streets, turn all

the music up, run through the streets with
   music, beautiful radios on
Market Street, they are brought here
   especially for you . . . Our brothers
are moving all over, smashing at jellywhite
   faces. We must make our own
World, man, our own world, and we can not
   do this unless the white man
is dead. Let's get together and kill him my   40
   man, let's get to gather the fruit
of the sun, let's make a world we want black
   children to grow and learn in
do not let your children when they grow
   look in your face and curse you by
pitying your tomish ways.

    I have difficulty responding to this poem *as poetry* because
of what I. A. Richards would call my "doctrinal adhesions."
Because of my beliefs, the implied anti-Semitism of "joosh,"
and the seeming exhortations to violence become a barrier
between me and the poem. But I must not treat it as a political
tract: the ultimate test of the poem as a poem is that established
by the poetic. Is its language at once excited and precise? Does
it evoke a range of meanings and engage me, attitudinally and
emotionally, in making meanings of the poem, in its re-
creation? Does it serve not so much to communicate the poet's
ideas to me as to cause me to experience the tumult and passion
of the ideas themselves?

    These questions were not asked by the judge who presided
over LeRoi Jones' trial following the Newark, New Jersey,
riots of 1967. He did not call in experts on poetics to testify
whether or not this is a poem. Instead, he accepted it as a
poem and saw in the poem only a mandate for action. He
decided that Jones' intention in writing the poem must have
been hortatory, actually to persuade the black people of
Newark to riot. Accordingly, the poem was called a "diabolical
prescription" by the judge, and Jones received a jail sentence
and a large fine.

    No poem—even what appears to be a "political" poem—is
a "prescription." Remember, a poem, like a dream, "never says:
'You ought,' or: 'This is the truth.'" The poem presents an
image, a vision. One of the chief dangers of intentionalism,

then, is that it tempts us to think of poems as serving *purposes*, as having reasons for being that are other than poetic. Whether the work is Yevgeny Yevtushenko's, Rudyard Kipling's, or Ezra Pound's, we pervert it as poetry if we assign anything other than a poetic meaning to it.

If intentionalism is so distinctly unhelpful in response to poetry, how then do we come to share in the "participation mystique"? How do we allow the poem to shape us as it shaped the poet? In Freud's terms, how do we enter the emotional attitude and mental constellation that provided the poet with the impetus to create? Our foray into the liabilities of an intentionalist poetic informs a concept of intent that will help us.

A distinction emerges that is crucial: on the one hand, we have *intentionalism* in response to poetry, which is untenable because it assumes we should inject nonpoetic dimensions (personal circumstances of the poet, motivational factors, and the like) into the process of response; on the other hand, in order to shape our response to a poem with some fidelity to the poet's own creative impulse, we must be able to imagine, sense, or perceive the *poetic intent* of the poem. We asked earlier what boundaries could possibly be placed on response, which our poetic demanded be associative, attitudinal, and emotional. The answer is that such response finds its range of possibility and its freedoms and restrictions of meanings within the poetic intent of any given poem.

Remembering my account, in Chapter I, of the making of "Lemming Song" may help to clarify the distinction. The poem can be responded to fully (that is, the reader can become re-creator) with no knowledge of why the poem was written. We do not have to know of the author's longtime interest in animal behavior, nor of the scientific article that prompted the poem. But full response requires that we consider reasons for the use of various words in the poem, like "thermostat," "triggers" and "cued"; it requires that we consider why the lines and stanzas break where they do; and it requires that we "know" why sex and death are so strongly linked in the poem. These have nothing to do with intention, but are integral to the work's poetic intent.

Poetic intent (hereafter, simply "intent") thus inheres in our coming to understand the decisions and choices we presume the poet to have made. In order to respond to a poem faithfully (that is, to distinguish those meanings that are more fully responsive to the poem from those that are more the product of some particular predisposition of the reader) we must be able to perceive the intent of the poem.

At some point during the process of response, the reader must, amid all his meaning-making, ask himself, "Is this meaning (or, are these meanings) in keeping with the intent of the poem, or is it primarily a meaning I'm bringing to the poem because of such-and-such an experience I've had?" This does not mean that the reader must renege on or deny his own emotional and attitudinal being. But he must balance his subjectivity with the effort to respond within the realm of the poem's intent.

How can we ever know the intent of a poem? Simply put, we cannot *know* it. However, we can train and discipline ourselves as readers to *sense* or intuitively *apprehend* a poem's intent. Responding to poetry, like making poems, is an art. As such, there are no absolute and unyielding criteria for measurement. But just as there is a discipline to the making of poems, a discipline comprising the balance between passion and precision, between freedom and constraint, so this same discipline applies to the process of response, to the making of meanings by the reader. The discipline does not reside in the kind of approach to poetry implicit in the exercise questions of textbooks. There are no right answers. But there is a technique.

We can identify two dimensions of the technique of response. One is to formulate for ourselves a poetic, an articulated and overt set of the assumptions, expectations, even demands, of poetry. The poetic must be at once firm enough to have definition and to be applied to poems without losing its integrity every time a given poem comes up with surprises, exceptions, or innovations that don't "fit" the poetic. When a poem doesn't fit, we must ask if our poetic is too narrow or if in fact we are confronted by something that we really don't think is a poem. For these really to be alternatives, the poetic must be flexible enough to adapt or amend itself to encompass the unfamiliar kind of poem. It must also be definitive enough to enable us to distinguish sham from truth, verse from poetry, cleverness from passion, an explosion of emotion from a work of art. The poetic we developed in the previous chapter may be able to stand us in good stead—we shall test it further as we progress.

This first dimension of technique is one to which a great deal of attention is usually paid, although I consider it to be the wrong kind of attention. Most readers are concerned with what a poem is; the problem is that they look for definitions of poetry to guide them rather than an organic account of process that describes how poetry works.

The second dimension of the technique of response is notably absent from most studies of poetry, whether they be private or undertaken as part of a poetry class. This entails, quite simply, that we make poems, that we ourselves write poetry. If we take the notion of intent in poetry seriously, how else are we to gain insight into the intent of a poem unless we have written poems? That we must do something ourselves in order to know how it functions seems so obvious a fact that it would hardly require mentioning were it not so consistently overlooked. In other words, I think the drama critic portrayed in the epigram beginning this chapter is clever but his statement is misleading. He can judge the omelette because *he* made it; it does not follow that he is a better judge of an egg than any hen.

In most of the activities of our lives, we know that to do is to know. Can we really comprehend the aching ankles of the five-year-old learning to ice skate if we have never skated ourselves? Can we understand what the runner means when he tells us he got a second wind if we have never run hard? Can we fully appreciate the workmanship of a fine sweater if we have never knitted? Comfortable in our street shoes, we can lend support to the novice skater, holding him up and offering encouragement. Having never run ourselves, we can thrill as we watch a comeback in the last lap of a mile race. We can wear the sweater, delighted by its soft texture, glowing colors, and intricate pattern. But in all these instances we cannot fully comprehend the process or the product unless we have done it ourselves.

Further, we acknowledge that those who do it will know more about it, since we defer to their insight. After the theater, a group of friends will inevitably pay special attention to the opinion of one of their number who himself has acted on the stage. When a moon rocket is launched, other television commentators give way to the observations of the former astronaut. Among sports announcers it is generally conceded that those who were or are themselves athletes are most fully able to understand what is going on in the minds and with the bodies of the men on the field. Many poets never write literary criticism, but those who do are listened to especially closely: Eliot, Pound, and William Carlos Williams have a special power as critics because they are also practitioners.

None of this is to say that we should feel inadequate in our response to something we have never done or can never do. Even though we have never painted, or written a novel or a play, our response to paintings, novels, and plays can certainly be insightful, emotionally powerful, and carefully considerate of the art form itself. I dare say a case could be made that some of the finest critics in the world are not themselves practitioners of the art. But I would suggest that even their criticism would benefit if they tried to do what they write so well.

Most of us will never be astronauts; most of us will never attempt to write a novel. But all of us can try to make a poem. The materials are at hand and the investment of time is comparatively short. Making poems, unlike driving racing cars, is not a luxury of the privileged few. On the contrary, it is an activity available to anyone engaged in a serious and disciplined effort to learn about poetry.

I do not think my suggestion that the reader of poetry ought himself to try to make a poem places an unfair burden on those who value poetry yet have never considered themselves as makers of poems. On the contrary, I hope this suggestion can be seen as creating an opportunity rather than an obstacle. Remember, I have said nothing of the quality of the poem to be created; I cannot urge too strongly or repeat too often that it is the process of making that is most important here. Further, the process of making a poem is similar to the process of meaning-making central to response to poetry. Just as we consider ourselves capable of responding to poetry (or of learning how we can respond to poetry), there is no reason why we cannot also consider ourselves capable of making poems (or of learning to be makers of poems).

Our object is to understand poetry as best we can. To do this, we have seen that we must learn to respond not only to the meaning-making potential of the poem and ourselves, but also to the intent integral to the poem. There is no other way to apprehend a poem's intent than by the empathetic process of judgment that depends on our being able to put ourselves in the mental and emotional "constellation" of the poet himself.

Our facility as the poem's re-creators will be enhanced by our knowledge of ourselves as creators.

As readers who are also poets, we shall be reversing the kind of role duality we examined in Chapter I, where it became apparent that the poet, as he makes the poem, must be able to put himself in the place of the reader. The poet has to be able to see his poem from the outside, looking in, in order to gauge the response he might elicit. We, in turn, must attempt to see the poem from the inside, looking from without, in order to gauge its intent. Our task can be measured by Raymond Carver's poem.

MORNING, THINKING OF EMPIRE

We press our lips to the enameled rims of the cups
And know this grease that floats
Over the coffee will one day stop our hearts.
Eyes and fingers drop onto silverware that is not
Silverware. Outside the window, waves beat against
The chipped white walls of the old city. Suddenly,
Your hands rise from the rough tablecloth
As if to prophesy. Your lips tremble . . .
To hell with the future, I want to say.
Our future lies deep in the afternoon.
It is a narrow street with a cart and driver,
A driver who looks at us and hesitates,
Then shakes his head. Meanwhile,
I coolly crack the egg of a fine Leghorn chicken.
Your eyes film. You turn from me and look across
The rooftops at the sea. Even the flies are still.
I crack the other egg.
Surely we have diminished one another.

There is nothing mysterious at least about the physical situation presented by the poem. Two people, probably a man and a woman, are having breakfast together, drinking their coffee and eating soft-boiled eggs. They are in an "old city" by the sea—the "cart and driver" suggest Europe and the Mediterranean. The central image (or, as described in Chapter I, the core metaphor) seems to be based on the prosaic event depicted and the portentous quality of "Empire" in the title and images like hearts stopping and hands rising to prophesy in the poem itself. The reader-poet who has himself attempted to make a poem of a glance from a loved one, of a remark by a stranger, of a strange feeling about what will happen to him that day, of any of the things Langer calls "unspeakable," will sense something about the intent of this poem and will know the difficulties it presented the poet. Poetry is in large part the process of putting the unspeakable into words, and that is what is going on in "Morning, Thinking of Empire."

The reader-poet will recognize the care with which the coffee-drinking and egg-cracking images are made. These things the poem can present overtly; they begin as simple physical acts. Yet they are made into more than that and they frame the heart of the poem—the hands rising, the lips trembling, damning the future with bravado. Having made poems himself, the reader will more readily recognize how meticulously this portrait of something felt but unspeakable between two people has been constructed.

Take simply "silverware that is not / Silverware." Again a prosaic detail; we are all familiar with the convention of calling forks and knives silverware whether they are made of silver or not. Yet here the poet has isolated that convention, transformed it into a small significant vision that reverberates through the whole. The reader, as poet, has worked to make the prosaic into the significant; silverware that is not silver will be understood by him.

Why is the poem entitled "Morning, Thinking of Empire," and how does having written poems equip the reader to answer this question? First and most obvious, the reader has had to make choices about the titles of his own poems. He knows the difference between a comparatively neutral title (for example, "Spring," "Love Song") and one that is potent, that contributes to the meanings of the poem. Neutral titles are essentially labels; often they are simply taken from the first line of the poem. The word "Empire," especially, repeated nowhere else in the poem, signifies that this title of itself contributes to the meanings of the poem. The effect of the title, then, is part of the intent of the poem. I suggest that having had to attend to his own titles, the reader will be more sensitive to this one, and will more readily recognize its effect in expanding the scope of the poem: what is going on between these two people is at once small and vast—the title signals this.

A possible meaning to be made of the poem is that the "Empire" is historical, and that these people, while break-fasting in a strange land, are brought by their surroundings to gloomy thoughts on the perishability of great empires like those of Rome and Egypt. Is this a maverick meaning, one untrue or at least secondary to the poem's intent? I think so. Further, I maintain that the reader who is also a poet will be able to recognize it as such because he will apprehend that the intent of the poem is to present the ineffable failure two people feel at that moment about what they have done with themselves. But why is the reader who has made poems any more likely to perceive this (if you agree with me about the intent) than one who has not? The answer lies in what was said earlier. The reader has himself tried to put the unspeak-able into words, he *senses* how it is being done here. He knows that the poet cannot say, "This problem we have is at once intimate and huge," but must rely on the evocative power of a title like "Morning, Thinking of Empire" to suggest the im-mensity of the failure experienced by the poem's protagonists.

"Surely we have diminished one another"—making poems himself will have taught the reader how difficult it is to end a poem (which we saw also in Chapter I). Is the final line "right"? I suspect that reader-poets will argue over this. What if the poem had ended with "I crack the other egg"? The reader would be left with the hard *crack* of the shell, a breaking that could symbolize all that has gone wrong. This side of the argument finds the last line too explicit; it states more than evokes and should therefore have been omitted. The other side might argue for the last line because without it too much is left open; without it the poet forfeits a degree of control over the meanings evoked by the poem. The last line thus can be said to epitomize the intent of the poem, for it leaves no doubt that the "Empire" is first and foremost one built by the two people, that the emotional currents are flowing directly between them, rather than being generated by time, place, or history.

I do not mean to suggest that there is only one meaning to the poem and that it is accessible to the poetry-writing reader alone. Nor do I mean to imply that having made one or several poems guarantees that a reader will respond more fully and more faithfully to the poems of others. The point is simply that I think the reader who is also a poet is more *likely* to be able to distinguish between idiosyncratic and integral meanings and is more likely to be sensitive to how the poem works. Having labored through the difficult process of making poems himself—and having had to be both poet and reader while so doing—he is likely to be more attentive to the process of poems written by others.

Concerning "Morning, Thinking of Empire" alone, I contend that having worked, himself, on poems will cause the reader to think as the poet might—about the details of imagery, about the function of the title, about the way the poem ends; in short, about the problems the poet faced in realizing the poem's intent. A reader who has never written a poem might do this also, but the reader-poet virtually has to.

Inspired by a Jacques Cousteau documentary film on the hippopotamus, and particularly by the way the hippos seemed virtually to dance on the river bottom, I wrote a poem called "How Hippos Make Love."

> In fat water
> fat hippos
> dance
> with soft flow
> like bread dough
> kneaded by fat
> fingers, slowly.
>
> They tiptoe
> so light
> the bottommud   10
> balloons
> them upward
> til their ears
> periscope.
>
> Coming down
> the buoyant male
> settles gently

> as a soap sud
> upon the broadest
> welcome: and this   20
> is how hippos make love.

A friend of mine asked me, after he and his wife had read the
poem several times and discussed it between themselves,
whether I intended the repetition of "fat" in the first stanza
or if I just couldn't think of another adjective. What a question! Of course I intended to repeat "fat" over and over in an
attempt to make the whole world of the poem exude fatness.

My friend is hardly a philistine—he and his wife are both
accomplished musicians and generally knowledgeable about
the arts. Yet he has never written a poem, a fact that makes
his question less absurd. Since he had never been engaged in
the process of choosing each word the way one does in making
a poem, he couldn't know how unequivocally intentional all
the words of this poem are. Whether or not the repetition of
"fat" works is another question. It may very well be that it
didn't for my friend. The strategy may fail insofar as "fat
water," "fat hippos," "fat fingers" do not evoke at least approximately the effect intended. But there is no question of the
conscious intent on my part.

Consider Keats' "Ode on a Grecian Urn"—particularly the
third stanza.

I

Thou still unravished bride of quietness,
  Thou foster-child of silence and slow time,
Sylvan historian, who canst thus express
  A flowery tale more sweetly than our rhyme:
What leaf-fringed legend haunts about thy shape
  Of deities or mortals, or of both,
    In Tempe or the dales of Arcady?
What men or gods are these? What maidens loth?
  What mad pursuit? What struggle to escape?
    What pipes and timbrels? What wild ecstasy?   10

II

Heard melodies are sweet, but those unheard
  Are sweeter; therefore, ye soft pipes, play on;
Not to the sensual ear, but, more endeared,

Pipe to the spirit ditties of no tone:
Fair youth, beneath the trees, thou canst not leave
   Thy song, nor ever can those trees be bare;
     Bold Lover, never, never canst thou kiss,
Though winning near the goal—yet, do not grieve;
   She cannot fade, though thou hast not thy bliss,
     For ever wilt thou love, and she be fair!   20

III

Ah, happy, happy boughs! that cannot shed
   Your leaves, nor ever bid the Spring adieu;
And, happy melodist, unwearièd,
   For ever piping songs for ever new;
More happy love! more happy, happy love!
   For ever warm and still to be enjoyed,
     For ever panting, and for ever young;
All breathing human passion far above,
   That leaves a heart high-sorrowful and cloyed,
     A burning forehead, and a parching tongue.   30

IV

Who are these coming to the sacrifice?
   To what green altar, O mysterious priest,
Lead'st thou that heifer lowing at the skies,
   And all her silken flanks with garlands drest?
What little town by river or sea shore,
   Or mountain-built with peaceful citadel,
     Is emptied of this folk, this pious morn?
And, little town, thy streets for evermore
   Will silent be; and not a soul to tell
     Why thou art desolate, can e'er return.   40

V

O Attic shape! Fair attitude! with brede
   Of marble men and maidens overwrought,
With forest branches and the trodden weed;
   Thou, silent form, dost tease us out of thought
As doth eternity: Cold Pastoral!
   When old age shall this generation waste,
     Thou shalt remain, in midst of other woe
Than ours, a friend to man, to whom thou say'st,
   "Beauty is truth, truth beauty,"—that is all
     Ye know on earth, and all ye need to know.   50

The (physical) center of this poem is laden with "happy," repeated over and over. If we could talk with Keats, we should hardly ask him if he intended this repetition or if it is a mistake. Understanding the intent of the repetition is crucial to apprehending the intent of the poem as a whole. One of the meanings I make of the poem is that of paradox, the great joy of the unfulfilled. The "Cold Pastoral" of the last stanza expresses the paradox most fully for me—that a warm and lustful scene, so full of passion and life, can also be cold, silent, and unchanging.

I put myself in the poet's place and see him at work, striving to evoke at once the austere dignity of the eternal urn and the flesh-and-blood delight of the scene painted on it. I sense that to do this he created a poem that starts off slowly, almost somberly, depicting the urn. It accelerates, builds to a crescendo in the third stanza. The poet cannot do enough to convey the exuberance of the scene he sees, both literally and in his imagination, created by the urn. In a sense, his presentation is of a happiness beyond happiness. The most eloquent expression of this can only be (paradoxically) the kind of inarticulateness born of awe that causes us to repeat the expression which we hope will approximate what we feel and wish to evoke in others. (In this context, I remember the line— "Wonderful! Wonderful! And yet more wonderful!")

There are no questions asked of the urn in the third stanza; instead, there are passionate exclamations by the narrative persona. With the resumption of question-asking—this I think distances the narrative persona from the urn—in the fourth stanza, the poem begins a deacceleration until broken by the upswing of the last stanza that culminates with the cry "Cold Pastoral!"

My apprehension of intent and the meaning-making evoked for me by Keats' "Ode" are integral. The meaning I make, that of interdependence between an eternal calm and an immediate passion, emerges from how I perceive the poem being made. The repetition of "happy," particularly relevant to my own poem, is just a beginning of the process of empathetic creation (or re-creation) that characterizes my response to the poem. I cannot say, "This is what Keats did," or "This is why he did such and such"; but I can imagine what he might have consciously striven to do and the reasons for it. It is this kind of imagining that can bring the respondent into the mental and emotional constellation of the artist.

The famous lines " 'Beauty is truth, truth beauty,'—that is all / Ye know on earth, and all ye need to know" must not—contrary to common practice—be treated as assertion. The tenets of our poetic advise us that poetry is not the statement of great ideas or principles, but a presentation of the experience of having the idea. Thus I do not put Keats' seeming proclamation to any test of logic. I do not ask if " 'Beauty is truth, truth beauty' " is true in any empirical or philosophical sense. An argument, philosophical or empirical, could wander inconclusively for days. And so it should. Keats is not saying that all that is ugly must be false, any more than he is saying all that is beautiful must be true. Such thoughts couldn't be further from the intent of these lines—or of the poem—as I perceive it. The poet is presenting an idea (or, perhaps more appropriately, a vision) born equally of his experience in making the poem and his imaginative response to the urn.

Thus we treat this as other than a poem if we find in Keats' lines a "Romantic manifesto," as do some critics and teachers. There is no manifesto of the Romantics here, any more than there is a manifesto of modern poets in MacLeish's "Ars Poetica," which we considered earlier—"A poem should not mean / But be." Both ideas or visions are "true" only insofar as they are true to the intent of the poem, if they succeed as part of the endings of poems in helping us to re-create for ourselves the experience of coming upon them, of conceiving them.

What does our notion of intent do for the dilemmas of response we discussed? Does a fresh start with "Elsie" (p. 78), or "The Sheep Child" (p. 81), or "On the Late Massacre in Piemont" (p. 91), approaching them with a strategy of empathetic re-creation, help us to distinguish idiosyncratic from faithful response?

The question is rhetorical. I am convinced that concern with the intent of these poems will discipline response in a way that makes the plastic cow clearly not viable in response to "Elsie." Nor will a rebirth-of-Christ meaning hold for "The Sheep Child." And Milton's poem presents the conquest of good over evil, rather than an arrogant injunction of vengeance.

Returning briefly to Williams' poem, we should ask ourselves why we, as reader-poets, would entitle that poem "Elsie." Apart from its meanings, the dominant images of the poem clearly are those of poverty-stricken rural America. If we were to choose a name in keeping with such images, what would be our choice? Although I personally know no one named Elsie, I can understand Williams' choice. In fact, I understand it better for not knowing any Elsie—my world is that of the university and the middle class. Moving back and forth between the images and meanings of the poem and its title, the appropriateness of the name "Elsie" becomes apparent to me. "Elsie" has a farm-girl aura, to which its unfashionableness contributes. It is slightly out of date, unfamiliar, and connotes a distant, rapidly diminishing, agrarian society. In deciding on "Elsie" myself—that is, trying to share the poet's mental and emotional constellation—I find no room for a meaning based on the Borden's trademark.

The Christ-reborn meaning of "The Sheep Child" is appealing because it is clever. But in its cleverness also lies its weakness. It lacks concern with poetic intent; it is a reader's game, seeing how far the poem's meanings can be stretched to encompass unlikely ones. I perceive the intent of the poem as a presentation of the myth of rural America. If this were not so, the poet would not so exclusively draw on the images and associations particular to American farm life. The barns and pastures, the soft-wooded trees and pinestraw, the foxes and dewy pastures, the wolves, hounds, and bean fields—put together, these all present American farm life, even without the explicit reference to the southern city of Atlanta, in the midst of farming country. If I were a poet working with a theme so universal as the Second Coming, I would not allow my images to be so particularized; on the other hand, if I were a poet who knew a part of this country well, and intended to make a poem of the land and its legends, I would attempt to present its particular images, sounds, smells—the "feel" of the countryside—as fully as possible. This the poet has done.

Further, I sense that the intent of the poem is to present the lives of the farm boys as much as it is to present the birth,

death, and life in legend of the sheep-child. The poem begins
and ends by talking about the lives of the farm boys, and the
closing presents the farm boys living out their days, mundanely
for the most part, but still haunted by the legend, by the possibility within themselves of the kind of union of which the
sheep-child was born. My poem on the rebirth of Christ—were
I to attempt one—could not end in this fashion. His Second
Coming would not be so localized and inauspicious as to leave
a bunch of farm boys to masturbatory fantasies and the ordinary upbringing of their families.

My empathetic re-creation of "On the Late Massacre in
Piemont" requires that I consider the effects of the persona's
imperative voice. Were I the poet, why would I choose to speak
to God in outright demands, or possibly even dare to command
God? In re-creating the poem, I "become" Milton. This does
not mean I will read political motivation into the poem—
reading the poem as a political tract perverts it, and assigning
extrapoetic motivation to the author smacks of intentionalism.

What I must try to do is to imagine why Milton, as poet,
not as politician, chose to write the sonnet as he did. In so
doing, I come to regard the imperative tone—"Avenge, O Lord,"
"Forget not"—as a carefully conceived rhetorical device. We
are not to take the commands literally; they exist to evoke
moral outrage and righteousness. The poet does not actually
believe he can command God. But he does believe he can inspire in his readers the same revulsion he feels toward the
massacre; he also believes he can offer hope—a moral vision
of a restoration of order, of a world in which such crimes will
not be tolerated. Hence it is the tone—not the literal content—
of the commands that is important. The one gives an Old
Testament quality to the poem. My empathetic re-creation leads
me to perceive the poet as prophet, inveighing against the evils
of the world, and of course addressing himself to God as well
as to his readers.

In pursuit of integrating principles for our poetic, a number of terms have been used to describe response to poems—
"self-experience" (Coleridge), "participation mystique" (Jung),
"the same emotional attitude, the same mental constellation"
(Freud), and "empathetic re-creation" (mine). They all lead
us to a single, fundamental precept: our response to poetry is

more likely to be at once fully explorative of meanings and capable of distinguishing among the fidelity of meanings if we ourselves have made poems. Response requires that we re-create the poem. We can be better re-creators for having been creators.

Our initial question was "How do we judge meanings made by the reader?" Our answer is in two parts. First, we cannot do so absolutely. Response is itself an art; or, if we reserve the term "art" for the creation of an original work, response is most certainly an intricate process in which there are no absolute standards for judgment. But, as a process, re-sponse can comprise better and worse strategies and methods. Thus the second part of our answer: having established a concept of poetic intent and a strategy for gauging that intent, we can attempt to discriminate among those responses that are more and less faithful to the intent of a given poem. In this lies the discipline of response. The reader must be able not only to let his imagination and emotions range widely among the meanings evoked by the poem, he must also be able to govern and shape the scope of his activity so it lies within the realm of the poem's intent. The discipline of response is what I have called empathetic re-creation. Re-creation itself is not enough, it must be tempered by the reader's conscious effort to empathize with the poet, to get into the poet's skin, to sense what the poet was trying to do in making that particular poem.

The poem, I have insisted, is not so much a product as a process. Our poetic has described the process as excited, pre-cise, evocative, presentational, full of meanings and generative of meaning-making. Empathetic re-creation is not a concept now to be superimposed on an already established poetic. It is rather to be interwoven through all the strands—every aspect of the poetic depends on it. To apprehend the excitement of language in poetry, to appreciate the precision with which a poem presents an image, to feel the power of evocation—all these are enhanced by our being able to re-create the poem empathetically, to engage ourselves imaginatively in its com-plete process, from inception to abandonment.

As empathetic re-creators, we might well try our skills and imaginations with this poem by John Dryden. How do we choose among meanings we can make of the "Grand Chorus" in particular?

A SONG FOR SAINT CECILIA'S DAY

NOVEMBER 22, 1687

I

From Harmony, from heavenly Harmony
    This universal frame began:
  When Nature underneath a heap
    Of jarring atoms lay
  And could not heave her head,
The tuneful voice was heard from high:
    Arise, ye more than dead!
Then cold, and hot, and moist, and dry
    In order to their stations leap,
    And Music's power obey.   10
From Harmony, from heavenly Harmony
    This universal frame began:
    From Harmony to Harmony
Through all the compass of the notes it ran,
The diapason closing full in Man.

II

What passion cannot Music raise and quell?
    When Jubal struck the chorded shell,
    His listening brethren stood around,
    And, wondering, on their faces fell
    To worship that celestial sound.   20
Less than a god they thought there could not dwell
    Within the hollow of that shell,
    That spoke so sweetly, and so well.
What passion cannot Music raise and quell?

III

    The trumpet's loud clangor
      Excites us to arms
    With shrill notes of anger
      And mortal alarms.
    The double double double beat
      Of the thundering drum   30
      Cries, "Hark! the foes come;
Charge, charge, 'tis too late to retreat!"

IV

    The soft complaining flute
    In dying notes discovers

The woes of hopeless lovers,
Whose dirge is whisper'd by the warbling lute.

V

Sharp violins proclaim
Their jealous pangs and desperation,
Fury, frantic indignation,
Depth of pains and height of passion   40
For the fair disdainful dame.

VI

But oh! what art can teach,
What human voice can reach
    The sacred organ's praise?
Notes inspiring holy love,
Notes that wing their heavenly ways
    To mend the choirs above.

VII

Orpheus could lead the savage race,
And trees unrooted left their place
    Sequacious of the lyre: 50
But bright Cecilia raised the wonder higher:
When to her organ vocal breath was given,
An Angel heard, and straight appear'd—
    Mistaking Earth for Heaven!

GRAND CHORUS

As from the power of sacred lays
    The spheres began to move,
And sung the great Creator's praise
    To all the blest above;
So, when the last and dreadful hour
This crumbling pageant shall devour,   60
The trumpet shall be heard on high,
The dead shall live, the living die,
And Music shall untune the sky.

5

RECONNAISSANCE

Here are the lyrics of two rock songs, "The Love You Save (May Be Your Own)" by Joe Tex, and "For What It's Worth" by Stephen Stills. Consider each separately and decide whether you would call either or both of these lyrics poetry.

THE LOVE YOU SAVE
(May Be Your Own)

People I've been misled
And I've been afraid
I've been hit in the head
And left for dead.
I've been abused,
And I've been accused
Been refused a piece of bread.

But I ain't never in my life before
Seen so many love affairs go wrong
As I do today.   10
I want you to stop!
Find out what's wrong.
Get it right, or just leave love alone
Because the love you save today
May very well be your own.

I've been pushed around.
I've been lost and found,
I've been given 'til sundown
To get out of town.
I've been taken outside,   20

And I've been brutalized
And I had to be always the one to smile
And apologize.

But I ain't never in my life before
Seen so many love affairs go wrong
As I do today.
I want you to stop!
Find out what's wrong.
Get it right, or just leave love alone
Because the love you save today   30
May very well be your own.

JOE TEX

FOR WHAT IT'S WORTH
There's something happenin' here.
What it is ain't exactly clear.
There's a man with a gun over there,
Tellin' me I've got to beware.
It's time we stop, children,
What's that sound?
Everybody look what's goin' down.

There's battle lines bein' drawn,
Nobody's right if everybody's wrong.
Young people speakin' their minds,   10
Gettin' so much resistance from behind.
It's time we stop, children,
What's that sound?
Everybody look what's goin' down.

What a field day for the heat.
A thousand people in the street,
Singin' songs and carryin' signs.
Mostly saying, "Hooray for our side."
It's time we stop, children,
What's that sound?   20
Everybody look what's goin' down.

Paranoia strikes deep,
Into your life it will creep.
It starts when you're always afraid,
Step out of line, the Man come
And take you away.
You better stop, hey,
What's that sound?
Everybody look what's goin' down.

STEPHEN STILLS
(for The Buffalo Springfield)

V

NEW USES FOR A POETIC: ROCK LYRICS AND FOUND POETRY

> Don't care to hear 'em play a tango,
> I'm in no mood to hear a mambo;
> It's 'way too early for a congo,
> So keep a-rockin' that piano.
> So I can hear some of that rock 'n' roll music,
> Any old way you choose it.
>
> CHUCK BERRY

We have developed a poetic that does not depend at all on the formal structures of poetry. It is independent of rhyme, verse form, intention, subject matter, and traditions of imagery, diction, and symbolism. It is wholly dependent on response, on the interaction between the language used and reaction of the respondent. As such, our poetic is an instrument not only for describing poetry but for discerning it as well. We might, for example, apply the poetic to an interesting or provocative sign in a store window advertising a spring fashion show, and reasonably ask ourselves whether the language of that sign constitutes poetry. If the language is at once precise and ex-cited; if it inspires us to make meanings; if we can, through empathetic re-creation, imagine a poetic intent in the language used—then we might well consider the sign in the window to be poetry, and unannounced poetry at that. We are then not only the readers but the discoverers of a poem.

A number of critics, most of them outside academe, have begun, in a not dissimilar way, to discover the poetry of rock music.[1] Books about the songs and their writers have titles

---

[1] I will use the term "rock" broadly to describe popular music from the 1950s to the present. The distinction between rock 'n' roll, folk-rock, and rhythm and blues is important musically—but not to a discussion of the lyrics as such.

like *The Poetry of Rock* and *New Poets/New Music*. Donovan Leitch is compared to Wordsworth, John Lennon to Joyce, and Bob Dylan to Walt Whitman.[2] Some textbooks on poetry have begun to include, albeit hesitantly, the lyrics of a few of the best-known "poetic" rock songs. The 1972 edition of Louis Simpson's *An Introduction to Poetry*,[3] for example, offers "Eleanor Rigby" and "Desolation Row" as the penultimate selections of its "Anthology of Poems."

The question of whether rock lyrics are in fact poetry remains at this moment unanswered. But there are broad assumptions made by those on both sides of the question. A book like A. Poulin's *Contemporary American Poetry*,[4] which ignores Dylan, Paul Simon, Arlo Guthrie, and Janis Ian, and sticks faithfully to poets like W. S. Merwin, Sylvia Plath, and Robert Lowell, quietly assumes that the lyricists are not poets. The counterassumption is not so quiet. The editors of *New Poets/New Music* state in no uncertain terms (in the second sentence of the book) that "these lyrics represent the mainstream of contemporary poetry." [5]

An anthology that is entitled *Contemporary American Poetry* and excludes Bob Dylan may be incomplete. But the declaration that the lyrics of Dylan and his contemporaries comprise the mainstream of contemporary poetry is unfounded. The editors of both kinds of books implicitly and overtly generalize broadly; they fail to examine both the poetic on which their assumptions are based and the lyrics themselves as poems or possible poems.

When Stephen Spender, the poet, and Frank Kermode, the critic, debate whether Bob Dylan is a poet or not, we might expect some articulation of poetic expectations or requirements to emerge.[6] But we are disappointed. Kermode seems to argue that Dylan is a poet because, like Shakespeare (and Beethoven), he has "four periods." The first three of Dylan's periods are "protest," "a more complex notion of the truth,"

---

[2] Richard Goldstein, ed., *The Poetry of Rock* (New York: Bantam Books, 1968), p. 11.
[3] Louis Simpson, ed., *An Introduction to Poetry*, 2nd ed. (New York: St. Martin's Press, 1972).
[4] A. Poulin, *Contemporary American Poetry* (Boston: Houghton Mifflin, 1971).
[5] John Schmittroth and John Mahoney, eds., *New Poets/New Music* (Cambridge, Mass.: Winthrop, 1970).
[6] "Bob Dylan: The Metaphor at the End of the Funnel," *Esquire* (May 1972), pp. 108–09, 118, 188.

and "musical experimentation and pastiche." [7] Kermode does not say what the fourth period is or will be; but after comparing Dylan to Shakespeare in this fashion, he offers other comparisons—Dylan has this in common with Rimbaud, that with Eliot, and yet another quality with Pound. Nowhere do we find a clear—much less a defensible—poetic.

On his side of the argument, Spender is if anything less persuasive. He contends that Dylan is not a true poet because, in sum: "The trouble is [the song lyrics] don't really come out of the front line, or the frontier, or poverty. They come out of the entertainment industry, and immense sums are being made." [8]

What we need is the use of an articulated poetic first of all. It is possible to read endlessly the articles written about the poetry of rock without ever finding out what the authors mean by poetry. [9] Next, the poetic must be viable; it cannot rely on traditional assumptions about poetry. I am surprised to find how many of the discoverers of the "new poetry" define poetry by outmoded criteria. Writing about Jacques Brel, Nat Shapiro tells us that the French singer's lyrics are undoubtedly poetry because of "his burning imagery, his brilliantly controlled rhythmic patterns, and his superb sense of dramatic construction." [10] John Mahoney uses a thematic argument to describe Leonard Cohen's lyrics as poetry, contending that the "religious imagery" and the "reevaluation of love" in Cohen's songs make him a "poet of the sacred and of the profane." [11] And Paul D. McGlyn argues that Donovan is a poet because his work falls within the tradition of poet as prophet. [12]

Such reasons don't hold, any more than do Spender's or Kermode's, given our poetic. We know that there is no traditional role for the poet, just as there is no specific subject matter that defines poetry. We have seen that, while qualities of imagery, rhythm, and drama may infuse poetry, they do not serve to characterize it any more than they characterize the novel or the short story, in which they can also be found. In light of such flaws in poetic theory, Richard Goldstein's ob-

[7] Ibid., pp. 109, 118.
[8] Ibid., p. 188.
[9] See also John Schmittroth's piece on Joni Mitchell in *New Poets/New Music*.
[10] Schmittroth and Mahoney, *New Poets/New Music*, p. 10.
[11] Ibid., pp. 22–24.
[12] Ibid., pp. 34–40.

servations in *The Poetry of Rock* seem more tenable. The title of his book notwithstanding, Goldstein merely flirts with the idea that rock lyrics are poetry. First he posits that "today, it is possible to suggest without risking defenestration that some of the best poetry of our time may well be contained within those slurred couplets [of rock lyrics]." But then Goldstein demurs, perhaps fearing after all that he *will* be thrown out of the window: "But do these lyrics really amount to art? . . . In a sense, assertions like these are the worst enemy of liberated rock. They enslave it with an artificial heritage." [13] This is equivocation of a high order, but Goldstein's book is among the better commentaries on the status of rock lyrics as poetry. That an intelligent critic is so ambivalent about his theme is symptomatic of the underlying uncertainty concerning the validity of the "new music" as "new poetry."

In addition to using an articulated and viable poetic as an instrument of discernment, we need to examine rock lyrics individually, just as we do poems. This may seem obvious, but the literature about rock lyrics has spun its wheels, so to speak, by applying full throttle even when the terrain is slippery. Rather than differentiating Chuck Berry from Stephen Stills, or Arlo Guthrie from Paul Simon, the champions of rock as poetry have lumped them together. Thus sound judgment and defensible argumentation have proved elusive.

We have a poetic (articulated and, I think, viable). So our task becomes that of examining the lyrics of individual songs. A point of clarification is in order before we begin, however: nothing in our investigation presumes that the lyricists themselves claim to be poets. Some do; many don't. Dylan's lines "a song is anything that can walk by itself / i am a songwriter. a poem is a naked person . . . some people say i am a poet" seem to sum up the situation of many rock lyricists. But whether or not the lyricist lays claim to poetry is irrelevant. Rock lyrics are a powerful artistic phenomenon of our time; in many aspects they would seem—on the surface—to be poetry; plenty of advocates and some of the authors assert that they are poetry: this, plus our own interest in poetry and the development of our poetic, provides the material for our query.

Chuck Berry, considered by most advocates to be the founding father of modern rock, wrote "Almost Grown."

[13] *The Poetry of Rock*, pp. 3, 11.

Yeah, I'm doing all right in school,
They ain't said I've broke no rule,
I ain't never been in Dutch,
I don't browse around too much;
Don't bother me, leave me alone,
Anyway I'm almost grown.

I don't run around with no mob,
I got myself a little job.
I'm gonna buy myself a little car,
I'll drive my girl in the park;   10
Don't bother me, leave me alone,
Anyway I'm almost grown.

I got my eye on a little girl,
Ah, she's really out of this world,
When I take her out to a dance,
She's gotta talk about romance;
Don't bother me, leave me alone,
Anyway I'm almost grown.

You know I'm still livin' in town,
But I done married and settled down,   20
Now I really have a ball,
So I don't browse around at all;
Don't bother me, leave me alone,
Anyway I'm almost grown.

These stanzas have meter, certainly, and interesting variations ("car" and "park," "girl" and "world") on a basic rhyme scheme. The language, even Coleridge would acknowledge, is excited, especially the refrain, "Don't bother me, leave me alone, / Anyway I'm almost grown." Furthermore, if the end of poetry is to produce pleasure, these stanzas succeed—the colloquialisms, the strong speech rhythms, and the insistence of the refrain make "Almost Grown" pleasurable to read or hear. Is it poetry?

I think the answer is no. "Almost Grown" is neither precise enough nor presentational enough to be characterized as poetry. To illustrate why I find lack of precision, consider the first line of the refrain, "Don't bother me, leave me alone." What does "Don't bother me" mean if not "leave me alone"?—half the line is redundant, since it adds nothing to the meaning of the lyric *as a poem*. Considered strictly as words to a song, or as verse, the phrase "leave me alone" can be justified rhythmically and also for the rhyme: "alone" and "grown." But what works in a song may not work in a poem; as we have seen, each word, each line of a poem must be its own justification as well as contributing to the meanings of the whole.

We can describe "I ain't never been in Dutch" similarly. The colloquial expression "in Dutch" is appealing, but the persona has already told us, "I'm doing all right in school, / They ain't said I've broke no rule." Not to belabor the obvious, it should be clear that these lyrics are simply not tight enough, or, in Coleridge's sense, precise enough, to be poetry.

It is also apparent that since making meanings is crucial to poetry, "Almost Grown" is not a poem. It states too much to be a poem; there is very little for the reader or listener to do by way of meaning-making or empathetic re-creation. "So I don't browse around at all" is mildly evocative—primarily because "browse" is suggestive of a nonchalant shopper—but the rest of the song simply tells a story, from school days through courtship to marriage.

With the poetic as our instrument, then, we find that "Almost Grown" has one of the qualities of poetry: excited language. It does not have the others. Because of the song's strong elements of rhythm and rhyme, it might be characterized as verse, but not poetry.

Two comments: One, it may appear that "Almost Grown" is too easy to dismiss as verse rather than poetry, that it is a straw man for arguments against rock as poetry. Yet among those who assert that rock lyrics are poetry, "Almost Grown" is an important historical example of the burgeoning of poetry in rock.[14] Two, it must be clear that any judgment made about lyrics as poetry cannot be construed as a judgment of the song (words and music combined). It may be that some of the best songs have those lyrics we can most readily decide are not poetry. We are not discussing music here, only the lyrics of songs presented linearly on a page or spoken, rather than sung, to us.

To underscore this second comment, we can look at the lyrics to "Heartbreak Hotel," by Mae Boren Axton, Tommy Durden, and Elvis Presley.

[14] Ibid., pp. 15–19.

Now, since my baby left me
I've found a new place to dwell,
Down at the end of Lonely Street
At Heartbreak Hotel.
I'm so lonely,
I'm so lonely,
I'm so lonely,
That I could die.

And tho' it's always crowded,
You can still find some room   10
For broken-hearted lovers
To cry there in the gloom
And be so lonely,
Oh, so lonely,
Oh, so lonely
They could die.

The bell hop's tears keep flowing,
The desk clerk's dressed in black.
They've been so long on Lonely Street,
They never will go back.   20
And they're so lonely.
Oh, they're so lonely,
They're so lonely
They pray to die.

So, if your baby leaves
And you have a tale to tell,
Just take a walk down Lonely Street
To Heartbreak Hotel,
Where you'll be so lonely,
And I'll be so lonely.   30
We'll be so lonely
That we could die.

This is a fine song; these lyrics are powerfully rhythmic, the
rhymes are neither forced nor trite, and the language is precise
—each word carries its weight as the lyric builds to the final,
despairing couplet, "We'll be so lonely / That we could die."

"Heartbreak Hotel" does not display the imprecision we
found in "Almost Grown." Further, the image created of the
hotel with its weeping bellhop, funereal desk clerk, and, of
course, woeful inmates is vivid. I even find that the denizens
of Heartbreak Hotel have the aura of Dante's damned, churning

in the underworld. Yet despite these qualities of the lyric, I
don't consider "Heartbreak Hotel" to be a poem. Like "Almost
Grown," it is discursive rather than presentational. There is
more statement than evocation. Apart from the associations
with Dante, I find that there is virtually no meaning-making,
no empathetic re-creation allowed by the lyrics. What we have
is the account—in song—of the fate of abandoned and dis-
consolate lovers. We cannot make meanings or imagine the
cause of the despair of those who patronize Heartbreak Hotel,
nor are we free to imagine what goes on there. It is all told
to us.

"Sally, Go 'Round the Roses" is quite a different kind of
lyric. One critic describes its refrain as like something from
Waiting for Godot, and observes that it is open to a "gaggle of
interpretations." [15]

> Sally, go 'round the roses.
> Sally, go 'round the roses.
> Sally, go 'round the roses.
> Sally, go 'round the pretty roses.
>
> The roses, they can't hurt you.
> No, the roses, they can't hurt you.
> The roses, they can't hurt you.
> No, the roses, they can't hurt you.
>
> Sally, doncha go, doncha go downtown.
> Sally, doncha go, doncha go downtown.   10
> The saddest thing in this whole wide world
> Is to see your baby with another girl.
>
> Sally, go 'round the roses.
> Sally, go 'round the roses.
> Sally, go 'round the roses.
> Sally, go 'round the pretty roses.
>
> They won't tell your secrets.
> They won't tell your secrets.
> They won't tell your secrets.
> No, the roses won't tell your secrets.   20
>
> Sally, baby, cry; let your hair hang down.
> Sally, baby, cry; let your hair hang down.

[15] Ibid., p. 34.

Sit and cry where the roses grow,
You can sit and cry and not a soul will know.

Sally go 'round the roses.

ZEL SANDERS and LONA STEVENS
(for the Jaynettes)

Nursery rhymes, religious epiphany, sexual mystery (possibly including lesbianism), and a vast tradition of symbolism based on the rose—these are all suggested by "Sally, Go 'Round the Roses."

The tension is obviously between the rose garden and "downtown." The roses of the song seem to be purely benevolent ones. I think of Burns' "O my Luve's like a red, red rose / That's newly sprung in June"; of Shakespeare's "A rose by any name would smell as sweet"; and also of Shakespeare's "Roses have thorns, and silver fountains mud" (see p. 87)—although Sally's roses appear to be thornless and incapable of hurt. The silent, healing effect of the roses is contrasted with the perils of "downtown," where evil is seen and secrets are not kept.

What kind of love affair is described? What are the "secrets" that inspire Sally's tears and that the roses will guard? I find it easy to reject the notion of lesbianism. There is enough precedent in rock themes to lead me to a more straightforward interpretation. Sally's man (her "baby") has left her and is with another woman. If Sally goes "downtown" she will see him with his new love—hence the advice of the song that she stay in the garden and shed her tears in silence among the roses. Although the roses and "let your hair hang down" mildly suggest Christian penitence, I tend to think that Sally's mourning, her "secrets," and her undone hair are simply the accoutrements of unrequited love—she is an abandoned woman in a wholly secular situation, rather than a species of saint or martyr.

Earlier, we distinguished between interpretations and meaning-making; this distinction will help us now to decide whether "Sally, Go 'Round the Roses" is a poem. Then we said that interpreting is a kind of "figuring out," whereas making meaning involves experiencing the various alternatives evoked by the poem. I suggest that "Sally, Go 'Round the Roses" is not a poem because it does not evoke meaning-making, although it does inspire interpretation. Like a puzzle, it confuses the reader and requires that he ponder alternative solutions in order to understand the lyrics. But unlike a poem, it does not create, or inspire the reader to create, the virtual, felt reality of possible meanings. Put more simply, these lyrics do not evoke enough meaning to be a poem.

The lyrics do not so much open up meaning as establish its perimeters. Rather than using the lyrics as a catapult into his own imaginative world, the reader simply fills in meaning. The nursery rhyme repetition is largely responsible for this limitation of the lyrics. "Sally, go 'round the roses," the line that is stated seven times in a song totaling twenty-five lines, contributes to a chanting effect but does not open possibilities of meaning. After a point (two lines repeated?) it is no longer evocative. The similar but less extreme repetitions of "The roses, they can't hurt you" and "They won't tell your secrets" impose the same limitations on meaning. We may conclude generally that poetry has less tolerance for repetition than song.

The shortcoming of "Almost Grown" and "Heartbreak Hotel"—as poems—is that they *tell* too much. "Sally, Go 'Round the Roses" is not a poem because it *presents* too little. There is not enough concrete imagery, detailed and developed as we move through the lyric, to afford us possibilities for our own experience. We are outside Sally, looking at her. We may have to figure out her situation, but we do not have to feel it.

The discursive nature of rock lyrics like "Almost Grown" and "Heartbreak Hotel" is by far the most common limitation when they are considered as poetry. It characterizes the songs of lyricists otherwise as dissimilar as Phil Spector ("To Know Him Is to Love Him"), Arlo Guthrie ("The Motorcycle Song," "Alice's Restaurant"), Johnny Cash ("I Walk the Line"), and Van Morrison ("Brown Eyed Girl"). The lyric can be forceful, vivid, and intensely rhythmical, and it can make use of simile or metaphor adroitly—but if it tells rather than presents, it is not poetry.

"Summer in the City," by John Sebastian, Mark Sebastian, and Steve Boone (for The Lovin' Spoonful), is an example of how far rock can go, to the borders of poetry, if you will, without being poetry.

Hot town,
Summer in the city.
Back o' my neck gettin' dirty and gritty.

Been down
Isn't it a pity;
Doesn't seem to be a shadow in the city.

All around
People lookin' half-dead,
Walkin' on the sidewalk hotter than a matchhead.

But at night it's a different world.   10
Go out and find a girl.
Come on, come on and dance all night;
Despite the heat, it'll be all right.

And babe,
Don't you know it's a pity
That the days can't be like the nights
In the summer in the city.

Cool town
Evening in the city
Dressed so fine and lookin' so pretty.   20

Cool cat,
Lookin' for a kitty;
Gonna look in every corner of the city.
Til I'm wheezin' like a bus stop
Running up the stairs
Gonna meet you on the rooftop.

This is genuinely masterful verse. The drive of the two-stress first lines ("Hot town," "Been down," "All around," "And babe," "Cool town," "Cool cat") of all but the middle stanza, the movement through time and mood, and the precise imagery combine to create a powerful whole. Descriptive impact is derived from both the attention to realistic detail—"Back o' my neck gettin' dirty and gritty," "Doesn't seem to be a shadow in the city"—and the use of simile—"Walkin' on the sidewalk hotter than a matchhead," "Til I'm wheezin' like a bus stop." We are there, on those streets, scorched and aware of the soot clinging to our skin. The idyll of evening cool, when people parade in new clothes, is in sharp contrast; yet like the humid, turgid heat, it is a real part of summer in the city.

The best line in the song, I think, is "Doesn't seem to be a shadow in the city." I cannot envision a more forceful image of merciless heat: I am at the bottom of a concrete canyon and yet there are no shadows; the sun, reflected on all sides, is inescapable. "Sidewalk hotter than a matchhead" is also a strong image, fashioned by simile. It partakes vaguely of a cliché (the street hot enough to fry an egg) but in itself is wholly original and combines not only a sense of heat but also of explosiveness. The hot matchhead may in an instant erupt into flame. What of "wheezin' like a bus stop"? The buses certainly wheeze, but the bus stop? Or perhaps we should imagine a passenger wheezing from his gallop down the block to catch the bus.

These fine lines are offset, when we consider the lyric as poetry, by lines that are essentially discursive rather than evocative, lines that are there solely to tell the story. A poem, in which every word, every line, must justify itself, cannot tolerate lines that are a transition between images rather than themselves evocative. In this song, "Go out and find a girl. / Come on, come on and dance all night" and "Running up the stairs / Gonna meet you on the rooftop" are such lines; they tell us what action is taking place but evoke nothing. These lines, and the several more like them, are what keep the lyrics from being poetry.

If the discursive element commonly limits the poetic possibility of rock lyrics, the phenomenon of an overly presentational lyric also occurs. This song, by Jim Morrison, of The Doors, may illustrate such a lyric.

HORSE LATITUDES

When the still sea conspires an armor
And her sullen and aborted
Currents breed tiny monsters,
True sailing is dead.

Awkward instant
And the first animal is jettisoned,
Legs furiously pumping
Their stiff green gallop,
And heads bob up
Poise
Delicate

> Pause
> Consent
> In mute nostril agony
> Carefully refined
> And sealed over.

In "Horse Latitudes," every line is presentational and evocative; I cannot find one that serves to convey information, that is primarily discursive. "And the first animal is jettisoned" may seem informational, but given its context—the fact that we are not told what kind of animal, from what the animal is jettisoned, or why—the line cannot be described as discursive. In a sense, the lyric is "pure" poetry.

As poetry, what meanings can we make of "Horse Latitudes"? A latitude is a region of the earth delineated by distance from the North and South poles. Or latitude can refer to a degree of freedom or permissibility granted within defined boundaries. Given the "still sea" of the first line of the lyric, I tentatively choose a geographic meaning for the title, although I cannot rule out that somehow the freedom of horses is also one of the meanings of the lyric.

Something is vitally wrong at sea—that much is clear. "Armor" suggests war; the currents are full of "tiny monsters"; sailing is no longer "true" and has somehow become perverted. But what is wrong and why? Animals are jettisoned, but what are they doing at sea anyway? Or are they sea animals? Readers to whom I have shown these lyrics as linear poetry invariably are befuddled. Some wonder if a boat has been attacked by a sea serpent. Others, given "horse" in the title and "tiny monsters" of the first stanza, think of sea horses and attempt a meaning in which a ship, sea horses, and hurricane collide. Significantly, most readers have given up, concluding that they cannot make meaning of the lyrics.

"Horse Latitudes" is a lyric that requires that the reader possess outside information. It provides us with an instance in which factual knowledge about the author's intention is required. (Remember, intention and poetic intent are not the same thing.) What Morrison knew when he wrote these lyrics —and what we are not likely to know when we read or hear them—is that Spanish galleons, en route to America, were sometimes forced by storms to toss their cargo overboard in order to lighten the vessel. Horses were among the cargo to be cast into the sea. The lyric can thus be seen as inspired by and presenting us with this awful event.[16]

Once we know these facts, meanings of "Horse Latitudes" spring into being. The first stanza presents the storm at sea; the second, the horses heaved into the water, their struggle and death. One meaning I make of "Horse Latitudes" is the sacrifice of beauty to crass survival. The "sullen" currents full of "tiny monsters" are all ugliness. The horses are helpless, noble, and immensely beautiful. The "Poise / Delicate / Pause" of their arched heads above the water, before succumbing "In mute nostril agony / Carefully refined" to death, epitomizes the fate of the beautiful pitted against the inexorable.

Other meanings, for me, involve my knowledge of the Spanish conquistadores. By all the accounts I have read, most of them were brutal men. They murdered and enslaved the natives of the New World; they were motivated by ambition of conquest and colonization. And they were greedy, eager to rape and pillage the people they found in America. From my bias against these Spaniards, another meaning can be made of the fate of the horses. The horses become emblematic of the fate of innocent, natural things at the hands of the conquistadores. The conquistadores, like the sea, are armored; they sweep relentlessly across the globe, leaving all indigenous life "In mute nostril agony."

But the Spaniards are never spoken of in the lyric. They are an absent presence. A reader more favorably inclined toward them, who sees them as true Christians bringing the New World religious salvation and the benefits of a more developed technology, is unhampered in making quite different meanings. For him, there may be visions of distraught sailors engaged in an agonizing duty. This meaning has the Spaniards no less victimized than the horses—men and horses both are caught in the sea's wrath, the survivors (if there are any after all) suffer as much as those who perish.

Another meaning does not involve humans at all. Indeed, as we have observed, there is no mention of them in the lyric itself. Thus the battle is wholly between the horses and the "tiny monsters" of the "sullen and aborted / Currents." Who

16 Ibid., p. 142.

wins? Perhaps the horses triumph in death, for theirs is the realm of grace and beauty. The sea is left to its own torments.

It should be apparent that as one reader, I consider the lyric of "Horse Latitudes" to be poetry. It is poetry because it is excited, precise, presentational, and evocative; as such it encourages meaning-making by the reader and engages him as co-poet in the act of empathetic re-creation. The poem, however, is flawed because it cannot stand alone, because it relies too heavily on a specific factual account that might as well be taken from a history book.

This is not, of course, to say that poets cannot assume some knowledge of history on the part of the reader. When we discussed the poet and his work in Chapter I, it became apparent that poets must cast themselves in the role of reader and must make decisions about what knowledge, associations, and imaginative power they can presume their readers will have. The author of "World War III," for example, assumed a historical awareness of the first and second world wars on the part of his readers, and made decisions about their response to a poem presenting the "unthinkable" next world war. But "Horse Latitudes," as far as I can tell by trying it out on a number of readers, assumes a too specific and esoteric knowledge of a historical event. A poem that requires a prose explanation in order for the reader to enter its world is weakened by its reliance on the doorman, no matter how sumptuous that world is once the reader is in it.

A similar problem may exist in © "A Whiter Shade of Pale."

> We skipped the light fandango
> And turned cartwheels cross the floor.
> I was feeling kind of seasick
> But the crowd called out for more.
> The room was humming harder
> As the ceiling flew away
> When we called out for another drink
> The waiter brought a tray
> And so it was that later
> As the miller told his tale   10
> That her face at first just ghostly
> Turned a whiter shade of pale.
>
> She said, "There is no reason,
> And the truth is plain to see,"

But I wandered through my playing cards
And would not let her be
One of sixteen vestal virgins
Who were leaving for the coast
And although my eyes were open
They might just as well been closed.   20
And so it was that later
As the miller told his tale
That her face at first just ghostly
Turned a whiter shade of pale.

KEITH REID and GARY BROOKER
(for Procol Harum)

    I first heard this song years ago, and have admired it ever since for the title. "A Whiter Shade of Pale," paler than pale— what a superb image! Hearing it on the radio, I had not the slightest idea what the song was about; I did, however, have a vague hunch that its meanings might require knowledge of some code or lexicon particular to the drug culture. (The Beatles' "Lucy in the Sky with Diamonds," for example, is often interpreted as being about LSD.) Seeing the lyrics of "A Whiter Shade of Pale" in the form of linear poetry does not provide me with any great assurance about its meanings except that I cannot find evidence that such meanings are accessible only to those familiar with drug terminology.

    The mad dance, the slight nausea, the clamoring crowd, the room "humming" and the ceiling flying away—the opening lines present a masterful setting for whatever is to follow. But what follows? A tale is told to a group sitting at a table; one of the party is terribly upset by what she hears. The second stanza would seem to involve some dialogue between the narrative persona of the poem and the distraught woman. The persona perhaps seduces her, rather than let her remain one of sixteen virgins on a journey. Then the experience is rounded out by another reference to the tale; it is told again, and again "That her face at first just ghostly / Turned a whiter shade of pale."

    The images, both those of the opening lines and later ones like "I wandered through my playing cards" and "sixteen vestal virgins / Who were leaving for the coast," are original and evocative. Yet what holds them together? The lyric has a narrative style to it—a story is being told—but there are links missing in the story. It becomes a puzzle.

Earlier, we criticized lyrics for including lines that served *merely* to tell a story. In poetry such lines vitiate the presentational strength of the whole. The opposite extreme—images presented without links that effect a cohesion of the whole— is no more tenable. The transitions, words or lines that unify the poem, must be there, but transition or unification cannot be their sole justification.

"A Whiter Shade of Pale" lacks cohesion. Instead of evoking meanings, it is, for me at least, simply something to figure out. Unlike "Horse Latitudes," it does not appear that a clue from without would release meanings in the lyric. One possible clue, for example, is that the lyric plays on "The Miller's Tale" of Chaucer's *Canterbury Tales*. This is certainly hinted at, since we have the unlikely figure (in a contemporary song) of a miller, and he is the one who tells a tale. Chaucer's miller narrates a tale of marital infidelity and of the undoing of both the cuckold and his young wife's two suitors. There is scarcely a more ribald and hilarious story in all of English literature—although episodes in Joyce's *Ulysses* may be its equal. This miller's tale could be what turns the woman's face "a whiter shade of pale." Yet it doesn't unleash meanings of the lyric as a whole. We still are left with a conundrum.

Chaucer's story has nothing to do with reason or truth. What are we to make of "She said, 'There is no reason, / And the truth is plain to see' "? Similarly, playing cards and vestal virgins don't figure in the Chaucer tale and are not illuminated by knowledge of "The Miller's Tale." Finally, the seeing-yet-blind image ("although my eyes were open / They might just as well been closed") remains just as incongruent and mystifying.

None of this is to say that "A Whiter Shade of Pale" doesn't succeed superbly as a song. I think it does. But it is not a poem, because it does not inspire us to make meanings, to engage in an empathetic re-creation of poetic intent.

One thing we can learn from the lyrics we've considered so far is that among the songs considered "rock" there is striking heterogeneity. Speaking of lyrics alone, we have found that some are verse (comprising language used discursively for the most part, although rhymed and metrical), others are

a mix of verse and poetry (comprising a genuinely presentational, evocative use of language interspersed with discursive
lines that serve "to tell the story"), and that some are almost
wholly imagistic (comprising a series of images that of themselves are evocative, but that, lacking discernible poetic intent,
fail to achieve a cohesive whole). Of this last group, "Horse
Latitudes" can become poetry for the reader once he is informed of a historical event; "A Whiter Shade of Pale," even
with information about Chaucer brought to the reader's attention, seems unlikely to be responded to as poetry.

It is time we examined a lyric that clearly can, of itself,
be considered poetry. "Suzanne," by Leonard Cohen, is, I think,
such a lyric.

> Suzanne takes you down
> To her place near the river.
> You can hear the boats go by,
> You can stay the night beside her,
> And you know that she's half-crazy
> But that's why you want to be there,
> And she feeds you tea and oranges
> That come all the way from China,
> And just when you mean to tell her
> That you have no love to give her,   10
> Then she gets you on her wave-length
> And she lets the river answer
> That you've always been her lover.
>
> And you want to travel with her,
> And you want to travel blind,
> And you know that she can trust you
> 'Cause you've touched her perfect body
> With your mind.
>
> And Jesus was a sailor
> When he walked upon the water   20
> And he spent a long time watching
> From a lonely wooden tower
> And when he knew for certain
> That only drowning men could see him,
> He said, "All men shall be sailors, then,
> Until the sea shall free them,"
> But he, himself, was broken
> Long before the sky would open.

Forsaken, almost human,
He sank beneath your wisdom   30
Like a stone.

And you want to travel with him,
And you want to travel blind,
And you think you'll maybe trust him
'Cause he touched your perfect body
With his mind.

Suzanne takes your hand
And she leads you to the river.
She is wearing rags and feathers
From Salvation Army counters,   40
And the sun pours down like honey
On our lady of the harbor;
And she shows you where to look
Among the garbage and the flowers.
There are heroes in the seaweed,
There are children in the morning,
They are leaning out for love,
And they will lean that way forever
While Suzanne, she holds the mirror.

And you want to travel with her,   50
You want to travel blind,
And you're sure that she can find you
'Cause she's touched her perfect body
With her mind.

This lyric, I am convinced, opens possibilities and op-
portunities of meaning-making; it is genuinely presentational
and evocative. There is no line, series of lines, or stanza that
serves merely as transition or to carry a story. The major shift
in the lyric is from Suzanne to Jesus; yet because I can perceive
a poetic intent that pervades the whole of the lyric, the shift
reveals meanings I can make, rather than confronting me with
a puzzle to solve.

There is so much of parallel structure and content in the
stanzas about Suzanne and Jesus that I readily make a meaning
that includes their comparison or even their co-identity. They
are both linked to the water, both are travelers who inspire
blind trust and love in others, both seem to have a prophetic
insight into the world. Being with Suzanne, being with Jesus,
and being with some mystical combination of both of them

(the shape of which depends on the meanings the reader makes) is an experience created by the reader and the poem—the reader becomes the "you" of the poem. We have already distinguished interpreting a poem from making meanings; "Suzanne" engages us so thoroughly as empathetic re-creators of its meanings that there is no question of our merely offering interpretations. Having just said that, I must amend it somewhat. The pronouns that shift in the second, fourth, and sixth stanzas break the spell of re-creation slightly for me. Consider the last two lines of those stanzas.

> II.   'Cause you've touched her perfect body
>   With your mind.
> IV.   'Cause he touched your perfect body
>   With his mind.
> VI.   'Cause she's touched her perfect body
>   With her mind.

I confess that my first several readings left me annoyed with the "you"-"he"-"she," "her"-"your"-"her" changes. They seemed simply clever and, in the worst sense, puzzling. So much depends on tracing down the transmutations of those pronouns that my engagement with poem as re-creator was threatened by a wholly intellectual kind of problem-solving. However, in later readings, I think I have gone beyond that and am able to integrate those lines into the meanings I make of the poem as a whole. In gross terms, these meanings involve ways of knowing. The first is knowing oneself by knowing the "perfect body" of another (Stanza II). The next is knowing another because he knows your own "perfect body." Finally, it is the paramount knowing that comes of knowing everything because one knows his own "perfect body."

Obviously the range of meanings that "Suzanne" can evoke is wide. The optimistic tenor of the meanings I make can be countered by pessimistic, even fatalistic, meanings. A reader might be strongly moved by the lines

> But he, himself, was broken
> Long before the sky would open.
> Forsaken, almost human,
> He sank beneath your wisdom
> Like a stone.

and find that Suzanne, like Christ, is a tragic messenger, that for all her truth, love, and charisma, the best she can do for those who are "leaning out for love" is to hold "the mirror." After all, the destiny of her followers—"And they will lean that way forever"—is not full of promise; it may even seem to some readers that the heroes and children are in a kind of purgatory, always yearning, forever unfulfilled.

The point, however, is not here to choose among meanings but to observe that "Suzanne" inspires empathetic re-creation and that many meanings can be made of it. It is clearly a work of presentational, rather than discursive, symbolism, and is poetry as well as song.

The Beatles' "A Day in the Life," written by John Lennon and Paul McCartney, is another song to which we can respond as poetry.

> I read the news today, oh boy,
> About a lucky man who made the grade
> And though the news was rather sad
> Well I just had to laugh
> I saw the photograph.
> He blew his mind out in a car
> He didn't notice that the lights had changed
> A crowd of people stood and stared
> They'd seen his face before
> Nobody was really sure   10
> If he was from the House of Lords.
>
> I saw a film today, oh boy,
> The English army had just won the war
> A crowd of people turned away
> But I just had to look
> Having read the book.
> I'd love to turn you on.
>
> Woke up, fell out of bed,
> Dragged a comb across my head
> Found my way downstairs and drank a cup,   20
> And looking up I noticed I was late.
> Found my coat and grabbed my hat
> Made the bus in seconds flat
> Found my way upstairs and had a smoke,
> Somebody spoke and I went into a dream.

> I read the news today, oh boy,
> Four thousand holes in Blackburn,
> Lancashire
> And though the holes were rather small
> They had to count them all   30
> Now they know how many holes it takes to fill the
>   Albert Hall.
> I'd love to turn you on.

There is no need to list the criteria again and go through them one by one with "A Day in the Life." The criteria are met, including the single most essential one, that of meaning-making potential. The lyrics of "A Day in the Life" do not tell a story, but the movement from news events to the personal details of the third stanza and back again to the newspapers is highly evocative. The reader must make connections, but there is plenty in the imagery and tone of the lyric as a whole to enable him to create meanings from the juxtapositions. The banal savagery of the world at large is somehow echoed in the banality of the speaker's life. Yet the speaker is a dreamer, not a savage; he has a smoke (marijuana?) that puts him— for a time at least—outside the brutal kingdom of news events.

For me, the most evocative line is stated only twice in the lyric, "I'd love to turn you on," and suggests a number of possible meanings. Is "you" a particular person, the world, or both? Is "I'd love to turn you on" a reaching out of love, an invitation to escape, or just an expression of boredom? I regard it as the one positive, active assertion by the persona. In all other respects he is simply a receiver of inputs: a reader of the newspaper, a moviegoer, and a smoker whose dreams are triggered by the voices of others. But given a drug meaning, "I'd love to turn you on" may not have positive implications. In this case, it is an invitation to escape; it means that the only way out of this mess of suicide, war, and industrial disaster is to get stoned. Again, we shall not work here to articulate what a legitimate range of meanings could be. As with "Suzanne," our purpose is to observe how and why the lyric can be responded to as poetry.

We have discussed the lyrics of eight rock songs. Our sample is admittedly small, yet I think it is representative of the poetic possibilities of rock 'n' roll. What we have learned from our study of "Almost Grown," "Heartbreak Hotel," "Sally, Go 'Round the Roses," "Summer in the City," "Horse Latitudes," "A Whiter Shade of Pale," "Suzanne," and "A Day in the Life" can be applied to the lyric of any song. A fair generalization, it seems to me, is that by examining the lyrics of rock songs individually and with an explicit poetic in mind, we will find that the majority of lyrics are not poetry but verse. We will also find, just as we have with "Horse Latitudes," "Suzanne," and "A Day in the Life," that a significant number of rock lyrics are not only poetry, but intriguing and emotionally powerful poetry at that. Among the lyricists not discussed who have written songs that are also poems, I include Paul Simon, Donovan Leitch, Willie Dixon, Bob Dylan, Tuli Kupferberg, Grace Slick, and Phil Ochs. But such lists are dangerous. The essential process is not categorical inclusion or exclusion; rather, it is to examine each work with care.

In at least one important way, our discussion of rock lyrics has served to further refine the poetic. In our earlier study of poetics and of specific poems we had seen how language could be used too discursively to affect the presentational ends of poetry. But we had not been confronted by the reverse phenomenon, that of language used so wholly presentationally that the work (lyric or poem) fails to cohere and becomes puzzling instead of evocative. "Horse Latitudes," singularly precise and intense—and yet thoroughly enigmatic until the reader is in possession of rather specialized historical knowledge—afforded us an example of total presentation. It presents rather than tells; but what we learned is that some telling is necessary, particularly if we are to bring to bear on the poem our knowledge of "grammar, logic, psychology and *good sense*," as Coleridge advises.

I suggest that our finding is cause to reconsider a dimension of the poetic. Perhaps Susanne Langer's invaluable contribution to it needs to be qualified slightly. Langer maintains that poetry more closely resembles presentational art, like music or painting, than it does other forms of discourse, because unlike discourse generally, poetry seeks to evoke rather than to make assertions. Langer's view is sound generally, and serves well to redress a balance too often weighted toward the side of the poem-as-statement or the poem-as-great-idea. But it is as a position on a scale that we must view Langer's contribution: poetry can no more be wholly presentational than it can be wholly discursive. It must be both, but its discursive function must always be supportive of its presentational, never supersede it.

If we push Langer's contention to its extreme, we can expect to find an equivalent in poetry to abstract painting. Yet there is no such equivalent, or, at least, not a tenable one. "Horse Latitudes" comes close. Like an abstract painting, it is intense, vivid, emotionally powerful, and self-conscious in the sense that we are aware of a creative imagination in the work. We do not ask of the painting, "What is it about?" and to some degree the question is also inappropriate when asked of a poem, since we have learned that a poem, strictly speaking, is not "about" anything that can be absolutely defined. None-theless, there is a degree—and I emphasize "degree"—to which we need to know what a poem is "about." When we learn that "Horse Latitudes" is "about" conquistadores and horses in a storm at sea, meanings unfold. But the poem is only "about" the conquistadores and their horses in the most superficial way—it is really "about" much more. It can almost be said that we need to know what a poem is "about" so we can dis-card that information and advance to the poem's more significant reaches. Again we see that response to poetry defies prescription. We must bring to our poetic well-tempered as-sumptions, inclinations and theoretical contentions—a poem cannot be described as being all of anything.

At the outset of this chapter I spoke of a new role for the reader of poetry. In addition to being the empathetic re-creator of acknowledged poems, he can be the discoverer of poems in material not officially designated or immediately discernible as poetry. The poetic is then used as an instrument not only to describe and evaluate, but also to discern un-announced poetry. We have been using the poetic this way in our study of rock lyrics. No single lyric was distinguished from the others by being labelled a poem; our task was to discern which lyrics among several might be poetry, and why.

Discovering unannounced poetry, what is commonly called "found" poetry, amid the welter of verbal and printed language to which we are constantly exposed, is a somewhat similar activity. The reader must bring an articulated and flexible poetic to bear on an utterance not formerly designated as poetry in order to see if it can be poetry. He discovers the poetry in the language; he discovers the poem.

An important difference between using the poetic as an instrument to discern the poetry of rock lyrics and discovering found poems is that in the latter instance the reader is more literally the maker of the poem. The words, lines, and stanzas of the lyrics were already assembled for us. The maker of the found poem usually has to select the words he will use from a larger number that will have nothing to do with the poem; then he creates sequences of lines and stanzas where none existed before. The maker of found poems is both reader-perceiver (discovering the poem in some utterance) and poet-reader (fashioning its form as a poem).

In terms of creative responsibility, found poems are not rightfully regarded as totally the poet's own, as are other kinds of poems. Yet the maker of a found poem is the poet. A common practice in publishing found poems reflects the ambiguity inherent in their genesis: the maker's name is printed with the found poem exactly where the poet's name is found for any other poem; yet it is also noted, usually in parentheses, that the poem is a found poem.

Here is a found poem I made from a student's evaluation of a course I taught on poetry. The student wrote a paragraph describing the variety of contexts in which poems had been presented to the class. Her prose read:

> At times the poet was known and present. At other times, the poet was present but anonymous. At still other times, the poet was unknown and absent.

My found poem is entitled "The Poet."

> At times
> The poet
> Was known
> And present.
>
> At other times
> The poet
> Was present
> But anonymous.

At still other times
The poet
Was unknown
And absent.

As can be seen, I haven't done anything to change the words or sentences of the prose. I have isolated them from their context (the student's paper), and arranged the words into very short lines and the sentences into three four-line stanzas. If this is a poem, the poem was lurking visibly behind the prose.

My rearrangement of the sentences into lines and stanzas is designed to heighten the effect of words and structure. "At times," "At other times," and "At still other times" are not of themselves stirring lines; yet I hoped that their placement as the first line of each of the stanzas would at once denote the sequence of events presented in the poem and evoke an almost mystical sense of time passing, evolving, coming, and going. "The poet," the second line of each stanza, is similarly designed to isolate and heighten the effect of what was simply the subject of the prose sentences. The shifts from "Was known / And present" to "Was present / But anonymous" to "Was unknown / And absent" speak for themselves.

Is "The Poet" a poem? As its maker, my view is perhaps biased in its favor. I think it is a poem because it has the potential to evoke a mildly mysterious and elusive sense of the poet, as if he were playing a game of hide-and-seek with the reader. The meaning-making it can inspire includes a practical description of what a reader might experience when reading a poem (sometimes feeling he knows the poet well; at other times, less well; and at still other times, not at all) and the more ethereal, even mystical, presentation of the poet. The poetic intent of "The Poet" certainly embraces this latter meaning. Other meanings could even include sociological and historical ones—at times poets are conspicuous societal forces; at other times, they hover on the fringes of society; and at still other times, they seem hardly a presence in the world of men.

To weave a tapestry of elaborate meanings from such a slender thread may appear to aggrandize the poem—"The Poet" is hardly an ambitious work. Yet in order to see the poem in the prose when I read it, I had to be aware of as much meaning-making potential as possible.

Here are a number of found poems, by Robert L. Peters and George Hitchcock, made from an old book called *Rats and How to Destroy Them*, by Mark Hovell. The creators of the poems have simply (or not so simply) lifted and rearranged the prose sentences they found in Hovell's text.

PRELUDE

In stables, cow-houses and
outbuildings
they were found to be
in large numbers
at all seasons.

They invaded the fowl-house
and carried off eggs.

They destroyed young poultry
in early spring.

The hedgerows were full   10
of their holes, and
they had undermined banks
around the ponds.

They gave the gardener no peace,
and dug up peas
and beans as soon as
they had been sown.

They ate their way
into the green-house.

Whatever the owner of the house   20
and those who worked there
may have thought of them

they appeared quite satisfied
with themselves

and their quarters must have been
all they desired

since they made no attempt
to leave them.

RESPONSIBILITIES

People
who live in the country
and have schoolboy sons
should not
leave the rats
for the boys
to kill
during their holidays;
they should
destroy them   10
at once.

People
who keep fowls
for amusement

but do not understand
the principles of
managing them

often throw food down
in the runs
in the evening   20

with the idea
that the early birds

will find in it
a substitute
for the first worm.

Such people succeed
in feeding
quite a large number
of rats.

Never   30
allow a rat
that can be killed
today
to live
till tomorrow.

THE MONGOOSE

The mongoose
is very abundant

and for regular trade
should be

obtainable in London
at one Pound a head.

It will kill
all kinds of small mammals
and birds.

The author very strongly
deprecates
turning a
mongoose loose
in town.

CODA

We shall always
have the rat
with us.

The makers of these found poems, Peters and Hitchcock, had an assist from the archaic oddities of Hovell's prose. But these were not enough in themselves to make the prose into poetry. An immense amount of the poetic possibility depends on the arrangement of the lines. An assertion as innocuous as "They ate their way / into the green-house," placed in the context of "Prelude," quivers with ominous reverberations; and so banal a prescription as "Never / allow a rat / that can be killed / today / to live / till tomorrow" becomes a delightful fillip at the end of "Responsibilities." The proclamation "We shall always / have the rat / with us" is notable because its poetic possibilities depend more on its position as the "Coda" of the series of poems than on anything inherent in itself as a three-line found poem.

I have seen found poems made from the content descriptions on a package of Dill's pipe cleaners ("strong * pliable * clean * full-bodied * absorbent"), from an advertisement for pornography, from a taxidermist's manual, from news bulletins. Currently I am considering making a found poem out of an advertisement for the Rolls-Royce Silver Shadow automobile. The advertisement announces two sides to the Rolls' impressiveness:

The Public Life. It's a working day, with very important people for your Silver Shadow Long-Wheelbase Sedan to indulge. Impress. Perhaps, even intimidate. Now the Rolls waits, ready. Ready to put prestige to work. To do the job it does best . . .

The Private Life. Now a day off. A day with the family. A day to give them self-esteem, to remind them of how far they've come. But more—to give them fun, excitement. Imagine, of all things, the joy of this great-hearted sedan turned loose from the sober responsibility to impress, impose, uphold . . .[17]

Is this a car or a sultan being spoken about? What versatility! To indulge, impress, intimidate; to give one's family self-esteem and remind them of how far they've come—if it were not for the dangerous ethos underlying all these promises, the advertisement would be funny. Surely a found poem lies in wait beneath the glossy prose.

No book on poetry that I know of discusses found poetry. After a considerable search, I am able to find one reference to it, in the glossary of Louis Simpson's *An Introduction to Poetry:*

Found Poetry.   A piece of writing that is read as poetry though it was not intended to be. Usually the poem is found in a passage of prose—it may be from a news item, advertisement, handbook, travel book, or catalogue—which is then divided into lines of verse. Most found poems, though not all, are satiric—the unexpected attention catching the writer off guard.[18]

As a glossary entry, this is a fair description, from the outside, of found poetry. It does not of course describe the process by which a poet-reader perceives the poem in the prose and makes the decisions that abstract it and transform it into poetry. Simpson is probably right that most found poems are satiric, and this may be a limitation inherent in the process by which found poems are made (I reassert my contention of Chapter I that process and product are inseparable).

But why should the scope of found poems be largely

[17] Rolls-Royce, Inc., 1972.
[18] *An Introduction to Poetry.*

limited to satire? I think our poetic will help us pursue this question. The poetic requires that a poem's language be excited, precise, evocative, and presentational; the found poems we have observed thus far succeed in all areas but one. They lack the kind of excitement of language of which Coleridge speaks, an excitement born of passionate feeling. Verse, as we have seen, also does not embody excitement. Found poetry is clearly not verse—it is far too evocative to be so conceived, and is independent of rhyme and meter—but it shares with verse a certain lack of intensity and a concomitant reliance on cleverness for its effect.

It might be argued that the satiric, clever nature of found poetry is simply the result of the prose chosen as its source. Perhaps if instead of catalogues, advertisements, and the like, we made a found poem of the finest prose, that poem would go beyond satire and be genuinely passionate. This in fact has been tried. The problem is that prose that is in its own right born of deep emotion and that inspires deep emotion in others does not lend itself to rearrangement as poetry. Our attempt earlier in the book to make poetry of a passage from Robert Coles' *Children of Crisis* (see p. 42) illustrates some of the liabilities of transforming serious prose into poetry. But *Children of Crisis* is expository rather than literary prose. For an example of literary prose made into poetry, we can turn to *A Stone, A Leaf, A Door*, a volume of poems, selected and arranged in verse by John S. Barnes, from the prose of Thomas Wolfe.

Here is a poem made from *Look Homeward, Angel.*

BEN

My Brother Ben's face, thought Eugene,
Is like a piece of slightly yellow ivory;
His high white head is knotted fiercely
By his old man's scowl;
His mouth is like a knife,
His smile the flicker of light across a blade.
His face is like a blade, and a knife,
And a flicker of light:
It is delicate and fierce,
And scowls beautifully forever,   10

And when he fastens his hard white fingers
And his scowling eyes
Upon a thing he wants to fix,
He sniffs
With sharp and private concentration
Through his long pointed nose.
Thus women, looking, feel a well of tenderness
For his pointed, bumpy, always scowling face:
His hair shines like that of a young boy—
It is crinkled and crisp as lettuce.   20

Wolfe's description is magnificent; we know how Eugene sees his brother, how others see him, and we ourselves are moved to our own vision of this taciturn, beautiful man. The description carries also the current of feeling that flows from Eugene to Ben. But a superb description does not make—by a rearrangement of lines—a superb poem. The prose is rightly responsible for a narrative link that in the poem becomes a shackle. "Thought Eugene" is the most glaring example of words used simply to tell what's going on, rather than to evoke. There is the repeated use of "is," an intransitive verb that the poem does not require, and all those "ands" that serve only to let us know we have come to the next item. In short, balance between discursive and presentational use of language is too heavily weighted on the side of the former for the prose to succeed as poetry.

One example is not proof that literary prose cannot be rearranged into good poetry. However, *A Stone, A Leaf, A Door* contains over one hundred and fifty such examples; and I have yet to discover a counterexample, either in that volume or elsewhere. The purpose here is not to prove that literary prose can't become poetry, but to discover principles involved in the poetic process. What we have discovered, I suggest, is that found poems are most often made from a particular kind of source (catalogues, advertisements, and the like), because this source is already of a presentational, rather than discursive, character. The material from which found poems are made imposes, in turn, limitations of scope on the found poems.

This is hardly to denigrate the role of found poems in the process of making and responding to poetry. On the contrary, because the processes of discovering and of making the poem are so closely aligned and so relatively accessible (compared with making a poem wholly, as described in Chapter I), the found poem, in addition to providing pleasure as poetry, affords us a fine model for testing and developing the tenets of our poetic.

Part of the intent of this chapter may now be seen as broadening our repertoire of poetic possibilities, as well as using and modifying our poetic. The rock lyrics and found poems we have considered require that we be open to the possibility of poetry that we might not otherwise consider. Further, we are likely to examine closely and even feel responsible for the poetry we find in such places, just as we might respond to a deer we discover feeding on a lawn in suburbia. Poetry is not just in poetry books—this is a simple notion but one which needs a vigorous defense and clear criteria for judgment.

6

RECONNAISSANCE

Choose a poem you like and type it on a sheet of paper, omitting the author's name. Give the poem to a friend to read, and talk with him or her about the poem until you feel that you both understand not only the poem but also each other's way of responding to it. In your conversation about the poem, try to encourage reasons on both your parts, rather than allowing assertions like "It's good" or "I don't like this line," to go unchallenged.

VI

SHARING POETRY

All art is collaboration.

JOHN SYNGE

Collaboration is at the core of poetry; and implicit in the preceding chapters has been a notion of collaboration between the poet and what I shall now call his "linguistic culture."

In its simplest form, the term linguistic culture designates a language common to a national or ethnic community and includes historical as well as current meanings of words, expressions, and literary symbols. (I use "meaning" in the spirit of Ogden and Richards, to refer to both the symbolic and the emotive uses of language.) As part of this concept of linguistic culture, I include subcultures of speakers and readers who use the common language but have also developed, within their subgroup, a special range of meaning for words, expressions, and literary symbols.

The poet collaborates with a linguistic culture in the first instance simply by writing in a given language. The language provides him with immediate communication on the symbolic level: "dog" is understood to refer to a four-legged, domesticated animal that barks. In its broader applications, the linguistic culture also affords the poet a fund of historical and literary symbols from which to draw emotive meaning—for example, Aesop's fable of the dog in the manger, or the myth of the dog that guards the gates of hell. Linguistic culture in the broader sense also provides the poet with contemporary idioms rich in meaning: "dog tired," "gone to the dogs," "dog days." Finally, the usages of a subgroup within the linguistic culture may offer further meaning: "What a dog I was with last night!"

We saw in the first chapter how the poet becomes one with his readers as he creates the poem. We may now recall that he identifies himself with the imagined reader not only as an individual, but also as a member of the same linguistic culture. Thus in "Lemming Song," I made assumptions and estimations of the linguistic culture that I, as poet, shared with my imagined and anticipated readers. I could assume they would know, symbolically, what a lemming is. Emotively, I assumed a range of meaning within the linguistic culture—the lemming as a symbol of madness, of suicidal impulse—on which I could draw. I also estimated that the linguistic culture of my readers would include knowledge of a specific literary figure, Walter Pater; and, as I noted in the chapter, that may have been a faulty assessment of the resources of the linguistic culture of my readers. It may also have been that I did not properly tap those resources; that is, my allusion to Pater should have been more explicit.

"World War III," the poem we examined in Reconnaissance 4, may now be seen as a poem that collaborates with both our general linguistic culture and with specific subcultures. As part of our linguistic culture generally, we can be assumed to be familiar with two world wars. Further, there has been enough talk of our potential for nuclear holocaust for the title, "World War III," to have powerful emotive meaning in itself. But the poet's usage goes beyond the common lexicon of the culture. He uses a G.I. expression, " 'This is the day the eagle craps' "; a military and political expression, "the American right wing"; and a term incorporating the vocabulary of modern physics, "fireball."

Since we are provided with an explanation of the G.I. expression ("You think of the euphemism for pay"), I assume the poetic intent of "World War III" is not to address an audience composed solely or primarily of soldiers. But no such background information accompanies the expression "the American right wing." My own cultural reference for the expression is political; I can clearly see it as the metaphorical description of a politically conservative extreme. A friend pointed out that the expression also describes an Air Force flight formation; his experience in the military provides him with a broader knowledge of our linguistic culture. Similarly, to apprehend that "old fireball" means both the sun and nuclear fission requires a linguistic culture that includes an awareness of recent developments in physics.

Yet I have said that I don't assume the poetic intent of this poem is to address an audience of soldiers. Nor do I assume it is directed at nuclear physicists. I think the poetic intent is, for the most part, to speak to readers like me—"lay readers" insofar as we are neither military personnel nor scientists.

My contention is based on the diction of the poem as a whole. There is enough in the poem, aside from these specific phrases, to provide the twentieth-century lay reader with access to the poem. The vocabulary is not arcane; the situation presented can be readily visualized by anyone who knows modern history and is aware of the sinister capability of recent technological and, perhaps, political trends. In short, there is enough "overlap" of "cultures" for our collaboration. This is not to say that a linguistic culture which includes the G.I.'s lingo and the physicist's slang does not enrich our responses to the poem.

Inclusion and exclusion by virtue of membership in a linguistic culture are a matter of degree; in any poem, there may be words, allusions, or historical references that fall outside our own linguistic culture. The question is how much is tolerable. I earlier criticized "Horse Latitudes" because I felt that too much specialized historical knowledge was required of the reader in order for him truly to collaborate with the poem. On the other hand, I did not raise this same objection to "On the Late Massacre in Piemont." Both poems make a presentation based on a specific historical event. Yet I suggest that in one instance ("Horse Latitudes") the poem is wholly inaccessible without knowledge of the event, while Milton's sonnet does not require us to be familiar with seventeenth-century history. Even without knowing that "stocks and stones" refers to graven images, or that the "triple tyrant" is the pope, there is enough in the poem with which I, from my linguistic culture, can collaborate. As I indicated earlier, I do not think the poem really concerns the Piemontese, the pope, or even the Reformation—its presentation is that of man's relationship to God, and of the interweaving of national ambition with divine sanction. Again, this is not to say that a broader linguistic culture, one that encompasses knowledge of Milton's England, would not enrich collaboration, and hence response. But the collaboration at the core of the poem derives first from dimensions of the poetry, not of the history.

"Black People!" by LeRoi Jones, which we looked at in another context in Chapter IV, assumes, through the entire poem, collaboration with a distinct subgroup and its linguistic culture. As a white, I am not part of that linguistic culture and therefore am excluded from collaboration—or, at the least, collaboration is exceedingly difficult. This does not mean I don't understand the vocabulary of the poem, or am ignorant of its specific references. On the contrary, as someone who grew up in and about Newark, New Jersey, I have been in the stores mentioned in the poem (Bamberger's, Klein's, Hahnes'), on the streets (Broad, Washington), and know something of the political figure (Frelinghuysen) who was powerful in the state.

But as much as I might try empathetically to re-create the poem, "Up against the wall mother / fucker this is a stick up!" cannot become "magic words" for me. Nor can I envision "the fruit of the sun" to be gained by "smashing at jellywhite faces." I am *not* saying that the poem advocates political action with which I disagree. Nor am I saying that Jones intends or does not intend to include me in his readership. As I have argued throughout this book, intentionalism and political motivation or effect play no role in the poetic I advocate. The poem's poetic intent—not its author's intentions or politics—directs it to a subgroup of the linguistic culture.

The poem is boldly addressed to black people. Its intent could not be clearer from the title alone. Further, the poem's diction includes a very specialized use of words and expressions: "whitey," "shit," "brothers," "my man," and "tomish ways." Certainly it is not only blacks who use the word "shit" or "brothers"; but the way these and other words are used in the poem expresses its intent—and I gauge that intent to be one of specific address to black people.

Finding the linguistic culture of "Black People!" virtually

alien, I have two choices. Since I cannot collaborate with it, I can decide that "Black People!" fails as a poem. Such a decision would be somewhat similar to the one I made about "Horse Latitudes," although the reasons for my cultural exclusion are different. It is also the kind of decision I have made when reading certain of Ezra Pound's "Cantos," especially when they contain long phrases in Italian, Latin, and Greek ("Canto IX" and "Canto XLVII" come most readily to mind). Alternatively, I can decide that the poem is not addressed to me, that it is not my place to judge it. In responding to "Black People!" I choose this latter course, for unlike "Horse Latitudes" or the "Cantos," "Black People!" clearly has the *poetic* intent of addressing itself to blacks. I can simply respect that intent as I perceive it.

Essentially, what we have is this: poetry is collaborative; one dimension of this collaboration requires that the language of the poem's "virtual life" make connection with the linguistic culture of the reader. The language of the poem includes everything that went into its making; the linguistic culture of the reader is everything he brings to the poem. It must be added that in response—response as a process—the reader's own linguistic culture can be broadened. It might even be argued further that a measure of a truly excellent poem is that response to it enlarges the scope of the reader's linguistic culture.

Earlier we learned that the dynamic of response is essentially the process of empathetic re-creation, itself a form of collaboration between the reader and the poem. We may now assert that a prerequisite for response, for any given instance of empathetic re-creation, is the presence of a linguistic culture in the poem with which the reader can collaborate, because his own relationship to the same linguistic culture meshes, at least to some degree, with that presented by the poem.

Thus I take Synge's assertion "All art is collaboration" to mean that art collaborates at once with the past and the future. Its past lies in the availability of language, symbols, and traditions; its future lies in the response of its readers, viewers, and hearers.

But there is yet another sense in which poetry can be collaborative. It can be collaborative because people *do* it together. This dimension of collaboration is perhaps less grand than the collaboration created by linguistic culture, but it is just as significant.

As we observed earlier, reading and writing poetry can be as private as a love letter, as secret as a diary, but it can also be something else. It can be a public, collaborative activity, and can be enriched by being so. There is no reason why a group cannot gather to respond to poems together and experience all the delight and creative energy of a quartet playing Mozart. And there is no reason why all poems must be written in solitary confinement; groups of poets can work creatively together, reviving an old literary tradition of collaborative poems and partaking of the modern phenomenon of collaboration as it is practiced in music, drama, and, to some extent, the visual arts.

We accept the idea that exciting jazz comes of spontaneous collaboration. Even classical music can be made this way, as Lucas Foss' Improvisation Ensemble has demonstrated. Is the same idea inimical to poetry?

Poetry, as we have seen, is not a "thing." It is a host of mutually supportive activities: making poems, developing a viable poetic, and responding to poems. To these, let us add a fourth activity, the sharing of poetry in all its active dimensions. Further, I suggest that, given the opportunity, people like to share the making of poems, their expectations of poetry, and the poems themselves. That is, people like to do these things if we can break down the usual restraints against doing them.

Creative-writing teachers commonly use strategies of collaboration as "loosening-up exercises" for their students. They will ask their students to make a group poem that builds as each person contributes a line. Or students will be instructed to make poems by using an anagram to provide the first letters of each line (for example, N-E-S-C-A-F-E); all the poems will have the same starting point and can be shared as soon as they are written. Another kind of collaboration occurs when each person writes a single line on his own; then the group puts all the lines together to make a poem.

Are these merely the "tricks" of clever teachers, or do they have some defensible rationale based on what poetry in fact is? For many years I considered the collaborative making of poems—group poems—as merely the device of a teacher confronted by inhibited or lethargic students; or, at best, it seemed a kind of parlor game about as significant as charades. But three observations made by Kenneth Koch, have caused me to reconsider.

Koch was "teaching" grade school children to write poetry. He discovered, first of all, that the children loved to make poems collaboratively. He asked each child to write a line beginning with "I wish"; then he collected all the lines, shuffled them, and read them aloud as one poem. Koch describes the children as "enormously excited by writing the lines and even more by hearing them read as a poem. They were talking, waving, blushing, laughing, and bouncing up and down." [1]

Koch also observed that the children preferred writing poems in class, among their fellows, to working on them alone at night:

> A surprising discovery I made at P.S. 61 was that children enjoyed writing poems at school more than at home. I had assumed that like grown-up writers they would prefer to be comfortable, quiet, and alone when they wrote, but I was wrong.... There was ... the fact of their all being in the room, writing together. No time for self-consciousness or self-doubts; there was too much activity: everyone was writing and talking and jumping around. And it was competitive in a mild and exhilarating way: it was what everyone was doing and everyone could do it. [2]

Finally, we have Koch's comment that collaborative endeavor led to later individual authorship of poems by the children:

> These collaborations almost always made the children want to make up, and usually to write, poems of their own. Composing a poem together is inspiring: the timid are given courage by braver colleagues; and ideas too good to belong to any one child are transformed, elaborated

---

[1] *Wishes, Lies and Dreams: Teaching Children to Write Poetry* (New York: Random House, 1970), p. 6.
[2] Ibid., pp. 28–29.

on, and topped...a subject is built up, starting with something rather plain and becoming deeper and more interesting in its elaboration.[3]

The title of Koch's book, *Wishes, Lies and Dreams*, describes the "themes" he assigned to his students. They were to write "wish poems," "lie poems," and "dream poems." Yet it seems to me that the title, and the notion of themes, is secondary to what the book is about. It is really about the collaborative making of and the shared response to poems. The children shouting out their poems for all to hear; the children piling lines and images one upon the next; the children inspiring each other as poets—this was the heart of Koch's teaching at P.S. 61 in New York City.

Here is a collaboration by an entire fifth grade. Koch taught the children the sestina form, provided the end words for the lines of the first stanza, and left the children to their collective imagination and delight.

HOORAY

My wonderful perplexity
Is so disjoint.
Words like that are not common
But they do have quite a wealth
Of meaning. Hooray! Hooray!
It's really fabulous.

It's a wonderful fabulous
Day! Let's have some perplexity.
It's time we got some hooray!
I think I'll just disjoint   10
Altogether. Look who's here! the wealth
Man! His visits aren't so common.

Today isn't so common
But tomorrow will be fabulous.
We want wealth
But getting wealth is a great perplexity.
I've got a disjoint.
My finger fell—hooray!

[3] *Ibid.*, p. 48.

It's time for lunch hooray
What do work and lunch have in common?   20
I'll go have something to eat in a disjoint
Restaurant. The food there was fabulous!
Food is a great perplexity.
Food is great wealth.

Here comes the Wealth
Parade! No one is going to say hooray.
Why that is is a great perplexity.
A parade isn't common
But it's fabulous.
The wealth man's float is going to disjoint!   30

Things like that are disjoint.
How should we distribute the wealth?
Distributing wealth is fabulous.
They're distributing wealth—hooray!
Distributing is so common
We'll distribute it with the perplexity.

The perplexity of the cat is disjoint.
It comes out in common with the wealth
Man. The people will say, "Hooray! it's fabulous!"

And here is a somewhat different collaborative poem, by
two students, Vivien Tuft and Fontessa Moore.

What's inside the moon?
    There's hot water inside.
What's the sky made of?
    It was made out of white snow.
If you cut the sun open what would you see?
    Terrible looking enemies.
When you write you look at your words have you thought
        of cutting open a letter to see what's inside?
    No. But if a person was crazy the answer would be yes.
What's inside colors?
    There's pink stars.
Where is the end of the universe?
    In back of the swimming pools.
How old is adventure?
    It is 60,000 years old.
Which color is older, black or white?
    Black because you can outline me.

Must the experience of poetry be different for adults than it was for the grade school children Koch describes? Instinctively, we are likely to answer that it must. It is difficult to visualize a group of adults writing down their poems and then clamoring, actually jumping around, for them to be heard. It is also hard to imagine adults putting aside their individual egos long enough to take genuine and deep pleasure in a group poem. (Most of my adult friends regard with scorn the very idea that creative work can be collective.) But there is evidence that contradicts this general impression.

For example, we have Dan Jones' account of his poetic collaboration with Dylan Thomas, a commentary worth quoting at some length:

> In poetry collaborations we always wrote alternate lines: I had the odd-numbered lines and Dylan the even-numbered, and we made it a rule that neither of us should suggest an alteration in the other's work. The poems, of which I still have about two hundred, are a different matter from the WBS [Warmly Broadcasting System, a satire on radio programming] fooling. It is still play, but it is what I would call serious play. The poetic style of Walter Bram, as we called ourselves, is bafflingly inconsistent: it is fragile, furious, laconic, massive, delicate, incantatory, cool, flinty, violent, Chinese, Greek, and shocking. One poem may begin "You will be surprised when I remain obdurate," and the next, "I lay under the currant bushes and told the beady berries about Jesus." Some of the poems are very, very beautiful; very. Especially those that tell of singularly gentle and godlike actions by the third person plural.
>
> They had come from the place high on the coral hills
> Where the light from the white sea fills the soil with
>   ascending grace.
> And the sound of their power makes motion as steep as
>   the sky,
> And the fruits of the great ground lie like leaves from a
>   vertical flower.
> They had come from the place; they had come and had
>   gone again

In the season of delicate rain, in a smooth ascension of
  grace.

  We had word obsessions: everything at one time was
"little" or "white"; and sometimes an adjective became
irresistibly funny in almost any connection: "innumerable
bananas," "wilful moccasin," "a certain Mrs. Prothero."
These word games and even the most facetious of our
collaborations had a serious experimental purpose, and
there is no doubt that they played an important part in
Dylan's early poetic development.[4]

The Jones/Thomas collaborations took place in the 1920s;
but lest we think them either dated or unique, we have a poem
from the very latest (as of this writing) edition of *Poetry*
magazine.

WHO HUNGERS FOR A FACE THAT FADES AWAY

Who hungers for a face that fades away?
The glacier slides, the hammers turn to knives.
A man is sketching frozen maps in clay.

The owl who breeds has nothing more to say.
The sleigh destroyed in an iceslide thrives.
Who hungers for a face that fades away?

Tundra in boots reminds him of decay.
He stabs, and the map bleeds, the map survives.
A man is sketching frozen maps in clay.

The fingerprint brands ice, what lines convey!
And the face etches shadow, melts, and dives.
Who hungers for a face that fades away?

The moonlight sags, sun sags where bruises lay.
Ice is the animal the oxhorn drives.
A man is sketching frozen maps in clay.

Ice plugs the caves that absent winds betray.
But where is the floating city death revives?
Who hungers for a face that fades away?
A man is sketching frozen maps in clay.

                                 PAUL NEMSER
                                 and MARK RUDMAN

[4] Constantine Fitz Gibbon, *The Life of Dylan Thomas* (Boston: Little, Brown, 1965),
p. 54, quoting Dan Jones.

Finally, let me offer this group poem, made recently by some friends of mine.[5]

THE BEEHIVE

The south wall buckled under it,
rock, leaf, mud, birdnest,
rocks stood up and clapped
the fortress of mud
next to the cast-off right hip
of a huladancer

lull tilt

North and South America fall off.
In their places sprout

                ripe melons.

The point is simply this: adults can and do make collaborative poems; we should think of the endeavor neither as a gimmick nor as strictly the province of schoolchildren. On the contrary, we might usefully regard the collaborative making of poems—either by co-poets or groups of poets—as opening up the ways in which poetry can be shared.

Jonathan Baumbach has edited a book entitled *Writers as Teachers/Teachers as Writers*, in which ten writers tell about their teaching. Every essay is different, but Baumbach announces in his introduction: "What it comes down to—and on this point all of the contributors to the book seem to agree —a writing class needs to be a community." [6]

In fact, not *every* contributor does stress the writing class as community. Wright Morris, for example, emphasizes "the privacy of [the writer's] calling," and says that, most of all, "he must rise and sing by himself." [7]

Several of those who speak of community as important to creating and talking about writing are not poets. Baumbach himself is a novelist who considers "gut reactions" essential to the sharing of literature among a community of people who

---

[5] Robert McDowell and Mark Jarman were the instigators within a group of nine people who made this poem.

[6] *Writers as Teachers/Teachers as Writers* (New York: Holt, Rinehart and Winston, 1970), p. 5.

[7] "The Word Between Them," in Baumbach, *Writers as Teachers/Teachers as Writers*, p. 201.

"write for each other." L. S. Simkes, a novelist and playwright, urges a highly personal interaction among his writing students. But it is not wholly coincidental, I think, that among the contributors to *Writers as Teachers/Teachers as Writers* it is the poets who most vigorously and eloquently conceive of community as integral to their endeavor as teachers-sharers of poetry.

(Let me note that in the rest of this chapter, I will use the terms "teacher" and "class" only as a convenience. They are not meant to limit the discussion to the classroom; it is an unfortunate fact that currently most talking about poetry, and writing about poetry, exist within the context of classrooms. I would as soon have "teacher" read "instigator" or "convener," and "class" read "group of persons talking about poetry.")

Here is George P. Elliott's comment on community:

> But sometimes, late in the semester, I would look forward to going into the same classroom with pleasure, charged up by the students' energy, their improvement, their sprouts of imagination. I did not talk much about this experience to other teachers, not wanting to seem boastful, fearing it might be illusory or a symptom of some sentimentality in myself. A Chaucer man helped me define it—the Chaucer men I have known tended to be wiser than most. You can tell a good class, he said, by the way it pulls together late in the term into a kind of community. He did not know how it came about or what he contributed to bringing it about ... but he felt, as I did and do, that only such a class can be called successful. This is an occasional community ... yet not only is the experience of such a fragile community a good in itself but also, as I believe, it heightens the experience of literature, which is among other things a form of communion.[8]

Elliott, like Koch, is sharing poetry with others. Elliott's students are in college rather than grade school, but for them too there is the crackle of excitement, of creative energy; and

[8] "Teaching Writing," in Baumbach, *Writers as Teachers/Teachers as Writers*, p. 47.

"communion" is as apt in describing the experience at P.S. 61 as it is for Elliott's students.

The poet Denise Levertov defines community as precisely the "atmosphere of sharing" that characterizes talking about poetry. Furthermore, as we hear her tell about one of the ways she shares poetry, we understand that it is the poetry itself that creates the community, no less than the participants of the group:

> I first tried out Muriel Rukeyser's wonderful idea of having a whole class read a poem one after another, without previous discussion—something which perhaps sounds boring but in fact turns out to be a sort of alchemical process, a process of filtering, refining, and intensification of understanding that is far more effective and moving than any mere analytical method can be. Usually the first one or two readers stumble and hesitate; the next two read with some confidence and facility; then a period of boredom and irritation may set in—probably most participants feeling they can't bear to hear those same words one more time; and then—subtly—that point is passed, and one finds oneself at a different level of response, finds oneself emerging into an intimate, sensuous comprehension of the poem that activates both intellect and imagination. I have never known it to fail.[9]

Earlier we spoke of poetry as performance; here, in Levertov's account, we have not only performance, but ensemble performance at that. As Kenneth Burke described response as a heaping up of attitudes, Levertov describes a heaping of attitudes through performance. Although there is no explicit dialogue among the respondents, each response (here the response is the performance) builds on those that have preceded it. Together, cumulatively, and by the subtle power the group builds, a "different level of response" is achieved.

Two observations: (1) Shared response of the sort Levertov recounts is in many ways the collective manifestation of the individual response we have explored throughout this book.

---

[9] "The Untaught Teacher," in Baumbach, *Writers as Teachers/Teachers as Writers*, p. 164.

Individual response ideally is built of the dynamic of attitudes evoked and played off each other; individual response is performance as the reader himself—silently or orally—brings the poem to life; individual response is an empathetic re-creation of the poem as the reader struggles to draw nearer his most viable conception of the poem's intent. All these dimensions of response can be replicated when poetry is shared; it may even be that they are fostered by group interaction. Certainly the kind of group involvement described by Koch, Elliott, and Levertov indicates that sharing poetry is in no way inimical to dimensions of response we most value. (2) Shared response, and the creation of a vital "occasional" community of respondents, derives as much from what poetry is as from strategies of group interaction. Another way of putting this is that the readers sharing poetry are not in an encounter group; they have not come together with the goal of interaction as their chief concern—the interaction is a function of the way we have discovered that poetry means. Since poetry evokes intensely personal and creative response, it follows that interaction among sharers of poetry will possess these characteristics.

Significantly, all these accounts—Koch's and each of the ten contributors to *Writers as Teachers/Teachers as Writers* —integrate making and responding. There is no such thing as a creative-writing class in which participants solely write. As we observed in Chapter I, the maker of the poem is also its reader, its very first reader. Role duality is integral to making poems, as it is, in a modified form, integral to responding to poems (the reader as re-creator). Within a group sharing poetry, all members can be both makers and readers; they write for each other, and, after the maker himself, the group is likely to be the first audience of a new work. This role duality of the sharers is part of the reason why the group talking about poetry must be a community. The sharing of poetry is total; the sharers come to be known to each other not only as readers but as makers.

What of the poetic? Do sharers of poetry develop a shared set of assumptions, expectations, and values concerning poetry? Does sharing poems impede or facilitate the individual in developing his own poetic?

First it must be said that sharing poetry hardly guarantees the development of an explicit, defensible poetic. A person can read innumerable poems over many years and never articulate a poetic—among sharers of poetry it may be less easy to do this, but it is possible. Levertov speaks of "discussions which failed, usually, to come to grips with anything, but slid off into purely subjective 'likes' and 'dislikes' because we had not established any evaluative standards." [10] One explanation of these failures, she suggests, is that the individual sharers did not know each other well enough really to get down to business, to become genuinely involved in the poems. But a similar cause can have a different effect, particularly among persons who have a formal background in English literature. Rather than failing "to come to grips with anything," the sharers of poetry can all too easily fail "to come to grips with" the poem at hand, substituting for its discussion a series of critical pronouncements like "The use of metaphor is striking," "This must be classified as a surrealist poem," or "I'd say he was influenced by Berryman." The discussants are echoing, in all likelihood, their previous training in literature.

We know that it is tempting to describe a poem's "topography" instead of plumbing its depths. Why does the poet use metaphor? What does it mean to say a poem is surrealistic? How can we ascertain—from the poem—what influenced or did not influence a poet as he made the poem? These are more basic and important questions.

Thus there are two ways, not unrelated, in which sharers of poems may fail actually to share a poem with each other. They may, at one end of the spectrum, indulge in purely subjective opinion—a voicing of "likes" and "dislikes." Or, with a kind of objectivity, the sharers may exchange critical pronouncements that say something about their knowledge of the history of English literature or of prosody. In both cases the sharers have not "come to grips with" fundamentals, what they actually believe poetry is or should be.

Attempts to share poetry without sharing poetics result in the kind of futility we saw in Chapter V, in Kermode and Spender's discussion of Bob Dylan. Each man shot a quiver full of critical arrows, but in all directions. There was no agreed on target.

I'm not sure whether kids like those with whom Koch worked or adults have an easier time integrating poetics into

[10] Ibid., p. 158.

the sharing of poetry. The kids are less likely to have preconceptions and prejudices, other than perhaps that poetry is
"hard." And they are also probably more willing to start from
scratch, with the acceptance—until they develop principles
which tell them otherwise—that anything can be poetry. But
we ought not to romanticize the virtues of naivete; there is
something to be said for the range of exposure adults have had
to poetry, and to life. The prior experience of adults with poetry
enables them to make comparative judgments. Their life ex-
periences provide them with a broader linguistic culture; for
example, adults are more likely than children to be aware of
the G.I. lingo used so evocatively in "World War III." And
while I consider most of what goes on in formal English
courses to work against an understanding of poetics, often
some standard, some notion of poetic principles, emerges between the lines of literary criticism. The adult will have the
beginnings of a poetic, unlike his younger counterpart; it is a
matter of enlarging the poetic, and making it explicit and
defensible.

Poetics, as much as any dimension of poetry, benefit by
being made public and collaborative. In fact, poetic assumptions and standards are so integral both to making poems and
to responding to poems that an explicit discussion of them is
essential to sharing poems. A "private" poetic is perhaps a
contradiction in terms. As soon as someone makes a poem,
that poem is a public declaration of at least a part of his poetic.
Similarly, as soon as someone says virtually anything *about a
poem* (as distinguished from commentary about its author or
history), he is expressing a poetic. The problem then is not so
much that poetics are not or cannot be part of sharing, but
that they need to be made an overt aspect of it rather than
continually lurking behind the discussion or being forced into
the open only in extremis ("Well, then, *what do you think*
poetry *is?*"

The dialogue of sharing fosters the development of a
poetic. In the making of poems, the community can provide
excitement, a sense of play, mild competition, and collaborative
forays into the imagination. In responding to poems, the community affords a broader interplay of attitudes, associations,
and meaning-making possibilities. In developing a poetic, the
community provides questions and challenges, and constitutes

a marketplace in which an idea or assumption must be explained, revised, defended, and, if possible, propagated. Just as the maker of poems needs the reader, so the reader needs other readers—not only to collaborate in the making of meanings but also to challenge the assumptions on which meanings and judgments are based.

Does this require that there be *one* poetic on which all the sharers of poetry must agree? The only fair way to answer this question is to equivocate: yes and no. There need to be agreed on ground rules; but, on the other hand, there also can be modifications once the rules themselves are made explicit. An analogy that comes to mind is that of squash, a game that has both an English and an American version. The two versions employ a slightly different ball, different court dimensions, and a different scoring system. Despite these variations, British squash players (and Indians and Pakistanis) can play the American game, and Americans can play the British version. In fact, the best players of American squash are usually Indians or Pakistanis who learned the British game first. There are essentials that are transferable.

Thus in using poetics. Differing concepts of precision, I suggest, can coexist among sharers of poetry, so long as some concept of precision in poetry is expressly valued by all the sharers. However, if two people attempt to share poetry and one of them considers precision important while the other holds the opposite value, there is obviously little sharing possible in the sense I use sharing. Then what we have is not two versions of squash, but a badminton player and a squash player trying to make a game. We can usefully recall the discussion of poetics between Coleridge and Wordsworth that we examined in Chapter II. There were keen differences between the two poetics; but Coleridge and Wordsworth shared a basic conception of excitement or passion in poetry with which they sought to replace the eighteenth century's emphasis on ornate language and clever expression.

The point of sharing a poetic is clearly not to exact unanimity of opinion among readers. Rather it is to assure that the readers be forced to consider what they value in poetry and why. Then, when these have been made explicit, a number of sharers can work with similar values or a respect for those who differ. In either case the end in mind is hardly that of

getting everyone to agree—we have seen that it is the differences in values and attitudes about poetry as much as consensus that heightens the dynamic of sharing it.

At the outset of this book, I described one of its intended
functions as that of "eliminating the middleman," the textbook
or teacher who more often than not comes between the reader
and poetry by requiring a response to the particular view of
the teacher or textbook rather than to poetry. While I still
perceive this as an important and necessary function, in writing
this last chapter my concept of "the middleman" has broadened. It is not just the teacher, or the literary critic, or the
Introduction to Poetry textbook that discourages a spontaneous
and joyous sharing of poetry—it is that poetry, like so much
of our culture and experience, has become institutionalized,
the province of special credential-giving organizations. The
obvious institution to name in this context is of course the
school; but the school is the product, I think, rather than
the originator, of a frame of mind that regards endeavors as
legitimate only if they are connected with or sponsored by
some institution. Hence we assume—all too readily—that if we
want to study poetry, we should take "a course"; if we want to
write poetry, we should enroll in "a workshop"; if we want
to listen to poetry, we should attend a reading by a prominent
poet.

The malaise affects virtually all aspects of our lives; and
spokesmen like Ivan Illich and Paul Goodman have expounded
at length on possible remedies for it at the societal level.[11]
But with poetry as such, it seems to me there is hope in making
actual the analogy I posited at the beginning of this chapter
between poetry and music. Of all the arts, music, I think, has
resisted becoming the province of experts and students, and
remains open to the kind of sharing about which we've been
talking. No matter how proficient the Budapest and the
Guarneri string quartets, the four players who meet every
Sunday night to make their own music experience joyous and
creative sharing. No matter how many Beatle and Rolling Stone
records have been sold, virtually every city and town has its

[11] Ivan Illich, *Deschooling Society* (New York: Harper & Row, 1970); Paul Goodman,
Growing Up Absurd (New York: Random House, 1960).

own rock groups. No matter how brilliant and famous Miles Davis is, amateur jazz combos blow their horns enthusiastically. From the front-porch bluegrass strummers to the local chamber musicians, music has retained an openness, an accessibility to the general populace, that I think is virtually unequaled in other art forms.

At the simplest level, this means that almost anyone feels he can pick up a harmonica and try a few chords, or that anyone with a bongo can thump away while a friend experiments with a recorder. Would that this were so with poetry, that each of us felt inclined to try out an image or a quatrain, to join someone in making an impromptu poem, to gather friends together to perform poems for each other. I am inclined to speculate that there is an inverse ratio between subjects taught in school and avocations pursued thereafter: English, with its unit on poetry, is generally required in schools and colleges; whereas few courses are available, much less required, in music-making and music appreciation. But there is another factor of which we should take account—music is almost always a collaborative venture; unaccompanied solo performances are the exception rather than the rule. Not only might music provide us with a model of sharing within art forms, but it suggests a strong link between the collaborative and performance aspects of an art and the accessibility of that art apart from institutional aegis.

The impulse behind this book may now be seen as basically that of exploring our own possibilities as much as those of poetry itself. We can be makers of poems, sensitive and imaginative readers of poems, discoverers of poems, and collaborators who share a variety of endeavors, from creating poems to developing poetic theories. The impulse is integrative; none of these roles is exclusive of the others.

The book does not presume to have discussed all the possibilities that inhere in poetry or in ourselves as we conduct our own reconnaissance into poems and poetics. But if the book succeeds, it will have raised new questions and possibilities that the reader will pursue well beyond these pages.

At the end of "Troilus and Criseyde," Chaucer bids farewell to his story with a charming envoy. While this work, unlike

Chaucer's "litel bok," aspires neither to "tragedye" nor "comedye," our subject has been "alle poesye":

> Go, litel bok, go, litel myn tragedye,
> Ther God thi makere yet, er that he dye,
> So sende myght to make in som comedye!
> But litel book, no makyng thow n'envie,
> But subgit be to alle poesye;
> And kis the steppes, where as thow seet pace
> Virgile, Ovide, Omer, Lucan, and Stace.

MORE POEMS

Stephen Spender

MY PARENTS KEPT ME FROM CHILDREN WHO WERE ROUGH

My parents kept me from children who were rough
Who threw words like stones and who wore torn clothes.
Their thighs showed through rags. They ran in the street
And climbed cliffs and stripped by the country streams.

I feared more than tigers their muscles like iron
Their jerking hands and their knees tight on my arms.
I feared the salt coarse pointing of those boys
Who copied my lisp behind me on the road.

They were lithe, they sprang out behind hedges
Like dogs to bark at my world. They threw mud
While I looked the other way, pretending to smile.
I longed to forgive them, but they never smiled.

Emily Dickinson

THE BAT IS DUN

The Bat is dun, with wrinkled Wings—
Like fallow Article—
And not a song pervade his Lips—
Or none perceptible.

His small Umbrella quaintly halved
Describing in the Air
An Arc alike inscrutable
Elate Philosopher.

Deputed from what Firmament—
Of what Astute Abode—
Empowered with what Malignity
Auspiciously withheld—

To his adroit Creator
Ascribe no less the praise—
Beneficent, believe me,
His Eccentricities—

Paul Laurence Dunbar
WE WEAR THE MASK

We wear the mask that grins and lies,
It hides our cheeks and shades our eyes,—
This debt we pay to human guile;
With torn and bleeding hearts we smile,
And mouth with myriad subtleties.

Why should the world be overwise,
In counting all our tears and sighs?
Nay, let them only see us, while
    We wear the mask.

We smile, but O great Christ, our cries
To Thee from tortured souls arise.
We sing, but oh, the clay is vile
Beneath our feet, and long the mile;
But let the world dream otherwise,
    We wear the mask.

William Butler Yeats
LEDA AND THE SWAN

A sudden blow: the great wings beating still
Above the staggering girl, her thighs caressed
By the dark webs, her nape caught in his bill,
He holds her helpless breast upon his breast.

How can those terrified vague fingers push
The feathered glory from her loosening thighs?
And how can body, laid in that white rush,
But feel the strange heart beating where it lies?

A shudder in the loins engenders there
The broken wall, the burning roof and tower
And Agamemnon dead.
                        Being so caught up,
So mastered by the brute blood of the air,
Did she put on his knowledge with his power
Before the indifferent beak could let her drop?

T. S. Eliot

THE LOVE SONG OF J. ALFRED PRUFROCK

> *S'io credesse che mia risposta fosse*
> *A persona che mai tornasse al mondo,*
> *Questa fiamma staria senza piu scosse.*
> *Ma perciocche giammai di questo fondo*
> *Non torno vivo alcun, s'i'odo il vero,*
> *Senza tema d'infamia ti rispondo.*

Let us go then, you and I,
When the evening is spread out against the sky
Like a patient etherized upon a table;
Let us go, through certain half-deserted streets,
The muttering retreats
Of restless nights in one-night cheap hotels
And sawdust restaurants with oyster-shells:
Streets that follow like a tedious argument
Of insidious intent
To lead you to an overwhelming question ...   10
Oh, do not ask, "What is it?"
Let us go and make our visit.

In the room the women come and go
Talking of Michelangelo.

The yellow fog that rubs its back upon the window-panes,
The yellow smoke that rubs its muzzle on the window-panes
Licked its tongue into the corners of the evening,
Lingered upon the pools that stand in drains,
Let fall upon its back the soot that falls from chimneys,
Slipped by the terrace, made a sudden leap,   20
And seeing that it was a soft October night,
Curled once about the house, and fell asleep.

And indeed there will be time
For the yellow smoke that slides along the street,
Rubbing its back upon the window-panes;
There will be time, there will be time
To prepare a face to meet the faces that you meet;
There will be time to murder and create,
And time for all the works and days of hands
That lift and drop a question on your plate;   30
Time for you and time for me,
And time yet for a hundred indecisions,
And for a hundred visions and revisions,
Before the taking of a toast and tea.

In the room the women come and go
Talking of Michelangelo.

And indeed there will be time
To wonder, "Do I dare?" and, "Do I dare?"
Time to turn back and descend the stair,
With a bald spot in the middle of my hair—   40
[They will say: "How his hair is growing thin!"]
My morning coat, my collar mounting firmly to the chin,
My necktie rich and modest, but asserted by a simple pin—
[They will say: "But how his arms and legs are thin!"]
Do I dare
Disturb the universe?
In a minute there is time
For decisions and revisions which a minute will reverse.

For I have known them all already, known them all:—
Have known the evenings, mornings, afternoons,   50
I have measured out my life with coffee spoons;
I know the voices dying with a dying fall
Beneath the music from a farther room.
     So how should I presume?

And I have known the eyes already, known them all—
The eyes that fix you in a formulated phrase,
And when I am formulated, sprawling on a pin,
When I am pinned and wriggling on the wall,
Then how should I begin
To spit out all the butt-ends of my days and ways   60
     And how should I presume?

And I have known the arms already, known them all—
Arms that are braceleted and white and bare
[But in the lamplight, downed with light brown hair!]
Is it perfume from a dress
That makes me so digress?
Arms that lie along a table, or wrap about a shawl.
     And should I then presume?
     And how should I begin?

                    .   .   .   .   .

Shall I say, I have gone at dusk through narrow streets   70
And watched the smoke that rises from the pipes
Of lonely men in shirt-sleeves, leaning out of windows? . . .

     I should have been a pair of ragged claws
Scuttling across the floors of silent seas.

                    .   .   .   .   .

And the afternoon, the evening, sleeps so peacefully!
Smoothed by long fingers,
Asleep ... tired ... or it malingers,
Stretched on the floor, here beside you and me.
Should I, after tea and cakes and ices,
Have the strength to force the moment to its crisis?   80
But though I have wept and fasted, wept and prayed,
Though I have seen my head [grown slightly bald] brought in
    upon a platter,
I am no prophet—and here's no great matter;
I have seen the moment of my greatness flicker,
And I have seen the eternal Footman hold my coat, and snicker,
And in short, I was afraid.

And would it have been worth it, after all,
After the cups, the marmalade, the tea,
Among the porcelain, among some talk of you and me,
Would it have been worth while,   90
To have bitten off the matter with a smile,
To have squeezed the universe into a ball
To roll it toward some overwhelming question,
To say: "I am Lazarus, come from the dead,
Come back to tell you all, I shall tell you all"—
If one, settling a pillow by her head,
    Should say: "That is not what I meant at all.
    That is not it, at all."

And would it have been worth it, after all,
Would it have been worth while,   100
After the sunsets and the dooryards and the sprinkled streets,
After the novels, after the teacups, after the skirts that trail
    along the floor—
And this, and so much more?—
It is impossible to say just what I mean!
But as if a magic lantern threw the nerves in patterns on a
    screen:
Would it have been worth while
If one, settling a pillow or throwing off a shawl,
And turning toward the window, should say:
    "That is not it at all,
    That is not what I meant, at all."   110

                        .   .   .   .   .

No! I am not Prince Hamlet, nor was meant to be;
Am an attendant lord, one that will do
To swell a progress, start a scene or two,
Advise the prince; no doubt, an easy tool,
Deferential, glad to be of use,
Politic, cautious, and meticulous:
Full of high sentence, but a bit obtuse;
At times, indeed, almost ridiculous—
Almost, at times, the Fool.

   I grow old ... I grow old ...   120
I shall wear the bottoms of my trousers rolled.

   Shall I part my hair behind? Do I dare to eat a peach?
I shall wear white flannel trousers, and walk upon the beach.
I have heard the mermaids singing, each to each.

   I do not think that they will sing to me.

   I have seen them riding seaward on the waves
Combing the white hair of the waves blown back
When the wind blows the water white and black.

   We have lingered in the chambers of the sea
By sea-girls wreathed with seaweed red and brown   130
Till human voices wake us, and we drown.

William Shakespeare
SONNET 73

That time of year thou mayst in me behold
When yellow leaves, or none, or few, do hang
Upon those boughs which shake against the cold,
Bare ruined choirs, where late the sweet birds sang.
In me thou see'st the twilight of such day
As after sunset fadeth in the west,
Which by and by black night doth take away,
Death's second self, that seals up all in rest.

In me thou see'st the glowing of such fire,
That on the ashes of his youth doth lie,
As the deathbed whereon it must expire,
Consumed with that which it was nourished by.
   This thou perceivest, which makes thy love more strong,
   To love that well which thou must leave ere long.

John Milton
ON HIS BLINDNESS

When I consider how my light is spent
   Ere half my days in this dark world and wide,
   And that one talent which is death to hide
   Lodged with me useless, though my soul more bent
To serve therewith my Maker, and present
   My true account, lest he returning chide,
   "Doth God exact day-labor, light denied?"
   I fondly ask. But Patience, to prevent
That murmur, soon replies, "God doth not need
   Either man's work or his own gifts. Who best
   Bear his mild yoke, they serve him best. His state
Is kingly: thousands at his bidding speed,
   And post o'er land and ocean without rest;
   They also serve who only stand and wait."

Theodore Roethke
MY PAPA'S WALTZ

The whiskey on your breath
Could make a small boy dizzy;
But I hung on like death:
Such waltzing was not easy.

We romped until the pans
Slid from the kitchen shelf;
My mother's countenance
Could not unfrown itself.

The hand that held my wrist
Was battered on one knuckle;
At every step you missed
My right ear scraped a buckle.

You beat time on my head
With a palm caked hard by dirt,
Then waltzed me off to bed
Still clinging to your shirt.

Robert Creeley

I KNOW A MAN

As I sd to my
friend, because I am
always talking,—John, I

sd, which was not his
name, the darkness sur-
rounds us, what

can we do against
it, or else, shall we &
why not, buy a goddamn big car,

drive, he sd, for
christ's sake, look
out where yr going.

Matthew Arnold
DOVER BEACH

The sea is calm tonight,
The tide is full, the moon lies fair
Upon the straits;—on the French coast the light
Gleams and is gone; the cliffs of England stand,
Glimmering and vast, out in the tranquil bay.
Come to the window, sweet is the night-air!
Only, from the long line of spray
Where the sea meets the moon-blanched land,
Listen! you hear the grating roar
Of pebbles which the waves draw back, and fling,   10
At their return, up the high strand,
Begin, and cease, and then again begin,
With tremulous cadence slow, and bring
The eternal note of sadness in.

Sophocles long ago
Heard it on the Aegean, and it brought
Into his mind the turbid ebb and flow
Of human misery; we
Find also in the sound a thought,
Hearing it by this distant northern sea.   20

The Sea of Faith
Was once, too, at the full, and round earth's shore
Lay like the folds of a bright girdle furled.
But now I only hear
Its melancholy, long, withdrawing roar,
Retreating, to the breath
Of the night-wind, down the vast edges drear
And naked shingles of the world.

Ah, love, let us be true
To one another! for the world, which seems   30
To lie before us like a land of dreams,
So various, so beautiful, so new,
Hath really neither joy, nor love, nor light,
Nor certitude, nor peace, nor help for pain;
And we are here as on a darkling plain
Swept with confused alarms of struggle and flight,
Where ignorant armies clash by night.

Albert Goldbarth

BODY MECHANICS

The hand: spread against the cloudless night, stars disappearing and reappearing among the fingers' quadrants; this is called the astrolabe, you can take it from your pocket and unfold it at arm's length; the suns collect in your palm, perhaps it's the gravity of your five pink half-moons; you wonder, are they rising? or setting? and sight the stars to chart direction, to see where you're going, eventually; where every body's going.

The eye: is pure acceptance; as if at the rim of the Disk Of Light, sun has been collected here, 93,000,000 miles away; and immersed, and broken inside the head with an infinite gentleness nothing else inside the head will ever break with; this is called the prism, you can open its lid and nothing lies; everything is its color; the joy of a summer afternoon's spectrum is known to you; we only forget the closing of eyes, and illuminations preceding sleep; the subtle lustre of ultraviolet, fading from an eyelash.

The body: in all of its organs, yours; temporal, opaque, delightful; that is, full of delight; and delight, defined as light-influenced; and influence in its original usage, that flow of ethereal powers between celestial bodies affecting ours; as in the park, we are deftly handling love beneath this June's entire moon, and we are hand in hand; as in the park, under August sun strokes, cops eyeing protestors, two separate visions, faced in a blind spot, eye to eye; we are doing, we are here to do; the body, and the body in activity is casting shadows, each body to its own extent; this is called the gnomon; it is this long, there is this much time.

Andrew Marvell

TO HIS COY MISTRESS

Had we but world enough, and time,
This coyness, lady, were no crime.
We would sit down, and think which way

To walk, and pass our long love's day.
Thou by the Indian Ganges' side
Shouldst rubies find; I by the tide
Of Humber would complain. I would
Love you ten years before the Flood,
And you should, if you please, refuse
Till the conversion of the Jews.   10
My vegetable love should grow
Vaster than empires, and more slow;
An hundred years should go to praise
Thine eyes, and on thy forehead gaze;
Two hundred to adore each breast,
But thirty thousand to the rest;
An age at least to every part,
And the last age should show your heart.
For, lady, you deserve this state,
Nor would I love at lower rate.   20
    But at my back I always hear
Time's winged chariot hurrying near;
And yonder all before us lie
Deserts of vast eternity.
Thy beauty shall no more be found,
Nor, in thy marble vault, shall sound
My echoing song; then worms shall try
That long-preserved virginity,
And your quaint honor turn to dust,
And into ashes all my lust: 30
The grave's a fine and private place,
But none, I think, do there embrace.
    Now therefore, while the youthful hue
Sits on thy skin like morning dew,
And while thy willing soul transpires
At every pore with instant fires,
Now let us sport us while we may,
And now, like amorous birds of prey,
Rather at once our time devour
Than languish in his slow-chapped power.   40
Let us roll all our strength and all
Our sweetness up into one ball,
And tear our pleasures with rough strife
Thorough the iron gates of life.
Thus, though we cannot make our sun
Stand still, yet we will make him run.

e. e. cummings
BUFFALO BILL'S DEFUNCT

Buffalo Bill's
defunct
            who used to
            ride a watersmooth-silver
                                    stallion
and break onetwothreefourfive pigeonsjustlikethat
                                                Jesus
he was a handsome man
                        and what i want to know is
how do you like your blueeyed boy
Mister Death

William Blake
LONDON

I wander thro' each charter'd street,
Near where the charter'd Thames does flow,
And mark in every face I meet
Marks of weakness, marks of woe.

In every cry of every Man,
In every Infant's cry of fear,
In every voice, in every ban,
The mind-forg'd manacles I hear.

How the Chimney-sweeper's cry
Every black'ning Church appalls;
And the hapless Soldier's sigh
Runs in blood down Palace walls.

But most thro' midnight streets I hear
How the youthful Harlot's curse
Blasts the new born Infant's tear,
And blights with plagues the Marriage hearse.

Robert Lowell

WAKING IN THE BLUE

The night attendant, a B.U. sophomore,
rouses from the mare's-nest of his drowsy head
propped on *The Meaning of Meaning.*
He catwalks down our corridor.
Azure day
makes my agonized blue window bleaker.
Crows maunder on the petrified fairway.
Absence! My heart grows tense
as though a harpoon were sparring for the kill.
(This is the house for the "mentally ill.")   10

What use is my sense of humor?
I grin at Stanley, now sunk in his sixties,
once a Harvard all-American fullback,
(if such were possible!)
still hoarding the build of a boy in his twenties,
as he soaks, a ramrod
with the muscle of a seal
in his long tub,
vaguely urinous from the Victorian plumbing.
A kingly granite profile in a crimson golf-cap,   20
worn all day, all night,
he thinks only of his figure,
of slimming on sherbet and ginger ale—
more cut off from words than a seal.
This is the way day breaks in Bowditch Hall at McLean's:
the hooded night lights bring out "Bobbie,"
Porcellian '29,
a replica of Louis XVI
without the wig—
redolent and roly-poly as a sperm whale,   30
as he swashbuckles about in his birthday suit
and horses at chairs.

These victorious figures of bravado ossified young.

In between the limits of day,
hours and hours go by under the crew haircuts
and slightly too little nonsensical bachelor twinkle
of the Roman Catholic attendants.
(There are no Mayflower
screwballs in the Catholic Church.)

After a hearty New England breakfast,   40
I weigh two hundred pounds
this morning. Cock of the walk,
I strut in my turtle-necked French sailor's jersey
before the metal shaving mirrors,
and see the shaky future grow familiar
in the pinched, indigenous faces
of these thoroughbred mental cases,
twice my age and half my weight.
We are all old-timers,
each of us holds a locked razor.   50

Robert Burns

TO A LOUSE,
ON SEEING ONE ON A LADY'S BONNET AT CHURCH

   Ha! where ye gaun, ye crowlin ferlie!
Your impudence protects you sairly:
I canna say but ye strunt rarely,
       Owre gawze and lace;
Tho' faith, I fear ye dine but sparely,
       On sic a place.

   Ye ugly, creepin, blastet wonner,
Detested, shunn'd, by saunt an' sinner,
How daur ye set your fit upon her,
       Sae fine a Lady!   10
Gae somewhere else and seek your dinner,
       On some poor body.

   Swith, in some beggar's haffet squattle;
There ye may creep, and sprawl, and sprattle,
Wi' ither kindred, jumping cattle,
       In shoals and nations;
Whare horn nor bane ne'er daur unsettle
       Your thick plantations.

Now haud you there, ye're out o' sight,
Below the fatt'rels, snug and tight,   20
Na faith ye yet! ye'll no be right,
            Till ye've got on it,
The vera tapmost, towrin height
            O' Miss's bonnet.

My sooth! right bauld ye set your nose out,
As plump an' gray as onie grozet:
O for some rank, mercurial rozet,
            Or fell, red smeddum,
I'd gie you sic a hearty dose o't,
            Wad dress your droddum!   30

I wad na been surpriz'd to spy
You on an auld wife's flainen toy;
Or aiblins some bit duddie boy,
            On's wylecoat;
But Miss's fine Lunardi, fye!
            How daur ye do't?

O Jenny dinna toss your head,
An' set your beauties a' abread!
Ye little ken what cursed speed
            The blastie's makin!   40
Thae winks and finger-ends, I dread,
            Are notice takin!

O wad some Pow'r the giftie gie us
To see oursels as others see us!
It wad frae monie a blunder free us
            An' foolish notion:
What airs in dress an' gait wad lea'e us,
            And ev'n Devotion!

Ezra Pound
A VIRGINAL

(1909)

No, no! Go from me. I have left her lately.
I will not spoil my sheath with lesser brightness,
For my surrounding air has a new lightness;
Slight are her arms, yet they have bound me straitly
And left me cloaked as with a gauze of ether;
As with sweet leaves; as with a subtle clearness.
Oh, I have picked up magic in her nearness
To sheathe me half in half the things that sheathe her.

No, no! Go from me. I have still the flavor,
Soft as spring wind that's come from birchen bowers.
Green come the shoots, aye April in the branches,
As winter's wound with her sleight hand she staunches,
Hath of the trees a likeness of the savor:
As white their bark, so white this lady's hours.

Margaret Atwood
GAME AFTER SUPPER

This is before electricity,
it is when there were porches.

On the sagging porch an old man
is rocking. The porch is wooden,

the house is wooden and grey;
in the living room which smells of
smoke and mildew, soon
the woman will light the kerosene lamp.

There is a barn but I am not in the barn;
there is an orchard too, gone bad,   10

its apples like soft cork
but I am not there either.

I am hiding in the long grass
with my two dead cousins,
the membrane grown already
across their throats.

We hear crickets and our own hearts
close to our ears;
though we giggle, we are afraid.

From the shadows around   20
the corner of the house
a tall man is coming to find us:

He will be an uncle,
if we are lucky.

Anonymous

LULLY, LULLEY

Lully, lulley, lully, lulley,
The faucon hath borne my make away.

He bare hym up, he bare hym down,
He bare hym into an orchard browne.

In that orchard there was an halle,
That was hanged with purpill and pall.

And in that hall there was a bede,
It was hanged with gold so rede.

And in that bed there lythe a knyght,
His woundis bledyng day and nyght.

By that bede side kneleth a may,
And she wepeth both nyght and day.

And by that bede side there stondith a ston,
Corpus Christi wretyn there on.

Wilfred Owen

DULCE ET DECORUM EST

Bent double, like old beggars under sacks,
Knock-kneed, coughing like hags, we cursed through sludge,
Till on the haunting flares we turned our backs,
And towards our distant rest began to trudge.
Men marched asleep. Many had lost their boots,
But limped on, blood-shod. All went lame, all blind;
Drunk with fatigue; deaf even to the hoots
Of gas-shells dropping softly behind.

Gas! GAS! Quick, boys!—An ecstasy of fumbling,
Fitting the clumsy helmets just in time,   10
But someone still was yelling out and stumbling
And flound'ring like a man in fire or lime.—
Dim through the misty panes and thick green light,
As under a green sea, I saw him drowning.

In all my dreams before my helpless sight
He plunges at me, guttering, choking, drowning.

If in some smothering dreams, you too could pace
Behind the wagon that we flung him in,
And watch the white eyes writhing in his face,
His hanging face, like a devil's sick of sin;   20
If you could hear, at every jolt, the blood
Come gargling from the froth-corrupted lungs,
Bitter as the cud
Of vile, incurable sores on innocent tongues,—
My friend, you would not tell with such high zest
To children ardent for some desperate glory,
The old Lie: Dulce et decorum est
Pro patria mori.

William Shakespeare

ULYSSES ON THE VIRTUES OF ORDER

Troy, yet upon his basis, had been down,
And the great Hector's sword had lacked a master,
But for these instances.
The specialty of rule hath been neglected;
And look, how many Grecian tents do stand
Hollow upon this plain, so many hollow factions.   80
When that the general is not like the hive
To whom the foragers shall all repair,
What honey is expected? Degree being vizarded,
Th' unworthiest shows as fairly in the mask.
The heavens themselves, the planets, and this center
Observe degree, priority, and place,
Insisture, course, proportion, season, form,
Office, and custom, in all line of order.
And therefore is the glorious planet Sol
In noble eminence enthroned and sphered   90
Amidst the other; whose med'cinable eye
Corrects the influence of evil planets,
And posts, like the commandment of a king,
Sans check, to good and bad. But when the planets
In evil mixture to disorder wander,
What plagues, and what portents, what mutiny,
What raging of the sea, shaking of earth,
Commotion in the winds, frights, changes, horrors,
Divert and crack, rend and deracinate
The unity and married calm of states   100
Quite from their fixture? O, when degree is shaked,
Which is the ladder of all high designs,
The enterprise is sick. How could communities,
Degrees in schools, and brotherhoods in cities,
Peaceful commerce from dividable shores,
The primogenity and due of birth,
Prerogative of age, crowns, scepters, laurels,
But by degree, stand in authentic place?
Take but degree away, untune that string,
And hark what discord follows. Each thing meets   110
In mere oppugnancy. The bounded waters
Should lift their bosoms higher than the shores
And make a sop of all this solid globe;
Strength should be lord of imbecility,
And the rude son should strike his father dead;
Force should be right, or rather right and wrong—

Between whose endless jar justice resides—
Should lose their names, and so should justice too.
Then everything include itself in power,
Power into will, will into appetite,   120
And appetite, an universal wolf,
So doubly seconded with will and power,
Must make perforce an universal prey
And last eat up himself. Great Agamemnon,
This chaos, when degree is suffocate,
Follows the choking.
And this neglection of degree it is
That by a pace goes backward with a purpose
It hath to climb. The general's disdained
By him one step below, he by the next,   130
That next by him beneath; so every step,
Exampled by the first pace that is sick
Of his superior, grows to an envious fever
Of pale and bloodless emulation;
And 'tis this fever that keeps Troy on foot,
Not her own sinews. To end a tale of length,
Troy in our weakness stands, not in her strength.

From *Troilus and Cressida*, Act I, Scene 3

Osage Indian Song

THE RISING OF THE BUFFALO MEN

I rise, I rise,
I, whose tread makes the earth to rumble.

I rise, I rise,
I, in whose thighs there is strength.

I rise, I rise,
I, who whips his back with his tail when in rage.

I rise, I rise,
I, in whose humped shoulder there is power.

I rise, I rise,
I, who shakes his mane when angered.

I rise, I rise,
I, whose horns are sharp and curved.

Translated by Francis Laflesche

William Blake

NEVER SEEK TO TELL THY LOVE

Never seek to tell thy love,
Love that never told can be;
For the gentle wind does move
Silently, invisibly.

I told my love, I told my love,
I told her all my heart;
Trembling, cold, in ghastly fears,
Ah! she doth depart.

Soon as she was gone from me,
A traveller came by,
Silently, invisibly:
He took her with a sigh.

Robert Sward

UNCLE DOG: THE POET AT 9

I did not want to be old Mr.
Garbage man, but uncle dog
Who rode sitting beside him.

Uncle dog had always looked
To me to be truck-strong
Wise-eyed, a cur-like Ford

Of a dog. I did not want
To be Mr. Garbage man because
All he had was cans to do.

Uncle dog sat there me-beside-him   10
Emptying nothing. Barely even
Looking from garbage side to side:

Like rich people in the backseats
Of chauffeur-cars, only shaggy
In an unwagging tall-scrawny way.

Uncle dog belonged any just where
He sat, but old Mr. Garbage man
Had to stop at everysingle can.

I thought. I did not want to be Mr.
Everybody calls them that first.   20
A dog is said, Dog! Or by name.

I would rather be called Rover
Than Mr. And sit like a tough
Smart mongrel beside a garbage man.

Uncle dog always went to places
Unconcerned, without no hurry.
Independent like some leashless

Toot. Honorable among Scavenger
Can-picking dogs. And with a bitch
At every other can. And meat: 30

His for the barking. Oh, I wanted
To be uncle dog—sharp, high fox-
Eared, cur-Ford truck-faced

With his pick of the bones.
A doing, truckman's dog
And not a simple child-dog

Nor friend to man, but an uncle
Traveling, and to himself—
And a bitch at every second can.

Paul Blackburn

THE PURSE-SEINE

Fierce luster of sun on sea, the gulls
                    swinging by,
        gulls flung by wind
aloft, hung clear and still before the
                    pivot
        turn
                    glide out
riding the wind as tho it were
                    the conditions of civilisation

But they are hungry too,   10
and what they do that looks so beautiful, is
        hunt.

The side of your face so soft, down, their cried falls, bitter
broken-wing graces crying freedom, crying carrion, and
we cannot look one another in the eye,
                that frightens, easier to face
the carapace of monster crabs along the beach. The empty
shell of death was always easier to gaze upon
than to look into the eyes of the beautiful killer. Never
                look a gull in the eye   20

Fit the 300-pound tom over the pursing lines, start it sliding
down the rope to close the open circle, bottom of the net,
                                                        weight
thudding down thru the sea

brass rings hung from the lead line come closer together, the
tom pushing the rings ahead of it, the purse line drawing thru
them, taking up the slack, the school sounding the fish streak-
                                                        ing
by toward that narrowing circle
                and out . . .

Waiting behind the skiff, birds sit on the sea, staring off, patient
        for what we throw them. We   30
                merely fight it, surf, and that other day. No
bed ever was until this, your face half-smiling down your
                                        swell of half-
sleep, eyes closed so tightly they will admit
                nothing but fear and stars. How can we
call all this our own? and shall we dare? admit the moon? full
bars of song from night birds, doors of the mind agape and
                                                swelling?
                Dream again
that orange slope of sand, we belting down it hand upon hand,
                                                the birds
                cry overhead

the sea   40
lies in its own black anonymity and we here on this bed
enact the tides, the swells, your hips rising toward me,
                waves break over the shoals, the
sea bird hits the mast in the dark and falls
with a cry to the deck and flutters off. Panic spreads, the
                night is long, no
        one sleeps, the net

is tight
we are caught or not, the tom sliding down ponderous
                    shall we make it?   50
                    The purse closes.

The beach is a playground, unsatisfactory, but we
pretending still it's play swim out too far, and reaching
back, the arms strain inward
Waters here are brown with sand, the land too close,
                    too close, we drown
                    in sight of
I love you and you love me . . .

John Donne

THE SUN RISING

      Busy old fool, unruly sun,
      Why dost thou thus,
Through windows, and through curtains call on us?
Must to thy motions lovers' seasons run?
      Saucy pedantic wretch, go chide
      Late school-boys, and sour prentices,
    Go tell court-huntsmen, that the King will ride,
    Call country ants to harvest offices;
Love, all alike, no season knows, nor clime,
Nor hours, days, months, which are the rags of time.   10

      Thy beams, so reverend, and strong
      Why shouldst thou think?
I could eclipse and cloud them with a wink,
But that I would not lose her sight so long:
      If her eyes have not blinded thine,
      Look, and tomorrow late, tell me,
    Whether both the Indias of spice and mine
    Be where thou left'st them, or lie here with me.
Ask for those kings whom thou saw'st yesterday,
And thou shalt hear, All here in one bed lay.   20

      She is all states, and all princes, I,
         Nothing else is.
   Princes do but play us; compared to this,
   All honour's mimic; all wealth alchemy.
      Thou sun art half as happy as we,
         In that the world's contracted thus;
      Thine age asks ease, and since thy duties be
      To warm the world, that's done in warming us.
   Shine here to us, and thou art everywhere;
   This bed thy centre is, these walls, thy sphere.   30

T. S. Eliot
JOURNEY OF THE MAGI

"A cold coming we had of it,
Just the worst time of the year
For a journey, and such a long journey:
The ways deep and the weather sharp,
The very dead of winter."
And the camels galled, sore-footed, refractory,
Lying down in the melting snow.
There were times we regretted
The summer palaces on slopes, the terraces,
And the silken girls bringing sherbet.   10
Then the camel men cursing and grumbling
And running away, and wanting their liquor and women,
And the night-fires going out, and the lack of shelters,
And the cities hostile and the towns unfriendly
And the villages dirty and charging high prices:
A hard time we had of it.
At the end we preferred to travel all night,
Sleeping in snatches,
With the voices singing in our ears, saying
That this was all folly.   20

Then at dawn we came down to a temperate valley,
Wet, below the snow line, smelling of vegetation,
With a running stream and a water-mill beating the darkness,
And three trees on the low sky.
And an old white horse galloped away in the meadow.
Then we came to a tavern with vine-leaves over the lintel,
Six hands at an open door dicing for pieces of silver,
And feet kicking the empty wine-skins.
But there was no information, and so we continued
And arrived at evening, not a moment too soon   30
Finding the place; it was (you may say) satisfactory.

All this was a long time ago, I remember,
And I would do it again, but set down
This set down
This: were we led all that way for
Birth or Death? There was a Birth, certainly,
We had evidence and no doubt. I had seen birth and death,
But had thought they were different; this Birth was
Hard and bitter agony for us, like Death, our death.
We returned to our places, these Kingdoms,   40
But no longer at ease here, in the old dispensation,
With an alien people clutching their gods.
I should be glad of another death.

Richard Eberhart
THE GROUNDHOG

In June, amid the golden fields,
I saw a groundhog lying dead.
Dead lay he; my senses shook,
And mind outshot our naked frailty.
There lowly in the vigorous summer
His form began its senseless change,
And made my senses waver dim
Seeing nature ferocious in him.
Inspecting close his maggots' might
And seething cauldron of his being,   10
Half with loathing, half with a strange love,

I poked him with an angry stick.
The fever rose, became a flame
And Vigour circumscribed the skies,
Immense energy in the sun,
And through my frame a sunless trembling.
My stick had done nor good nor harm.
Then stood I silent in the day
Watching the object, as before;
And kept my reverence for knowledge 20
Trying for control, to be still,
To quell the passion of the blood;
Until I had bent down on my knees
Praying for joy in the sight of decay.
And so I left; and I returned
In Autumn strict of eye, to see
The sap gone out of the groundhog,
But the bony sodden hulk remained.
But the year had lost its meaning,
And in intellectual chains 30
I lost both love and loathing,
Mured up in the wall of wisdom.
Another summer took the fields again
Massive and burning, full of life,
But when I chanced upon the spot
There was only a little hair left,
And bones bleaching in the sunlight
Beautiful as architecture;
I watched them like a geometer,
And cut a walking stick from a birch. 40
It has been three years, now.
There is no sign of the groundhog.
I stood there in the whirling summer,
My hand capped a withered heart,
And thought of China and of Greece,
Of Alexander in his tent;
Of Montaigne in his tower,
Of Saint Theresa in her wild lament.

William Wordsworth
THE WORLD IS TOO MUCH WITH US

The world is too much with us; late and soon,
Getting and spending, we lay waste our powers:
Little we see in Nature that is ours;
We have given our hearts away, a sordid boon!
The Sea that bares her bosom to the moon;
The winds that will be howling at all hours,
And are up-gathered now like sleeping flowers;
For this, for everything, we are out of tune;
It moves us not.—Great God! I'd rather be
A Pagan suckled in a creed outworn;
So might I, standing on this pleasant lea,
Have glimpses that would make me less forlorn;
Have sight of Proteus rising from the sea;
Or hear old Triton blow his wreathèd horn.

William Shakespeare
SONNET 116

Let me not to the marriage of true minds
Admit impediments. Love is not love
Which alters when it alteration finds,
Or bends with the remover to remove:
O, no! it is an ever-fixèd mark,
That looks on tempests and is never shaken;
It is the star to every wandering bark,
Whose worth's unknown, although his height be taken.
Love's not Time's fool, though rosy lips and cheeks
Within his bending sickle's compass come;
Love alters not with his brief hours and weeks,
But bears it out even to the edge of doom.
   If this be error, and upon me proved,
   I never writ, nor no man ever loved.

Sir Philip Sidney
LEAVE ME, O LOVE

Leave me, O love which reachest but to dust;
And thou, my mind, aspire to higher things;
Grow rich in that which never taketh rust,
Whatever fades but fading pleasure brings.
Draw in thy beams, and humble all thy might
To that sweet yoke where lasting freedoms be;
Which breaks the clouds and opens forth the light,
That doth both shine and give us sight to see.
O take fast hold; let that light be thy guide
In this small course which birth draws out to death,
And think how evil becometh him to slide,
Who seeketh heaven, and comes of heavenly breath.
   Then farewell, world; thy uttermost I see;
   Eternal Love, maintain thy life in me.

William Shakespeare
SONNET 54

Oh, how much more doth beauty beauteous seem
By that sweet ornament which truth doth give!
The rose looks fair, but fairer we it deem
For that sweet odor which doth in it live.
The canker blooms have full as deep a dye
As the perfumèd tincture of the roses,
Hang on such thorns, and play as wantonly
When summer's breath their maskèd buds discloses.
But for their virtue only is their show,
They live unwooed and unrespected fade,
Die to themselves. Sweet roses do not so.
Of their sweet deaths are sweetest odors made.
   And so of you, beauteous and lovely youth,
   When that shall vade, by verse distills your truth.

Adrian Keith Smith

RAIN

The rain screws up its face
and falls to bits.
Then it makes itself again.
Only the rain can make itself again.

Robert Frost

THE MOST OF IT

He thought he kept the universe alone;
For all the voice in answer he could wake
Was but the mocking echo of his own
From some tree-hidden cliff across the lake.
Some morning from the boulder-broken beach
He would cry out on life, that what it wants
Is not its own love back in copy speech,
But counter-love, original response.
And nothing ever came of what he cried
Unless it was the embodiment that crashed   10
In the cliff's talus on the other side,
And then in the far-distant water splashed,
But after a time allowed for it to swim,
Instead of proving human when it neared
And someone else additional to him,
As a great buck it powerfully appeared,
Pushing the crumpled water up ahead,
And landed pouring like a waterfall,
And stumbled through the rocks with horny tread,
And forced the underbrush—and that was all.   20

Maxine Kumin

THE PAWNBROKER

The symbol inside this poem is my father's feet
which, after fifty years of standing behind
the counter waiting on trade,
were tender and smooth and lay on the ironed sheet,
a study of white on white, like a dandy's shirt.
A little too precious; custom-made.
At the end of a day and all day Sunday they hurt.
Lying down, they were on his mind.

The sight of his children barefoot gave him a pain
—part anger, part wonder—as sharp as gravel   10
inside his lisle socks.
Polacks! he said, but meant it to mean
hod carriers, greenhorns, peasants; not ghetto Poles
once removed. *Where are your shoes? In hock?*
I grew up under the sign of those three gold balls
turning clockwise on their swivel.

Every good thing in my life was secondhand.
It smelled of having been owned before me by
a redcap porter whose ticket
ran out. I saw his time slip down like sand   20
in the glass that measured our breakfast eggs. At night
he overtook me in the thicket
and held me down and beat my black heart white
to make the pawnbroker's daughter pay.

On Saturday nights the lights stayed lit until ten.
There were cops outside on regular duty to let
the customers in and out.
I have said that my father's feet were graceful and clean.
They hurt when he turned the lock
on the cooks and chauffeurs and unlucky racetrack touts   30
and carwash attendants and laundresses and stock-
room boys and doormen in epaulets;

they hurt when he did up accounts in his head
at the bathroom sink
of the watches, cameras, typewriters, suitcases, guitars,
cheap diamond rings and thoroughbred
family silver, and matched them against the list
of hot goods from Headquarters,
meanwhile nailbrushing his knuckles and wrists
clean of the pawnticket stains of purple ink.   40

Firsthand I had from my father a love ingrown
tight as an oyster, and returned it
as secretly. From him firsthand
the grace of work, the sweat of it, the bone-
tired unfolding down from stress.
I was the bearer he paid up on demand
with one small pearl of selfhood. Portionless,
I am oystering still to earn it.

Not of the House of Rothschild, my father, my creditor
lay dead while they shaved his cheeks and blacked his
    mustache.   50
My lifetime appraiser, my first prince whom death unhorsed
lay soberly dressed and barefoot to be burned.
That night, my brothers and I forced

the cap on his bottle of twenty-year-old scotch
and drank ourselves on fire beforehand
for the sacrament of closing down the hatch,
for the sacrament of easing down the ways
my thumblicking peeler of cash on receipt of the merchandise,
possessor of miracles left unredeemed on the shelf
after thirty days,   60
giver and lender, no longer in hock to himself,
ruled off the balance sheet,
a man of great personal order
and small white feet.

Samuel Taylor Coleridge

KUBLA KHAN

In Xanadu did Kubla Khan
A stately pleasure-dome decree:
Where Alph, the sacred river, ran
Through caverns measureless to man
    Down to a sunless sea.
So twice five miles of fertile ground
With walls and towers were girdled round:
And there were gardens bright with sinuous rills,
Where blossomed many an incense-bearing tree;
And here were forests ancient as the hills,   10
Enfolding sunny spots of greenery.

But oh! that deep romantic chasm which slanted
Down the green hill athwart a cedarn cover!
A savage place! as holy and enchanted
As e'er beneath a waning moon was haunted
By woman wailing for her demon-lover!
And from this chasm, with ceaseless turmoil seething,
As if this earth in fast thick pants were breathing,
A mighty fountain momently was forced:
Amid whose swift half-intermitted burst   20
Huge fragments vaulted like rebounding hail,
Or chaffy grain beneath the thresher's flail:
And 'mid these dancing rocks at once and ever
It flung up momently the sacred river.
Five miles meandering with a mazy motion
Through wood and dale the sacred river ran,
Then reached the caverns measureless to man,
And sank in tumult to a lifeless ocean:
And 'mid this tumult Kubla heard from far
Ancestral voices prophesying war!   30

    The shadow of the dome of pleasure
    Floated midway on the waves;
    Where was heard the mingled measure
    From the fountain and the caves.
It was a miracle of rare device,
A sunny pleasure-dome with caves of ice!

    A damsel with a dulcimer
    In a vision once I saw:
    It was an Abyssinian maid,
    And on her dulcimer she played,   40
    Singing of Mount Abora.
    Could I revive within me
    Her symphony and song,
    To such a deep delight 'twould win me,
That with music loud and long,
I would build that dome in air,
That sunny dome! those caves of ice!
And all who heard should see them there,
And all should cry, Beware! Beware!
His flashing eyes, his floating hair!   50
Weave a circle round him thrice,
And close your eyes with holy dread,
For he on honey-dew hath fed,
And drunk the milk of Paradise.

Robert Hayden

THE WHIPPING

The old woman across the way
    is whipping the boy again
and shouting to the neighborhood
    her goodness and his wrongs.

Wildly he crashes through elephant ears,
    pleads in dusty zinnias,
while she in spite of crippling fat
    pursues and corners him.

She strikes and strikes the shrilly circling
    boy till the stick breaks   10
in her hand. His tears are rainy weather
    to woundlike memories:

My head gripped in bony vise
    of knees, the writhing struggle
to wrench free, the blows, the fear
    worse than blows that hateful

Words could bring, the face that I
    no longer knew or loved . . .
Well, it is over now, it is over,
    and the boy sobs in his room,   20

And the woman leans muttering against
    a tree, exhausted, purged—
avenged in part for lifelong hidings
    she has had to bear.

David Swanger

HIGHER ECONOMICS

From *The Term Structure of Interest Rates*, by Jacob B. Michaelsen
(New York: Intext Educational Publishers, 1973).

Hedgers stay in their preferred habitat.
Speculators are willing to depart from it.

It may prove useful
to call these latter
"arbitrageurs."

Arbitrageurs then will depart
from their preferred habitat
but only for a price.

They are averse to risk.
They are most liquid
in their preferred habitat.

Wallace Stevens

PETER QUINCE AT THE CLAVIER

I

Just as my fingers on these keys
Make music, so the selfsame sounds
On my spirit make a music, too.

Music is feeling, then, not sound;
And thus it is that what I feel,
Here in this room, desiring you,

Thinking of your blue-shadowed silk,
Is music. It is like the strain
Waked in the elders by Susanna.

Of a green evening, clear and warm,   10
She bathed in her still garden, while
The red-eyed elders, watching, felt

The basses of their beings throb
In witching chords, and their thin blood
Pulse pizzicati of Hosanna.

II

In the green water, clear and warm,
Susanna lay.
She searched
The touch of springs,
And found   20
Concealed imaginings.
She sighed,
For so much melody.

Upon the bank, she stood
In the cool
Of spent emotions.
She felt, among the leaves,
The dew
Of old devotions.

She walked upon the grass,   30
Still quavering.
The winds were like her maids,
On timid feet,
Fetching her woven scarves,
Yet wavering.

A breath upon her hand
Muted the night.
She turned—
A cymbal crashed,
And roaring horns.   40

III

Soon, with a noise like tambourines,
Came her attendant Byzantines.

They wondered why Susanna cried
Against the elders by her side;

And as they whispered, the refrain
Was like a willow swept by rain.

Anon, their lamps' uplifted flame
Revealed Susanna and her shame.

And then, the simpering Byzantines
Fled, with a noise like tambourines.   50

IV

Beauty is momentary in the mind—
The fitful tracing of a portal;
But in the flesh it is immortal.
The body dies; the body's beauty lives.
So evenings die, in their green going,
A wave, interminably flowing.
So gardens die, their meek breath scenting
The cowl of winter, done repenting.
So maidens die, to the auroral
Celebration of a maiden's choral.   60
Susanna's music touched the bawdy strings
Of those white elders; but, escaping,
Left only Death's ironic scraping.
Now, in its immortality, it plays
On the clear viol of her memory,
And makes a constant sacrament of praise.

Diane Wakoski

THE EMPRESS

She took the bone from her arm.
This music frenzied the wild gazelles
and the milk pigs running
under the high arches of her feet
and past her heavy black-budded breasts.
Taking this instrument
to
file
the words
in her   10
shawl, spilling
out in dis-
order/ honing each
syllable
till the screeching
became a har-
mony, till the buzz

became small on the smooth edge
of a word,
she set herself 20
a simple task. But the music in her own
armbone was so loud
she set the thicket
within her
running. Arm bone. Arm bone. Arm bone.
The arm bone sings. The arm bone sings.
And the gazelle leap under her armpits.
The small pigs snuffle and run past
lips. The birds caw, caw.
What noise, 30
as she only makes
a word.
Commotion for
every syllable.

LeRoi Jones/Imamu Amiri Baraka

PREFACE TO A TWENTY VOLUME
SUICIDE NOTE

Lately, I've become accustomed to the way
The ground opens up and envelops me
Each time I go out to walk the dog.
Or the broad edged silly music the wind
Makes when I run for a bus—

Things have come to that.

And now, each night I count the stars,
And each night I get the same number.
And when they will not come to be counted
I count the holes they leave.

Nobody sings anymore.

And then last night, I tiptoed up
To my daughter's room and heard her
Talking to someone, and when I opened
The door, there was no one there . . .
Only she on her knees,
Peeking into her own clasped hands.

W. H. Auden

IN MEMORY OF W. B. YEATS

d. Jan. 1939

I

He disappeared in the dead of winter:
The brooks were frozen, the airports almost deserted,
And snow disfigured the public statues;
The mercury sank in the mouth of the dying day.
O all the instruments agree
The day of his death was a dark cold day.

Far from his illness
The wolves ran on through the evergreen forests,
The peasant river was untempted by the fashionable
    quays;
By mourning tongues   10
The death of the poet was kept from his poems.

But for him it was his last afternoon as himself,
An afternoon of nurses and rumours;
The provinces of his body revolted,
The squares of his mind were empty,
Silence invaded the suburbs,
The current of his feeling failed: he became his
    admirers.

Now he is scattered among a hundred cities
And wholly given over to unfamiliar affections;
To find his happiness in another kind of wood   20
And be punished under a foreign code of conscience.
The words of a dead man
Are modified in the guts of the living.

But in the importance and noise of tomorrow
When the brokers are roaring like beasts on the floor
    of the Bourse,
And the poor have the sufferings to which they are fairly
    accustomed,
And each in the cell of himself is almost convinced of his
    freedom;
A few thousand will think of this day
As one thinks of a day when one did something slightly
    unusual.
O all the instruments agree   30
The day of his death was a dark cold day.

II

You were silly like us: your gift survived it all;
The parish of rich women, physical decay,
Yourself; mad Ireland hurt you into poetry.
Now Ireland has her madness and her weather still,
For poetry makes nothing happen: it survives
In the valley of its saying where executives
Would never want to tamper; it flows south
From ranches of isolation and the busy griefs,
Raw towns that we believe and die in; it survives,   40
A way of happening, a mouth.

III

Earth, receive an honoured guest;
William Yeats is laid to rest:
Let the Irish vessel lie
Emptied of its poetry.

Time that is intolerant
Of the brave and innocent,
And indifferent in a week
To a beautiful physique,

Worships language and forgives   50
Everyone by whom it lives;
Pardons cowardice, conceit,
Lays its honours at their feet.

Time that with this strange excuse
Pardoned Kipling and his views,
And will pardon Paul Claudel,
Pardons him for writing well.

In the nightmare of the dark
All the dogs of Europe bark,
And the living nations wait,   60
Each sequestered in its hate;

Intellectual disgrace
Stares from every human face,
And the seas of pity lie
Locked and frozen in each eye.

Follow, poet, follow right
To the bottom of the night,
With your unconstraining voice
Still persuade us to rejoice;

With the farming of a verse   70
Make a vineyard of the curse,
Sing of human unsuccess
In a rapture of distress;

In the deserts of the heart
Let the healing fountain start,
In the prison of his days
Teach the free man how to praise.

Dylan Thomas

FERN HILL

Now as I was young and easy under the apple boughs
About the lilting house and happy as the grass was green,
   The night above the dingle starry,
     Time let me hail and climb
   Golden in the heydays of his eyes,
And honoured among wagons I was prince of the apple towns
And once below a time I lordly had the trees and leaves
     Trail with daisies and barley
   Down the rivers of the windfall light.

And as I was green and carefree, famous among the barns   10
About the happy yard and singing as the farm was home,
   In the sun that is young once only,
     Time let me play and be
   Golden in the mercy of his means,
And green and golden I was huntsman and herdsman, the
        calves
Sang to my horn, the foxes on the hills barked clear and cold,
     And the sabbath rang slowly
   In the pebbles of the holy streams.

All the sun long it was running, it was lovely, the hay
Fields high as the house, the tunes from the chimneys, it was
air   20
   And playing, lovely and watery
      And fire green as grass.
   And nightly under the simple stars
As I rode to sleep the owls were bearing the farm away,
All the moon long I heard, blessed among stables, the nightjars
   Flying with the ricks, and the horses
      Flashing into the dark.

And then to awake, and the farm, like a wanderer white
With the dew, come back, the cock on his shoulder: it was all
   Shining, it was Adam and maiden,   30
      The sky gathered again
And the sun grew round that very day.
So it must have been after the birth of the simple light
In the first, spinning place, the spellbound horses walking
warm
   Out of the whinneying green stable
      On to the fields of praise.

And honoured among foxes and pheasants by the gay house
Under the new made clouds and happy as the heart was long,
   In the sun born over and over,
      I ran my heedless ways,   40
   My wishes raced through the house high hay
And nothing I cared, at my sky blue trades, that time allows
In all his tuneful turning so few and such morning songs
   Before the children green and golden
      Follow him out of grace,

Nothing I cared, in the lamb white days, that time would
take me
Up to the swallow thronged loft by the shadow of my hand,
   In the moon that is always rising,
      Nor that riding to sleep
   I should hear him fly with the high fields   50
And wake to the farm forever fled from the childless land.
Oh as I was young and easy in the mercy of his means,
      Time held me green and dying
   Though I sang in my chains like the sea.

Paul Simon
THE SOUND OF SILENCE

Hello darkness my old friend,
I've come to talk with you again,
Because a vision softly creeping,
Left its seeds while I was sleeping
And the vision that was planted in my brain
Still remains within the sound of silence.

In restless dreams I walked alone,
Narrow streets of cobble stone
'Neath the halo of a street lamp,
I turned my collar to the cold and damp   10
When my eyes were stabbed by the flash of a neon light
That split the night, and touched the sound of silence.

And in the naked light I saw
Ten thousand people maybe more,
People talking without speaking,
People hearing without listening,
People writing songs that voices never share
And no one dares disturb the sound of silence.

"Fools!" said I, "You do not know
Silence like a cancer grows.   20
Hear my words that I might teach you
Take my arms that I might reach you."
But my words like silent raindrops fell
And echoed, in the wells of silence.

And the people bowed and prayed
To the neon God they made,

And the sign flashed out its warning
In the words that it was forming.
And the sign said:
        "The words of the prophets are written   30
          on the subway walls and tenement halls"
And whispered in the sounds of silence.

Thomas Hardy

H A P

If but some vengeful god would call to me
From up the sky, and laugh: "Thou suffering thing,
Know that thy sorrow is my ecstasy,
That thy love's loss is my hate's profiting!"

Then would I bear it, clench myself, and die,
Steeled by the sense of ire unmerited;
Half-eased in that a Powerfuller than I
Had willed and meted me the tears I shed.

But not so. How arrives it joy lies slain,
And why unblooms the best hope ever sown?
—Crass Casualty obstructs the sun and rain,
And dicing Time for gladness casts a moan. . . .
These purblind Doomsters had as readily strown
Blisses about my pilgrimage as pain.

Robert Hershon

SPITTING ON IRA ROSENBLATT

It was a great pleasure
spitting on Ira Rosenblatt
a fine forbidden thing
denied me by his mother
and my mother to ensure
that I would pass my Sundays
spitting on Ira Rosenblatt

He in the alley, I on the wall
spitting on Ira Rosenblatt's
hair and face and shoulders   10
each time he tried to escape
It was a fine thing to torment him
such a sweet and industrious pleasure
spitting on Ira Rosenblatt

Working up the spittle, a duty:
spitting on Ira Rosenblatt
I spit in the toilet these days
There is no one left to torment that way
not that willing and straightforward way
How pleasant Sundays were, high on a wall   20
spitting on Ira Rosenblatt

Edmund Waller

GO, LOVELY ROSE

Go, lovely rose,
Tell her that wastes her time and me,
    That now she knows,
When I resemble her to thee,
    How sweet and fair she seems to be.

Tell her that's young,
And shuns to have her graces spy'd,
    That hadst thou sprung
In desarts, where no men abide,
    Thou must have uncommended dy'd.   10

Small is the worth
Of beauty from the light retir'd;
    Bid her come forth,
Suffer her self to be desir'd,
    And not blush so to be admir'd.

Then die, that she,
The common fate of all things rare,
    May read in thee;
How small a part of time they share,
    That are so wondrous sweet and fair.   20

James Dickey

FALLING

> *A 29-year-old stewardess fell ... to her death tonight*
> *when she was swept through an emergency door*
> *that suddenly sprang open.... The body ... was*
> *found ... three hours after the accident.*
> —*New York Times*

The states when they black out and lie there rolling
    when they turn
To something transcontinental   move by   drawing
    moonlight out of the great
One-sided stone hung off the starboard wingtip   some
    sleeper next to
An engine is groaning for coffee   and there is faintly
    coming in
Somewhere the vast beast-whistle of space. In the galley
    with its racks
Of trays   she rummages for a blanket   and moves
    in her slim tailored
Uniform to pin it over the cry at the top of the door. As
    though she blew

The door down with a silent blast from her lungs
    frozen   she is black
Out finding herself   with the plane nowhere and her
    body taking by the throat
The undying cry of the void   falling   living
    beginning to be something   10
That no one has ever been and lived through
    screaming without enough air
Still neat   lipsticked   stockinged   girdled by
    regulation   her hat
Still on   her arms and legs in no world   and yet
    spaced also strangely
With utter placid rightness on thin air   taking her
    time   she holds it
In many places   and now, still thousands of feet from
    her death she seems
To slow   she develops interest   she turns in her
    maneuverable body

To watch it. She is hung high up in the overwhelming
    middle of things in her
Self   in low body-whistling wrapped intensely   in
    all her dark dance-weight

Coming down from a marvellous leap   with the
    delaying, dumfounding ease
Of a dream of being drawn   like endless moonlight to
    the harvest soil   20
Of a central state of one's country   with a great
    gradual warmth coming
Over her   floating   finding more and more breath
    in what she has been using
For breath   as the levels become more human
    seeing clouds placed honestly
Below her left and right   riding slowly toward them
    she clasps it all
To her and can hang her hands and feet in it in peculiar
    ways   and
Her eyes opened wide by wind, can open her mouth as
    wide   wider and suck
All the heat from the cornfields   can go down on her
    back with a feeling
Of stupendous pillows stacked under her   and can
    turn   turn as to someone
In bed   smile, understood in darkness   can go away
    slant   slide
Off tumbling   into the emblem of a bird with its wings
    half-spread   30
Or whirl madly on herself   in endless gymnastics in
    the growing warmth
Of wheatfields rising toward the harvest moon.   There
    is time to live
In superhuman health   seeing mortal unreachable
    lights far down   seeing
An ultimate highway with one late priceless car probing
    it   arriving
In a square town   and off her starboard arm the
    glitter of water catches
The moon by its one shaken side   scaled, roaming
    silver   My God it is good
And evil   lying in one after another of all the positions
    for love
Making   dancing   sleeping   and now cloud wisps
    at her no
Raincoat   no matter   all small towns brokenly
    brighter from inside
Cloud   she walks over them like rain   bursts out
    to behold a Greyhound   40
Bus shooting light through its sides   it is the signal
    to go straight

Down like a glorious diver   then feet first   her skirt
      stripped beautifully
Up   her face in fear-scented cloths   her legs
      deliriously bare   then
Arms out   she slow-rolls over   steadies out
      waits for something great
To take control of her   trembles near feathers
      planes head-down
The quick movements of bird-necks turning her head
      gold eyes   the insight-
eyesight of owls blazing into the hencoops   a taste for
      chicken overwhelming
Her   the long-range vision of hawks enlarging all
      human lights of cars
Freight trains   looped bridges   enlarging the
      moon racing slowly
Through all the curves of a river   all the darks of the
      midwest blazing   50
From above. A rabbit in a bush turns white   the
      smothering chickens
Huddle   for over them there is still time for
      something to live
With the streaming half-idea of a long stoop   a
      hurtling   a fall
That is controlled   that plummets as it wills   turns
      gravity
Into a new condition, showing its other side like a
      moon   shining
New Powers   there is still time to live on a breath
      made of nothing
But the whole night   time for her to remember to
      arrange her skirt
Like a diagram of a bat   tightly it guides her   she
      has this flying-skin
Made of garments   and there are also those sky-divers
      on TV   sailing
In sunlight   smiling under their goggles   swapping
      batons back and forth   60
And He who jumped without a chute and was handed
      one by a diving
Buddy. She looks for her grinning companion   white
      teeth   nowhere
She is screaming   singing hymns   her thin human
      wings spread out
From her neat shoulders   the air beast-crooning to

her   warbling
And she can no longer behold the huge partial form of
      the world   now
She is watching her country lose its evoked master shape
      watching it lose
And gain   get back its houses and peoples
      watching it bring up
Its local lights   single homes   lamps on barn roofs
      if she fell
Into water she might live   like a diver   cleaving
      perfect   plunge

Into another   heavy silver   unbreathable
      slowing   saving   70
Element: there is water   there is time to perfect all
      the fine
Points of diving   feet together   toes pointed
      hands shaped right
To insert her into water like a needle   to come out
      healthily dripping
And be handed a Coca-Cola   there they are   there
      are the waters
Of life   the moon packed and coiled in a reservoir
      so let me begin
*To plane across the night air of Kansas   opening my
      eyes   superhumanly*
*Bright   to the dammed moon   opening the natural
      wings of my jacket*
*By Don Loper   moving like a hunting owl toward the
      glitter of water*
One cannot just *fall   just tumble screaming all that
      time   one must* use
It   she is now through with all   through all
      clouds   damp   hair   80
Straightened   the last wisp of fog pulled apart on her
      face like wool revealing
New darks   new progressions of headlights along dirt
      roads   from chaos

And night   a gradual warming   a new-made,
      inevitable world of one's own
Country   a great stone of light in its waiting waters
      hold   hold out
For water: who knows when what correct young woman
      must take up her body
And fly   and head for the moon-crazed inner eye of

midwest   imprisoned

Water   stored up for her for years   the arms of her
    jacket slipping

Air up her sleeves to go   all over her? What final
    things can be said

Of one who starts out sheerly in her body in the high
    middle of night

Air   to track down water like a rabbit where it lies
    like life itself   90

Off to the right in Kansas? She goes toward   the
    blazing-bare lake

Her skirts neat   her hands and face warmed more and
    more by the air

Rising from pastures of beans   and under her
    under chenille bedspreads

The farm girls are feeling the goddess in them struggle
    and rise brooding

On the scratch-shining posts of the bed   dreaming of
    female signs

Of the moon   male blood like iron   of what is really
    said by the moan

Of airliners passing over them at dead of midwest
    midnight   passing

Over brush fires   burning out in silence on little hills
    and will wake

To see the woman they should be   struggling on the
    rooftree to become

Stars: for her the ground is closer   water is nearer
    she passes   100

It   then banks   turns   her sleeves fluttering
    differently as she rolls

Out to face the east, where the sun shall come up from
    wheatfields   she must

Do something with water   fly to it   fall in it
    drink it   rise

From it   but there is none left upon earth   the
    clouds have drunk it back

The plants have sucked it down   there are standing
    toward her only

The common fields of death   she comes back from
    flying to falling

Returns to a powerful cry   the silent scream with
    which she blew down

The coupled door of the airliner   nearly   nearly
    losing hold

Of what she has done   remembers   remembers the
    shape at the heart
Of cloud   fashionably swirling   remembers she
    still has time to die   110
Beyond explanation. Let her now take off her hat in
    summer air the contour
Of cornfields   and have enough time to kick off her
    one remaining
Shoe with the toes   of the other foot   to unhook
    her stockings
With calm fingers, noting how fatally easy it is to
    undress in midair
Near death   when the body will assume without effort
    any position
Except the one that will sustain it   enable it to rise
    live
Not die   nine farms hover close   widen   eight of
    them separate, leaving
One in the middle   then the fields of that farm do the
    same   there is no
Way to back off   from her chosen ground   but she
    sheds the jacket
With its silver sad impotent wings   sheds the bat's
    guiding tailpiece   120
Of her skirt   the lightning-charged clinging of her
    blouse   the intimate
Inner flying-garment of her slip in which she rides like
    the holy ghost
Of a virgin   sheds the long windsocks of her stockings
    absurd
Brassiere   then feels the girdle required by
    regulations squirming
Off her: no longer monobuttocked   she feels the girdle
    flutter   shake
In her hand   and float   upward   her clothes
    rising off her   ascending
Into cloud   and fights away from her head the last
    sharp dangerous shoe
Like a dumb bird   and now will drop in   SOON
    now will drop

In like this   the greatest thing that ever came to
    Kansas   down from all
Heights   all levels of American breath   layered in
    the lungs from the frail   130

Chill of space to the loam where extinction slumbers in
    corn tassels thickly
And breathes like rich farmers counting: will come
    among them after
Her last superhuman act   the last slow careful passing
    of her hands
All over her unharmed body   desired by every sleeper
    in his dream:
Boys finding for the first time their loins filled with
    heart's blood
Widowed farmers whose hands float under light covers
    to find themselves
Arisen at sunrise   the splendid position of blood
    unearthly drawn
Toward clouds   all feeling something   pass over
    them as she passes
Her palms over *her* long legs   *her* small breasts
    and deeply between
Her thighs   her hair shot loose from all pins
    streaming in the wind   140
Of her body   let her come openly   trying at the last
    second to land
On her back   This is it   THIS
                All those who find her impressed
In the soft loam   gone down   driven well into the
    image of her body
The furrows for miles flowing in upon her where she
    lies very deep
In her mortal outline   in the earth as it is in cloud   can
    tell nothing
But that she is there   inexplicable   unquestionable
    and remember
That something broke in them as well   and began to
    live and die more
When they walked for no reason into their fields to
    where the whole earth
Caught her   interrupted her maiden flight   told her
    how to lie   she cannot
Turn   go away   cannot move   cannot slide off it
    and assume another   150
Position   no sky-diver with any grin could save her
    hold her in his arms
Plummet with her   unfold above her his wedding silks
    she can no longer
Mark the rain with whirling women that take the place

of a dead wife
Or the goddess in Norwegian farm girls   or all the
    back-breaking whores
Of Wichita. All the known air above her is not giving up
    quite one
Breath   it is all gone   and yet not dead   not
    anywhere else
Quite   lying still in the field on her back   sensing
    the smells
Of incessant growth try to lift her   a little sight left
    in the corner
Of one eye   fading   seeing something wave   lies
    believing
That she could have made it   at the best part of her
    brief goddess   160
State   to water   gone in headfirst   come out
    smiling   invulnerable
Girl in a bathing-suit ad   but she is lying like a
    sunbather at the last
Of moonlight   half-buried in her impact on the earth
    not far
From a railroad trestle   a water tank   she could see
    if she could
Raise her head from her modest hole   with her
    clothes beginning
To come down all over Kansas   into bushes   on the
    dewy sixth green
Of a golf course   one shoe   her girdle coming down
    fantastically
On a clothesline, where it belongs   her blouse on a
    lightning rod:
Lies in the fields   in *this* field   on her broken back
    as though on
A cloud she cannot drop through   while farmers
    sleepwalk without   170
Their women from houses   a walk like falling toward
    the far waters
Of life   in moonlight   toward the dreamed eternal
    meaning of their farms
Toward the flowering of the harvest in their hands
    that tragic cost
Feels herself go   go toward   go outward
    breathes at last fully
Not   and tries   less   once   tries   tries
    AH, GOD—

William Carlos Williams
THIS IS JUST TO SAY

I have eaten
the plums
that were in
the icebox

and which
you were probably
saving
for breakfast

Forgive me
they were delicious
so sweet
and so cold

William Shakespeare
O MISTRESS MINE

O mistress mine, where are you roaming?
O, stay and hear; your true love's coming,
　　That can sing both high and low.
Trip no further, pretty sweeting;
Journeys end in lovers meeting,
　　Every wise man's son doth know.

What is love? 'Tis not hereafter;
Present mirth hath present laughter;
　　What's to come is still unsure:
In delay there lies no plenty;
Then come kiss me, sweet and twenty!
　　Youth's a stuff will not endure.

From *Twelfth Night*, Act II, Scene 2

Anne Sexton

LETTER WRITTEN ON
A FERRY CROSSING
LONG ISLAND SOUND

I am surprised to see
that the ocean is still going on.
Now I am going back
and I have ripped my hand
from your hand as I said I would
and I have made it this far
as I said I would
and I am on the top deck now,
holding my wallet, my cigarettes,
and my car keys   10
at two o'clock on a Tuesday
in August of 1960.

Dearest,
although everything has happened,
nothing has happened.
The sea is very old.
The sea is the face of Mary,
without miracles or rage
or unusual hope,
grown rough and wrinkled   20
with incurable age.

Still,
I have eyes.
These are my eyes:
the orange letters that spell
"ORIENT" on the life preserver
that hangs by my knees,
the cement lifeboat that wears
its dirty canvas coat,
the faded sign that sits on its shelf   30
saying "KEEP OFF."
Oh, all right, I say,
I'll save myself.

Over my right shoulder
I see four nuns
who sit like a bridge club,
their faces poked out
from under their habits,

as good as good babies who
have sunk into their carriages.   40
Without discrimination,
the wind pulls the skirts
of their arms.
Almost undressed,
I see what remains:
that holy wrist,
that ankle,
that chain.

Oh, God,
although I am very sad,   50
could you please
let these four nuns
loosen from their leather boots
and their wooden chairs
to rise out
over this greasy deck,
out over this iron rail,
nodding their pink heads to one side,
flying four abreast
in the old-fashioned side stroke,   60
each mouth open and round,
breathing together
as fish do,
singing without sound.

Dearest,
see how my dark girls sally forth,
over the passing lighthouse of Plum Gut,
its shell as rusty
as a camp dish,
as fragile as a pagoda   70
on a stone,
out over the little lighthouse
that warns me of drowning winds
that rub over its blind bottom
and its blue cover—
winds that will take the toes
and the ears of the rider
or the lover.

There go my dark girls;
their dresses puff   80
in the leeward air.

Oh, they are lighter than flying dogs
or the breath of dolphins;
each mouth opens gratefully,
wider than a milk cup.
My dark girls sing for this:
They are going up.

Here are my four dark girls.
See them rise
on black wings, drinking   90
the sky, without smiles
or hands
or shoes.
They call back to us
from the gauzy edge of paradise,
good news, good news.

Gerard Manley Hopkins

THE WINDHOVER:

To Christ Our Lord

I caught this morning morning's minion, king-
   dom of daylight's dauphin, dapple-dawn-drawn Falcon, in his
     riding
Of the rolling level underneath him steady air, and striding
High there, how he rung upon the rein of a wimpling wing
In his ecstasy! then off, off forth on swing,
   As a skate's heel sweeps smooth on a bow-bend: the hurl and
     gliding
   Rebuffed the big wind. My heart in hiding
Stirred for a bird,—the achieve of, the mastery of the thing!

Brute beauty and valour and act, oh, air, pride, plume, here
   Buckle! AND the fire that breaks from thee then, a billion
Times told lovelier, more dangerous, O my chevalier!

   No wonder of it: shéer plód makes plough down sillion
Shine, and blue-bleak embers, ah my dear,
   Fall, gall themselves, and gash gold vermilion.

James Wright

THE JEWEL

There is this cave
In the air behind my body
That nobody is going to touch:
A cloister, a silence
Closing around a blossom of fire.
When I stand upright in the wind,
My bones turn to dark emeralds.

Ray Durem

AWARD

A Gold Watch to the FBI
Man who has followed
me for 25 years.

Well, old spy
looks like I
led you down some pretty blind alleys,
took you on several trips to Mexico,
fishing in the high Sierras,
jazz at the Philharmonic.
You've watched me all your life,
I've clothed your wife,
put your two sons through college.
what good has it done?   10
the sun keeps rising every morning.
ever see me buy an Assistant President?
or close a school?
or lend money to Trujillo?
ever catch me rigging airplane prices?
I bought some after-hours whiskey in L.A.
but the Chief got his pay.
I ain't killed no Koreans
or fourteen-year-old boys in Mississippi.
neither did I bomb Guatemala,   20

or lend guns to shoot Algerians.
I admit I took a Negro child
to a white rest room in Texas,
but she was my daughter, only three,
who had to pee.

D. H. Lawrence

SNAKE

A snake came to my water-trough
On a hot, hot day, and I in pyjamas for the heat,
To drink there.

In the deep, strange-scented shade of the great dark
   carob-tree
I came down the steps with my pitcher
And must wait, must stand and wait, for there he was at
   the trough before me.

He reached down from a fissure in the earth-wall in the
   gloom
And trailed his yellow-brown slackness soft-bellied down,
   over the edge of the stone trough
And rested his throat upon the stone bottom,
And where the water had dripped from the tap, in a
   small clearness,   10
He sipped with his straight mouth,
Softly drank through his straight gums, into his slack
   long body,
Silently.

Someone was before me at my water-trough,
And I, like a second comer, waiting.

He lifted his head from his drinking, as cattle do,
And looked at me vaguely, as drinking cattle do,
And flickered his two-forked tongue from his lips, and
   mused a moment,
And stooped and drank a little more,
Being earth-brown, earth-golden from the burning bow-
   els of the earth   20
On the day of Sicilian July, with Etna smoking.

The voice of my education said to me
He must be killed,
For in Sicily the black, black snakes are innocent, the
   gold are venomous.

And voices in me said, If you were a man
You would take a stick and break him now, and finish
   him off.

But must I confess how I liked him,
How glad I was he had come like a guest in quiet, to
   drink at my water-trough
And depart peaceful, pacified, and thankless,
Into the burning bowels of this earth?   30

Was it cowardice, that I dared not kill him?
Was it perversity, that I longed to talk to him?
Was it humility, to feel so honoured?
I felt so honoured.

And yet those voices:
If you were not afraid, you would kill him!

And truly I was afraid, I was most afraid,
But even so, honoured still more
That he should seek my hospitality
From out the dark door of the secret earth.   40

He drank enough
And lifted his head, dreamily, as one who has drunken,
And flickered his tongue like a forked night on the air,
   so black,
Seeming to lick his lips,
And looked around like a god, unseeing, into the air,
And slowly turned his head,
And slowly, very slowly, as if thrice adream,
Proceeded to draw his slow length curving round
And climb again the broken bank of my wall-face.
And as he put his head into that dreadful hole,   50
And as he slowly drew up, snake-easing his shoulders,
   and entered farther,
A sort of horror, a sort of protest against his withdraw-
   ing into that horrid black hole,
Deliberately going into the blackness, and slowly draw-
   ing himself after,
Overcame me now his back was turned.

I looked round, I put down my pitcher,
I picked up a clumsy log
And threw it at the water-trough with a clatter.

I think it did not hit him,
But suddenly that part of him that was left behind con-
    vulsed in undignified haste,
Writhed like lightning, and was gone   60
Into the black hole, the earth-lipped fissure in the wall-
    front,
At which, in the intense still noon, I stared with fasci-
    nation.

And immediately I regretted it.
I thought how paltry, how vulgar, what a mean act!
I despised myself and the voices of my accursed human
    education.

And I thought of the albatross,
And I wished he would come back, my snake.

For he seemed to me again like a king,
Like a king in exile, uncrowned in the underworld,
Now due to be crowned again.   70

And so, I missed my chance with one of the lords
Of life.
And I have something to expiate;
A pettiness.

Julius Lester

PARENTS

(*The New York Times*—February 7, 1968)

Linda failed to return home from a dance Friday night.
On Saturday
she admitted she had spent the night
with an Air Force lieutenant.

The Aults decided on a punishment
that would "wake Linda up."
They ordered her
to shoot the dog
she had owned about two years.
On Sunday,   10
the Aults and
Linda
took the dog into the desert
near their home.
They
had the girl
dig a shallow grave.
Then
Mrs. Ault
grasped the dog between her hands and   20
Mr. Ault
gave
his daughter
a .22 caliber pistol
and told her
to shoot the dog.

Instead,
the girl
put the pistol
to her right temple   30
and shot herself.

The police said
there were no charges
that could be filed
against the parents
except possibly

cruelty
to
animals.

Alfred, Lord Tennyson

THE EAGLE

He clasps the crag with crooked hands;
Close to the sun in lonely lands,
Ring'd with the azure world, he stands.

The wrinkled sea beneath him crawls;
He watches from his mountain walls,
And like a thunderbolt he falls.

David Wagoner

THE LABORS OF THOR

Stiff as the icicles in their beards, the Ice Kings
Sat in the great cold hall and stared at Thor
Who had lumbered this far north to stagger them
With his gifts, which (back at home) seemed scarcely human.

"Immodesty forbids," his sideman Loki
Proclaimed throughout the preliminary bragging,
And reeled off Thor's accomplishments, fit for Sagas
Or a seat on the bench of the gods. With a sliver of beard

An Ice King picked his teeth: "Is he a drinker?"
And Loki boasted of challengers laid out   10
As cold as pickled herring. The Ice King offered
A horn-cup, long as a harp's neck, full of mead.

Thor braced himself for elbow and belly room
And tipped the cup and drank as deep as mackerel,
Then deeper, reaching down for the halibut
Till his broad belt buckled. He had quaffed one inch.

"Maybe he's better at something else," an Ice King
Muttered, yawning. Remembering the boulders
He'd seen Thor heave and toss in the pitch of anger,
Loki proposed a bout of lifting weights.   20

"You men have been humping rocks from here to there
For ages," an Ice King said. "They cut no ice.
Lift something harder." And he whistled out
A gray-green cat with cold, mouseholey eyes.

Thor gave it a pat, then thrust both heavy hands
Under it, stooped and heisted, heisted again,
Turned red in the face and bit his lip and heisted
From the bottom of his heart—and lifted one limp forepaw.

Now pink in the face himself, Loki said quickly
That heroes can have bad days, like bards and beggars,   30
But Thor of all mortals was the grossest wrestler
And would stake his demigodhood on one fall.

Seeming too bored to bother, an Ice King waved
His chilly fingers around the mead-hall, saying,
"Does anyone need some trifling exercise
Before we go glacier-calving in the morning?"

An old crone hobbled in, foul-faced and gamy,
As bent in the back as any bitch of burden,
As gray as water, as feeble as an oyster.
An Ice King said, "She's thrown some boys in her time."   40

Thor would have left, insulted, but Loki whispered,
"When the word gets south, she'll be at least an ogress."
Thor reached out sullenly and grabbed her elbow,
But she quicksilvered him and grinned her gums.

Thor tried his patented hammerlock takedown,
But she melted away like steam from a leaky sauna.
He tried a whole Nelson; it shrank to half, to a quarter,
Then nothing. He stood there, panting at the ceiling,

"Who got me into this demigoddiness?"
As flashy as lightning, the woman belted him   50
With her bony fist and boomed him to one knee,
But fell to a knee herself, as pale as moonlight.

Bawling for shame, Thor left by the back door,
Refusing to be consoled by Loki's plans
For a quick revision of the Northodox Version
Of the evening's deeds, including Thor's translation

From vulnerable flesh and sinew into a dish
Fit for the gods and a full apotheosis
With catches and special effects by the sharpest gleemen
Available in an otherwise flat season.   60

He went back south, tasting his bitter lesson,
Moment by moment, for the rest of his life,
Believing himself a pushover faking greatness
Along a tawdry strain of misadventures.

Meanwhile, the Ice Kings trembled in their chairs
But not from the cold—they'd seen a man hoist high
The Great Horn-Cup that ends deep in the ocean
And lower all Seven Seas by his own stature;

They'd seen him budge the Cat of the World and heft
The pillar of one paw, the whole north corner;   70
They'd seen a mere man wrestle with Death herself
And match her knee for knee, grunting like thunder.

INDEX
of Poets, Titles, and First Lines

A 4
B 5
C 6
D 7
E 8
F 9
G 0
H 1
I 2
J 3